Gt Marlow

Dorchester

Wallingford

Streatley

Goring

Pangbourne

Maple-
durham

Reading

Henley

Wargrave

Sonning

Gt Marlow

Cookham

Maidenhead

Bray

Taplow

Windsor

WRITING
THE THAMES

WRITING THE THAMES

CHRISTINA HARDYMENT

Bodleian Library
UNIVERSITY OF OXFORD

First published in 2016 by the Bodleian Library
Broad Street, Oxford OX1 3BG

www.bodleianshop.co.uk

ISBN 978 1 85124 450 8

Cover design by Dot Little at the Bodleian Library
Designed and typeset in 12 on 15 Monotype Fournier
by illuminati, Grosmont
Printed and bound by Great Wall Printing Co. Ltd., Hong Kong
on 120 gsm IKPP W/F

British Library Catalogue in Publishing Data
A CIP record of this publication is available from the British Library

CONTENTS

ACKNOWLEDGEMENTS are due to the most helpful librarians of the London Library and the Bodleian Library. Samuel Fanous, Head of Bodleian Publishing, made everything possible by giving his blessing to the whole idea. Finding pictures was huge fun, especially with the help of Leanda Shrimpton, who bettered many of my suggestions. Janet Phillips was a most supportive, sensitive and discerning editor. Meredith Ramsbotham and Fran Yorke accompanied me on several fact-finding trips, most notably on the *Waveney* paddle steamer. Brian and Mary Coates shared their deep knowledge of the river with me. Thanks, too, to Philip Tabor, who groped manfully with my original chaotic and over-long draft, and to Peter Snow, always a fine sounding board as to structure. John Eade, to whom I dedicate the book, not only provided the best possible database of material about the Thames on his website, but read and commented on the text, and has been an unendingly patient source of information.

Christina Hardyment, Oxford, 2016

NOTE ON THE TEXT Some archaic spellings in quotations have been modernised for ease of reading.

INTRODUCTION

The quiet of an age-old river is like the slow turning of pages
of a well-loved book.

Robert Gibbings, Till I End My Song, 1957

THE Thames caught me early. As a child, it was my play-
ground. When we lived high on Richmond Hill in the early
1950s I collected sticklebacks in a jam jar from a tiny backwater
near Richmond Lock, and walked down to cross Richmond Bridge
to get a bus to school in Hampton. When I was nine, we moved
to Pope's Avenue, near Strawberry Hill. I biked across Teddington
Lock to get to Richmond Park with a gang of friends. I skated
every week at Richmond's riverside ice rink, and tobogganed
down the thrillingly steep Terrace Gardens towards the river
below on a white enamelled drip tray purloined from our gas oven.
I mused on the river's ever-rolling stream from the vantage point
of L'Auberge, a fashionable coffee bar above Richmond Bridge.
I was courted in Marble Hill Park, danced to the Rolling Stones
on Eel Pie Island, and learnt to sail at Tamesis Sailing Club,
near Kingston.

Working in London, I crossed the river twice a day; its brown-
green muscled stream seemed an elsewhere place, an offer of
escape that I had no means of taking. After moving to Wiltshire
I learnt to windsurf in the gravel pits that flank the tiny stream
of the Thames at Ashton Keynes, and skated along its tributary
the Kennet from Burbage to Devizes. For the last thirty years

I have lived in Oxford, a city characterised more for me by its waterways than its university. I acquired *Gipsy*, a British Moth sailing dinghy kept on Port Meadow, and *Dulcibella*, a camping punt, which is moored for the summer on the river above Bablockhythe. I windsurfed on Port Meadow when it flooded, and contrived an ice-surfer when the flood froze hard enough to skate on. I have explored the 'Stripling Thames' from Lechlade to Oxford under sail in *Gipsy*, and punted from Oxford to Cricklade in *Dulcibella*. Oars have never appealed, but I steered a traditional skiff aptly named *Run Softly* downstream from Godstow to the Perch Inn. I've talked literature in a Dutch barge moored near Pinkhill Lock, swum among water lilies above Inglesham, and walked the river's banks for miles with my dog Leo, who never chases sheep or cows but rejoices in putting up flocks of geese on the water meadows. I know the downstream waters less well, but I've raced Thames barges from Maldon and Rochester, explored the Kent shore from Gravesend to Reculver, and taken the rakish and elegant *Waveney*, a beautifully restored 1940s paddle steamer, from Tower Pier to Southend.

My collection of books about the river has grown steadily through the years. It seemed natural to justify extending it even further by uniting my love of 'literary geography' with my love of the Thames in a book that would celebrate the river's long literary tradition, resurrecting little-known gems, and recommending the best of the prose and poetry that pay it homage. But how to approach such an amorphous and potentially endless subject? I didn't want to follow the usual authorial canter listing Interesting Facts from source to sea, or from sea to source, or to write a chronological history of the river's literature. Nor could I pretend to have discovered a Grand Unifying Theory such as Peter Ackroyd's chosen thread of sacredness, or Patrick Wright's eloquent championing of the dockers and the people of the neglected estuarial reaches, and blanket criticism of the 'heritage industry'. I'm not a great believer in all-embracing theories or sweeping generalisations. It seems to me that the Thames has had all manner of meanings to those who have known it across the centuries; nor are its heroes and villains distinct types. For me the river is partly about 'contemplative recreation', forgetting reality lost in a book in my punt, or planning ambles along as yet unvisited reaches, and partly about action. River sailing is, said the Edwardian Olympic sailor Linton Hope, as tricky to master as fly-fishing; it is also on occasion decently perilous (swept sideways in a punt into hawthorn bushes by a brutally fast stream, knocked out by a violent swing of my sailing dinghy's boom).

In the end I chose seven groupings to illustrate how writers have viewed the river through the lenses of their own times and their personal predilections. 'Liquid History' takes four instances of history being made and written about. 'Topographers and Tourists' tells of the early topographers and the literary conceits they adopted, and of the 'Home Tourists' who explored the river in search of the picturesque. 'Writers' Retreats' shows how many great writers found literary inspiration in living beside the river, and wove it into their books. 'Messing About in Boats' records the various ways that people escaped from everyday life on its waters. The social interest and richness of the early material led me to limit myself on the whole to books written during the Victorian and Edwardian heyday of holidaying on the Thames; I have, however, included the most notable twentieth-century author-explorers in the bibliography, and used the delightful endpapers from Walter Higgins's *Father Thames* (1924) to help readers to find locations along the river. 'Naturalists on the Thames' celebrates those who opened the eyes of their contemporaries to the wonders of the river's aquatic and riparian flora and fauna. 'Dead in the Water' is the sombre story of those who came to grief in its waters both in fact and in fiction. 'Rhyming the River' offers verses galore, both inspired and absurd. To round the book off, I survey the new directions being taken by today's Thames-obsessed writers.

ONE

LIQUID HISTORY

'THE St Lawrence is water, the Mississippi is muddy water, but the Thames is liquid history', declared the Liberal MP John Burns proudly when a visiting American sneered at the puny size of his beloved river in 1929. Burns knew a great deal about the Thames, especially the importance of London River, as seamen call the Thames between the estuary and the city. He was a dedicated trade unionist who married the daughter of a Battersea shipwright, and led the 1889 dock strike. One of the three Woolwich ferries still bears his name. Although Winston Churchill had little time for the independent radical MP's political opinions, he echoed his view of the Thames when he called it 'the golden thread of our nation's history'. Hilaire Belloc expanded on the idea in *The Historic Thames* (1907): 'The fundamental character which has lent the Thames its meaning in English history … is twofold', he wrote. 'A river affords a permanent means of travel and a river also forms an obstacle and a boundary'. In his magisterial volume *Thames, Sacred River* (2007), Peter Ackroyd calls it 'a museum of Englishness' which 'embodies the history of the nation'.

Visual proof of the early importance of the Thames appears in the famous Gough Map of Britain. The cartographer who drew it in the 1350s made rivers much more prominent than roads. He

The Thames and its tributaries are exceptionally prominent in the fourteenth-century map of Britain known as the Gough map, after Richard Gough, who gave it to the Bodleian Library in 1809.

arranged his map with east at the top and showed a wide Thames estuary welcoming in travellers and trade from Europe with open, if marshy, arms. The message is clear. The Thames is England's most important artery. Thirty miles inland, at the first point at which the river could be securely bridged, is London, a position which made it, in Churchill's succinct phrase, 'the emporium of England'. Upstream of the capital the river's winding western reaches and its tributaries north and south enabled wherries and barges piled high with goods to reach the heart of England, and to carry back the economic wealth of the fertile southern counties to the capital and hence the world.

Good roads were few and far between. Although some of the Roman legacy of straight stone-made ways endured, land routes were made hazardous by potholes and highwaymen, and wagons were cumbersome and prone to break down. Boats were slow in comparison to a fast horseman, but they were on the whole sure, and could offer safe accommodation at night, if there was no monastery or inn at the river's edge. At the time of the Gough Map, the Thames was tidal as far as Staines, and voyages were planned to benefit from the rising or ebbing stream.

Time and again the Thames has witnessed history in the making, as such historians of the river as Jonathan Schneer and Mick Sinclair have ably described. During the centuries before and after the Gough Map, the river was an important link between strategic strongholds such as Oxford, Wallingford, Windsor and the Tower of London. Its banks and bridges were parleying points for warring sides in times of civil unrest. Its estuary was lined with defences against invasion by sea. In London, waterborne pageants celebrated royal coronations, weddings (famously that of Charles II to Catherine of Braganza) and the funerals of such national heroes as Nelson and Churchill with impressive pomp, but they are recorded better in art than in literature. However, four enduringly famous occasions inspired both contemporary and later writers and poets: the crossing of the Thames by the Romans in 54 BCE and 43 CE, the signing of Magna Carta at Runnymede in 1215, Queen Elizabeth I's defiant stand at Tilbury against the Spanish Armada in 1588 and London's great frost fair of 1683–4.

CAESARS AND THE THAMES

> [H]e ordered an elephant, an animal till then unknown to the Britons, to enter the river first, mailed in scales of iron, with a tower on its back, on which archers and slingers were stationed.
>
> Polyaenus, *Stratagems of War*, c.163 CE

The earliest mention of the Thames in written history is in Julius Caesar's *Commentaries on the Gallic Wars*, which he reticently phrased in the third person. When he attempted to invade Britain in 55 BCE, storms destroyed so many of his ships that he retreated. A year later he was more successful, but on heading north discovered that the Thames was a serious barrier.

> The river can be forded in one place only, and that with difficulty. When he had arrived there, he perceived that numerous forces of the enemy were marshalled on the other bank of the river; the bank was also defended by sharp stakes fixed in front, and stakes of the same kind fixed under the water were covered by the river. These things being discovered from [some] prisoners and deserters, Caesar, sending forward the cavalry, ordered the legions to follow them immediately. But the soldiers advanced with such speed and such ardour, though they stood above the water by their heads only, that the enemy could not sustain the attack of the legions and of the horse, and quitted the banks, and committed themselves to flight. (Book V)

The tale was embroidered gloriously 200 or so years later, when the Macedonian rhetorician Polyaenus added an elephant to Caesar's forces.

When Caesar's passage over a large river in Britain was
disputed by the British king Cassivellaunus, at the head of
a strong body of cavalry and a great number of chariots,
he ordered an elephant, an animal till then unknown to the
Britons, to enter the river first, mailed in scales of iron, with
a tower on its back, on which archers and slingers were
stationed. If the Britons were terrified at so extraordinary
a spectacle, what shall I say of their horses? Amongst the
Greeks, the horses fly at the sight of an unarmed elephant;
but armoured, and with a tower on its back, from which
missiles and stones are continually hurled, it is a sight too
formidable to be borne. The Britons accordingly with their
cavalry and chariots abandoned themselves to flight, leaving
the Romans to pass the river unmolested, after the enemy
had been routed by the appearance of a single beast. (Book 8)

In his *Britannia* (1586), William Camden identifies the crossing as
Coway Stakes, 3 miles east of Chertsey. There, he writes,

the Romans entered with so much intrepidity into the river
up to their chins, that the Britons could not stand the shock,
but abandoned the banks and fled. I cannot be mistaken in
this, the river being scarce six feet deep hereabouts, and the
place now called from these stakes 'Coway Stakes'.

Camden quotes Bede as saying that 'Remains of these are still
to be seen, and it is evident, at first sight, that each of them is of
the thickness of a man's thigh, covered with lead, and made fast
in the bed of the river.' Camden also opines that Polyaenus had
confused Caesar's campaign with that of the Emperor Claudius,
who may well have brought at least one elephant as well as four
legions to Britain ninety years later, in 43 CE. Claudius was
bringing reinforcements to Aulus Plautius, who had made some
inroad into Kent, defeating Caractacus, and driving the Britons
back to the Thames 'at a point near where it empties into the
ocean and at flood-tide forms a lake'. Because the Britons knew
the ways of the river, they crossed easily enough. Plautius had

Could this elephant denarius celebrating some kind of triumph, now in the Ashmolean Museum, have been minted to mark Caesar's crossing to Britain with elephants?

with him a squad of Batavians who were trained to swim in full armour and succeeded in following them across, and more Romans found a bridge upstream. But the fight was inconclusive, with the Britons vanishing into the marshes, leaving the Romans to flounder blindly through the swamps. Plautius summoned help, and Claudius set out through Gaul for Britain with what Dio Cassius described as 'extensive equipment, including elephants'. Cassius tells us that Claudius met up with Plautius, crossed the Thames, and captured Colchester, but he does not mention elephants again at all.

Robert Graves elaborates on the idea of Claudius having elephants with him in *Claudius the God* (1935). Chapters 18 to 21 envisage Claudius bringing both elephants and camels with him in a strengthened ship, landing at Richborough, crossing the Thames in London with them, and launching an assault on Colchester, headquarters of Caractacus. Once it is taken, Claudius enters, travelling 'on elephant-back like an Indian prince'. In recent tourist-minded times, Colchester has made the most of the romantic linking of their city with pachyderms, though the mayor has not yet processed through the city on one of the four ivory-trade orphans that now amble happily around Colchester Zoo.

Elephants crossing the Thames at London are better than nothing. But Caesar's elephant at Coway Stakes might just be more than a legend. One classical scholar has argued that it is possible that Julius Caesar did have an elephant with him. 'Towards the end of 55 BCE, Pompey had given Rome its first stone theatre and commemorated its opening by games in which twenty African elephants did battle with African hunters' wrote C.E. Stevens in *History Today* (1959). 'How easy to let [Caesar] have an elephant.' If he did, it would explain the mystery of a silver denarius that was in wide circulation during the next ten years which shows an elephant trampling a serpent – symbol, says Stevens, of the ocean. Underneath, the single word 'CAESAR' is boldly stamped. It has to be said that Stevens had a penchant for romance: he was after all one of the Inklings, the Oxford literary group around J.R.R. Tolkien and C.S. Lewis.

Although the Chertsey elephant may be mythical, and Coway Stakes merely the remains of a weir, the legend that it was the scene of Caesar's crossing has proved persistent in the popular imagination. Victorian tourists certainly saluted it as such. Still angry about the many unfriendly 'No Mooring' signs he and his boating chums encounter on their way to Coway, Jerome K. Jerome writes tartly:

> At 'Corway Stakes' – the first bend above Walton Bridge
> – was fought a battle between Caesar and Cassivelaunus.
> Cassivelaunus had prepared the river for Caesar, by planting
> it full of stakes (and had, no doubt, put up a notice-board).
> But Caesar crossed in spite of this. You couldn't choke
> Caesar off that river. He is the sort of man we want round
> the backwaters now.

Preventing invaders from negotiating the Thames remained a challenge for centuries. Opportunities for crossing the river were inquired into by scouts and spies, as were the defences erected at bridges and fords. Shallow-keeled Viking fleets sailed surprisingly far upstream: the Danes got to Fulham in Alfred's time, and the *Anglo-Saxon Chronicle* states in 1016 'Cnut came with 160 sixty ships, and Ealdorman Eadric with him, over the Thames into Mercia at Cricklade, and then turned into Warwickshire, in which they burned and killed all that they came to.' Having got my camping punt up to Cricklade only with much huffing and puffing and grating on the gravelly bottom, I have my doubts about this. It is true that the river was much reduced by the creation of the Thames Severn Canal in the late eighteenth century, but even so it seems more likely that, as most historians have argued, the reference was to an army made up of the crews from 160 ships marching to Cricklade on foot, and so to Warwickshire.

In times of civil war, the Thames also had a role as a barrier, as in the 1387 Battle of Radcot Bridge between the forces of Richard II's champion Robert de Vere, Earl of Oxford and Duke of Ireland, and those of the Earl of Derby, afterwards Henry IV. John Stow's account of the fight makes it clear that chivalry was not to the fore.

> Stout Thomas Molyneux, [de Vere's] captain, prepared himself for the battle, and though wearied after fighting entered the River. Sir Thomas Mortimer knight exhorted him to come up, or else he would shoot him through in the river: 'If I do come up', saith Thomas Molyneux, 'wilt thou save my life?' 'I do make no such promise', saith he, 'but either come up, or thou shalt straight die for it. To whom he answered, suffer me to come up and let me fight either with thee or some other, and die like a man.' As he came up, the knight caught him by the helmet, and plucked it off his head, and straightways with his dagger struck him into the brains.

Charles I's nephew Prince Rupert of the Rhine (1619–1682), hero of innumerable romances, fights off Cromwell's forces at Radcot Bridge in 1645 and defeats a parliamentary force twice his size at Brentford in 1642. He is the hero of Margaret Irwin's *The Stranger Prince*, who makes him a great river-lover.

Rupert was watching the stream below glinting here and there through the trees in the slanting light of the evening sun behind him. In the lazy warmth, a strange inertia fell on him ... He thought ... of bathes he had had in English rivers – the smell of bedstraw hot in the sun as now, then the plunge into cool, earthy water under overhanging branches, into shadows deep as a cave – a kingfisher flashing blue past him in the sunlight beyond the shade – a trout that he had caught in his hand – a moorhen's nest with eight speckled eggs, and the leaves of yellow flags pulled and interwoven by the hen into a hiding place over it.

Finally, a mere half-century ago, the World War II concrete defences known as pillboxes were constructed along the right (northerly) bank of the Upper Thames between Lechlade and Radcot, and between Abingdon and Reading, in case the Germans invaded. Their story is told in William Foot's *The Battlefields That Nearly Were: Defended England 1940* (2006).

KING JOHN AND THE BARONS

At Runnymede, at Runnymede,
What say the reeds at Runnymede?

Rudyard Kipling, *The Reeds of Runnymede*, 1922

Literary history was unarguably made beside the Thames with the signing and sealing at Runnymede of Magna Carta in June 1215. The river had already been the scene of gatherings significant to the establishment of parliamentary democracy. The great Saxon king Alfred (871–901) held a witan, a gathering of the chief men in the kingdom, at Shifford, today a remote hamlet on the north bank of the river 6 miles south of Witney. The gnomic *Proverbs of Alfred* declare that

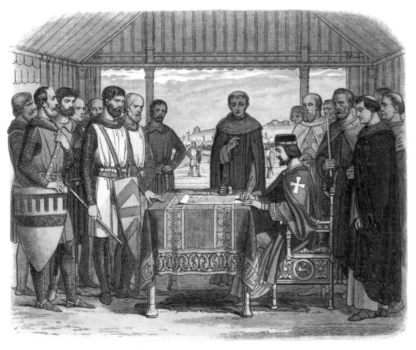

History was literally made on the Thames in 1215, when King John signed Magna Carta at Runnymede. Illustration by Richard Doyle for James Doyle's *Chronicle of England* (1864).

At Shifford many thanes were set;
There book-learned bishops met.
Earls and knights, all awesome men.
And Alfric, wise in lawsome ken:
There too England's own darling,
England's shepherd, England's king,
Alfred! them he truly taught
To live in duty as they ought.

Alfred had other connections with the Thames. He was born in nearby Wantage, and he established his capital on the Thames at Reading. Literature celebrates his role as the father of England's navy. G.A. Henty's *The Dragon and the Raven* (1921) describes how Alfred decides 'to build a fleet which may, when they again invade us, take its station near the mouth of the Thames and fall upon the vessels bringing stores and reinforcements'. The *Dragon* 'is a splendid ship, and does credit alike to King Alfred's first advice, to the plans of the Italian shipbuilders, and to the workmanship and design of the shipwright of Exeter'.

It has also been claimed that the Thames had a role in the limitation to royal power admitted by the Danish King Canute (994–1035). He established a royal palace at Thorney Island, Westminster, which was at high tide cut off from the mainland by the branched mouth of the Tyburn River. With all the resourcefulness of the publicists of Colchester, a Palace of Westminster fact sheet claims that the tidal Thames outside the palace was the scene of Canute's famous attempt to turn the tide. Where this idea comes from, I can't discover, although a line in the Skaldic poem *Knútsdrápa* does celebrate Canute's renown as 'driver of the leaping steed of the roller on Thames' bank'.

As its Anglo-Saxon name (*runieg*, meeting; *mede*, meadow) attests, Runnymede had been the scene of open-air witans since the time of Alfred the Great. It was a good place to meet, halfway between the royal citadel of Windsor and Staines, the next downstream bridge over the Thames. The outcome of the meeting on 15 June 1215 was the sealing under oath of 'Magna Carta Libertatum' by King John. Brokered by the Archbishop of Canterbury Stephen Langton, the 'great charter of the liberties of England' established limitations on the power of the king and is the single most famous historical document in the history of common and constitutional law, influencing struggles for freedom and democracy ever after. The earliest literary record of it is thought to be a Latin poem in the thirteenth-century *Melrose Chronicle*. 'A new state of things begun in England; such a strange affair as had never been heard; for the body wishes to rule the head, and the people desired to be masters over the king' are its opening words.[1] Magna Carta itself included a mention of the Thames, in the form of a clause saying that kiddels (fish weirs) must be removed from the River Thames and the Medway so that they can be used freely as thoroughfares.

Subsequently many poets and novelists were fired by the occasion. Looking down on Runnymede from Cooper's Hill, Sir John Denham declared:

My eye, descending from the hill, surveys
Where Thames amongst the wanton valleys strays ...
Here was that Charter sealed wherein the crown
All marks of arbitrary power lays down.
Tyrant and slave, those names of hate and fear,
The happier style of king and subject bear...

'Cooper's Hill', 1642

Mark Akenside (1721–1770) made a plea 'For a Column at Runnymede':

Thou, who the verdant plain dost traverse here
While Thames among his willows from thy view
Retires; O stranger, stay thee, and the scene
Around contemplate well. This is the place
Where England's ancient barons, clad in arms
And stern with conquest, from their tyrant king
(Then rendered tame) did challenge and secure
The charter of thy freedom.

When Jerome K. Jerome's boat reaches Runnymede, he offers a long and tongue-in-cheek imagining of the laying of the 'great cornerstone of England's temple of liberty'. Here are tasters from it.

As we looked out upon the river in the morning sunlight,
we could almost fancy that the centuries between us and that
ever-to-be-famous June morning of 1215 had been drawn
aside, and that we, English yeomen's sons in homespun cloth,
with dirk at belt, were waiting there to witness the writing
of that stupendous page of history, the meaning whereof was
to be translated to the common people some four hundred
and odd years later by one Oliver Cromwell, who had deeply
studied it. ...

The river down to Staines is dotted with small craft and boats and tiny coracles – which last are growing out of favour now, and are used only by the poorer folk. Over the rapids, where in after years trim Bell Weir lock will stand, they have been forced or dragged by their sturdy rowers, and now are crowding up as near as they dare come to the great covered barges, which lie in readiness to bear King John to where the fateful Charter waits his signing. …

The rumour has run round that slippery John has again escaped from the Barons' grasp, and has stolen away from Duncroft Hall with his mercenaries at his heels, and will soon be doing other work than signing charters for his people's liberty.

Not so! This time the grip upon him has been one of iron, and he has slid and wriggled in vain. Far down the road a little cloud of dust has risen, and draws nearer and grows larger, and the pattering of many hoofs grows louder, and in and out between the scattered groups of drawn-up men, there pushes on its way a brilliant cavalcade of gay-dressed lords and knights. And front and rear, and either flank, there ride the yeomen of the Barons, and in the midst King John.

In 1911, Rudyard Kipling supplied a bouncy ballad about Runnymede for C.R.L. Fletcher's *A School History of England*.

At Runnymede, at Runnymede,
What say the reeds at Runnymede?
The lissom reeds that give and take,
That bend so far, but never break,
They keep the sleepy Thames awake
With tales of John at Runnymede.

At Runnymede, at Runnymede,
Oh, hear the reeds at Runnymede:
'You musn't sell, delay, deny,
A freeman's right or liberty.
It wakes the stubborn Englishry,
We saw 'em roused at Runnymede!

When through our ranks the Barons came,
With little thought of praise or blame,
But resolute to play the game,
They lumbered up to Runnymede;
And there they launched in solid line
The first attack on Right Divine,
The curt uncompromising "Sign!"
They settled John at Runnymede.

'At Runnymede, at Runnymede,
Your rights were won at Runnymede!'

GLORIANA AT TILBURY

And to barge upon the water,
   being King Henry's royal daughter,
She did go with trumpets sounding,
   and with dubbing drums apace,
Along the Thames that famous river,
   for to view the camp a space.

Thomas Deloney, 1588

When Philip of Spain launched his Armada in 1588, England was prepared for battle. During 1587, shipbuilders had toiled mightily, and every available fighting man was armed and drilled.

By the time that the Armada arrived in July, fleets had been massed on the south coast. Off Plymouth, Sir Francis Drake and Sir Thomas Howard successfully engaged the cumbersome Spanish galleons in nimbler, deftly handled ships, most famously the *Revenge* (whose sinking in 1591 is the subject of a legendary poem by Tennyson) and *Ark Royal*. The Spanish struggled eastwards up the Channel to escort the Duke of Parma's army waiting in Flanders across the North Sea. The Thames estuary was the nation's most vulnerable place, and thousands of English troops began to mass at Tilbury, where the river narrows. Elizabeth decided to join them. The spirit of the occasion was splendidly captured in a 1798 tract, *The names of the nobility, gentry and others who contributed to the defence of the country in 1588.*

> It was a pleasant sight to behold the soldiers as they marched towards Tilbury, their cheerful countenances, courageous words and gestures, dancing and leaping wheresoever they came; and in the camp their most felicity was hope of fight with the enemy, where oft-times divers rumours ran of their foes approach, and that present battle would be given them; then were they as joyful at such news as if lusty giants were to run a race.

Elizabeth's arrival in the royal barge was described by an eye-witness, the novelist and balladeer Thomas Deloney (c.1543–1600).

> On the eighth of August she, from faire St James took her way:
> With many Lords of high degree, in princely robes and rich array...
> Her faithful soldiers great and small, as each one stood within his place:
> Upon their knees began to fall, desiring God to save her Grace.
> For joy whereof her eyes was filled, that the water down distilled.
> Lord blesse you all my friends (she said) but do not kneel so much to me:
> Then sent she warning to the rest, they should not let such reverence be.
> Then casting up her Princely eyes, unto the hill with perfect sight:
> The ground all covered, she espies, with feet of armed soldiers bright.
> Whereat her royal heart so leaped, on her feet upright she stepped.
> Tossing up her plume of feathers, to them all as they did stand:
> Cheerfully her body bending, waving of her royal hand.

Queen Elizabeth I exultant, armed and ready to defend her realm. The camp at Tilbury is below her; so is the intrepid English fleet tackling the portly galleons of the Spanish Armada. Engraving by Thomas Cecill (1625).

The parade of strength in front of the queen took place just outside the village on a plateau of high ground near the windmill. Next morning, the queen, 'an armed Pallas', spoke to the troops. It is generally acknowledged that her speech was her own work, and a triumph of rhetorical oratory. 'Certainly I have had many learned teachers who laboured diligently to make me erudite', she had boasted in Latin twenty years earlier in Oxford. Her exact words are harder to ascertain. Two early records of this speech survive. One is in much faded lettering on an early-seventeenth-century painting in Gaywood church, Norfolk.

Now for Queen & for the kingdom I have been your Queen in Peace in war, neither will I bid you go & Fight, but come & let us Fight the battle of the Lord. For what are these proud Philistines that they should Revile the host of the Living God. It may be they will challenge my sex. For that I am a woman so may I charge their mould for that they are but men whose breath is in their nostrils and if God do not charge England with the sins of England we shall not need to fear what Rome or Spain can do against us, whom is but An army of Flesh whereas trusting in the Lord our God to Fight our battles & to help us it skills not Greatly if all the devils in hell be against us.

There are echoes of this in a sermon by William Leigh which was printed in 1612, but delivered earlier.

The Queen spoke in these or like words: 'Come on now my companions at arms, and fellow Soldiers, in the field, now for the Lord, for your Queen, and for the kingdom. For what are these proud Philistines, that they should revile the Host of the living God? I have been your Prince in peace, so will I be in war; neither will I bid you go and fight, but come and let us fight the battle of the Lord. The enemy perhaps may challenge my sex for that I am a woman, so may I likewise charge their mould for that they are but men, whose breath is in their nostrils, and if God do not charge England with the sins of England, little do I fear their force. We commend your prayers, for they will move the heavens, so do we your powerful preaching, for that will shake the earth of our earthly hearts and call us to repentance, whereby our good God may relieve us, and root up in mercy his deferred judgements against us, only be faithful and fear not. Si deus nobiscum quis contra nos?[2]

However, the most quoted version of her speech is in a letter from Dr Leonel Sharp, who had been at Tilbury as the Earl of Leicester's chaplain. Polished up somewhat from the version he hastily wrote as she spoke, he sent it to the Duke of Buckingham in 1623.

My loving people,

We have been persuaded by some that are careful of our safety, to take heed how we commit ourselves to armed multitudes, for fear of treachery; but I assure you I do not desire to live to distrust my faithful and loving people. Let tyrants fear, I have always so behaved myself that, under God, I have placed my chiefest strength and safeguard in the loyal hearts and good-will of my subjects; and therefore I am come amongst you, as you see, at this time, not for my recreation and disport, but being resolved, in the midst and heat of the battle, to live and die amongst you all; to lay down for my God, and for my kingdom, and my people, my honour and my blood, even in the dust. I know I have the body but of a weak and feeble woman; but I have the heart and stomach of a king, and of a king of England too, and think foul scorn that Parma or Spain, or any prince of Europe, should dare to invade the borders of my realm; to which rather than any dishonour shall grow by me, I myself will take up arms, I myself will be your general, judge, and rewarder of every one of your virtues in the field. I know already, for your forwardness you have deserved rewards and crowns; and We do assure you in the word of a prince, they shall be duly paid you.[3]

Whatever Elizabeth actually said, she reinforced her position as an adored goddess. Events soon proved her favoured by Olympus, for the assembled troops never had to go into combat. A week before Elizabeth arrived at Tilbury, the Armada had been seriously damaged by fireships filled with explosives, a trick borrowed from the Dutch. Drake and Howard then closed in and inflicted more damage. And while Deloney's ballad, registered at the Stationer's Office within twenty-four hours of the queen's visit, was being printed and distributed around London, storms blew up, and the crippled Spanish ships were chased northwards by Drake and Howard as far as the Firth of Forth.

The poet James Aske rose to the occasion almost as quickly as Thomas Deloney, with 'Elizabetha Triumphans', a 1,200-word epic recording the victory which was published in late 1588. In a nice conceit, the first letter of each line spells out his title:

E Elizabeth sole Rectrix of this Land,
L Long time with thee hath reigned happy peace:
I In all thy deeds assisteth Pallas' hand,
Z Zenobia-like thy fame shall never cease.
A All other souls throughout the wondrous world
B Behold and see thy sweet prosperity:
E Even by thy force of late they soon were thrall'd,
T That falsely bragged of their deity.
H Honor, with Peace, Prosperity, and Fame,
A Accord with thee, and highly praise thy name.
T Triumph (O English people), leap for joy,
R Redouble oft the lauding song ye sing,
I In praise of her, who banisheth annoy.
U Unto Jehovah's altars offerings bring,
M Myrrh, Frankincense, with every sweetest flower:
P Play on your timbrels, let your comets sound;
H Heave up your hands to Him that giveth power,
A And did of late your threatening foes confound.
N No traitors be, but honour still her name,
S Sithence for her sake Jehovah wrought the same.

Elizabeth's appearance at Tilbury, 'clad all in white velvet with a silver cuirass embossed with a mythological design, and in her right hand a silver truncheon chased in gold',[4] had an echo in Edmund Spenser's Britomart, warlike goddess of chastity in *The Faerie Queen* (1590). The mythic quality of the occasion increased as time went on. The 1633 rewrite of Thomas Heywood's play *If You Know Not Me, You Know Nobody* substituted yet another version of Elizabeth's Tilbury speech for the single line ('A maiden queen will be your General') in its 1605 original.

> ... here we fix our foot.
> Not to stir back, were we sure here t'encounter
> With all the Spanish vengeance threaten'd us,
> Came it in Fire and Thunder. Know my Subiects

Your Queen hath now put on a Masculine spirit,
To tell the bold and daring what they are,
Or what they ought to be ...
Nor let the best prov'd soldier here disdain
A woman should conduct an host of men.
Oh I could wish them landed, and in view
To bid them instant battle ere march farther
Into my land, this is my vow, my rest;
I'll pave their way with this my virgin breast.

Let us end with Thomas Babington Macaulay's unfinished poem 'Armada', which begins with a stirring description of beacons being lit all over England to alert Britons to their peril, climaxing in London.

The sentinel on Whitehall gate looked forth into the night,
And saw o'erhanging Richmond Hill that streak of blood-red
    light.
Then bugle's note and cannon's roar the death-like silence
    broke,
And with one start, and with one cry, the royal city woke.
At once on all her stately gates arose the answering fires;
At once the wild alarum clashed from all her reeling spires;
From all the batteries of the Tower pealed loud the voice of fear;
And all the thousand masts of Thames sent back a louder cheer.

England was not always so lucky. On 10 June 1667, the two great diarists of the day both recorded their reaction to news of the Dutch invasion of the estuary of the Thames and the Medway. Samuel Pepys arose to the news that

the Dutch are come up as high as the Nore; and more
pressing orders for fireships. W. Batten, W. Pen, and I to St.
James's; where the Duke of York gone this morning betimes,
to send away some men down to Chatham. So we three to
White Hall, and met Sir W. Coventry, who presses all that
is possible for fire-ships. So we three to the office presently;
and thither comes Sir Fretcheville Hollis, who is to command

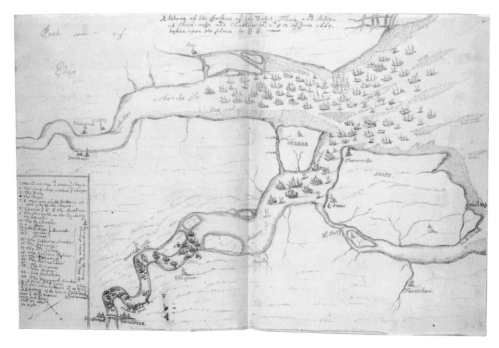

In June 1667 John Evelyn sketched this view of the Dutch heading up the Thames and into the Medway as he had seen it 'from the hill above Gillingham', and sent it to Samuel Pepys.

them all in some exploits he is to do with them on the enemy in the River. So we all down to Deptford, and pitched upon ships and set men at work: but, Lord! to see how backwardly things move at this pinch, notwithstanding that, by the enemy's being now come up as high as almost the Hope [Hope Reach, between the Medway and Tilbury].

John Evelyn, less immediately concerned with naval matters, recorded on the same day that he went

To London, alarmed by the Dutch, who were fallen on our fleet at Chatham, by a most audacious enterprise, entering the very river with part of their fleet, doing us not only disgrace, but incredible mischief in burning several of our best men-of-war lying at anchor and moored there, and all this through our unaccountable negligence in not setting out our fleet in due time.

This alarm caused me, fearing the enemy might venture up the Thames even to London (which they might have done with ease, and fired all the vessels in the river, too), to send away my best goods, plate, etc., from my house [Sayes Court at Deptford] to another place. The alarm was so great that it put both country and city into fear, panic, and consternation, such as I hope I shall never see more; everybody was flying, none knew why or whither.

FROSTIANA

Thousands and Thousands to the River flocks
Where mighty flakes of Ice do lie like Rocks.
There may you see the Coaches swiftly run,
As if beneath the ice were Waters none.
And shoals of People every where there be
Just like to Herrings in the brackish Sea

Great Britain's Wonder, 1684

Writers loved describing winters so severe that the Thames became a solid rather than a liquid highway. In a special appendix on frost fairs at the end of his 1840 *The Thames and Its Tributaries, or Rambles among the Rivers*, Charles Mackay lists those mentioned in the early chronicles.

In the year 250 the Thames was frozen over for nine weeks; in 291 for six weeks; in 401 for two months; in 558 for six weeks; in 695 also for six weeks, when booths were built, and a market held upon the ice; in 827 for nine weeks; in 908 for two months; in 923 for thirteen weeks; in 998 for five weeks; in 1063 for fourteen weeks; in 1114 for four weeks; in 1207 for eleven weeks. In 1434–5 the frost lasted from November 24th to February 10th, the Thames being passable on foot from London to within a mile of Gravesend; in 1565 the frost lasted six weeks; in 1683 thirteen weeks. In 1716 a fair was held on the Thames for several days; again in 1739; then in 1778; and lastly, in 1814.

The Thames in London had a carnival air during the freeze frost of 1683–4, with streets of stalls on the ice. *Frost Fair at Temple Stairs 1684*, by Abraham Hondius.

He gives no sources, but has clearly read the Elizabethan chronicler Raphael Holinshed (1529–1580), quoting his eyewitness account of the frost in 1565.

On the 21st of December began a frost, which continued so extremely that on New Year's Eve people went over and along the Thames on the ice from London Bridge to Westminster. Some played at football as boldly there as if it had been on dry land. Diverse of the Court, being there at Westminster, shot daily at Pricks [targets] set upon the Thames, and the people went on the Thames in greater numbers than in any street of the City of London.

Most talked of and written about was the thirteen-week frost of
1683–4. The cold was so intense that full-grown trees split apart,
with 'noises as loud as the firing of musketry' (Mackay). John
Evelyn noted in his diary that 'coaches plied from Westminster
to the Temple, and from several other stairs to and fro, as in
the streets, sleds, sliding with skates, a bull-baiting, horse and
coach-races, puppet-plays and interludes, cooks, tippling, and
other lewd places, so that it seemed to be a bacchanalian triumph,
or carnival on the water.' He described *Landskip*, a painting of
the fair which came with a key to all the events. He also saw a
printing press set up on the ice printing personalised souvenirs of
the frost. Its owner, George Croom, who had a sense of humour,
printed this rhyming advertisement:

To the print-house go,
Where Men the art of Printing soon do know,
Where, for a Teaster, you may have your name
Printed, hereafter for to show the same;
And sure, in former Ages, ne'er was found
A Press to print, where men so oft were drown'd![5]

One ticket, made for King Charles II, had a jocular hint that Princess Anne was pregnant, printing as it did 'Hans in Kelder' (Jack in Cellar) under the names of her and her husband.

The fullest prose account of the frozen Thames was the anonymous *An historical account of the late great frost, in which are discovered in several comical relations the various humours, loves, cheats, and intrigues of the town as the same were managed upon the river of Thames during that season*. Published at the Black Swan, Chancery Lane, in 1684, it described how the river became 'the only scene of pleasure in and about London'.

A whole street of booths, contiguous to each other,
was built from the Temple Stairs to the barge-house in
Southwark, which were in-habited by traders of all sorts,
which usually frequent fairs and markets, as those who
deal in earthenwares, brass, copper, tin, and iron, toys and
trifles; and besides these, printers, bakers, cooks, butchers,
barbers, coffee-men, and others ...
 Nor was the trade only amongst such who were fixt in
booths, but also all sorts of cries which usually are heard
in London streets, were there; the hawkers with their
news, the costermonger with his fruit, the wives with
their oysters, pies, and gingerbread, and such like. Nor
was there any recreation in season which could not be
found there, with more advantage than on land; such as
foot-ball play, nine-pins, cudgels, bull and bear-baiting,
and others which on the occasion was more ordinary,
as sliding in skates, chairs, and other devices, such
as were made of sailing-boats, chariots, and carrow-
whimbles ...

And in all places smoking fires on the solid waters,
roasting, boiling, and preparing food for the hungry and
liquors for the thirsty; eating, drinking, and rejoicing.

Stories of the gullible being fleeced by rogues and what Mackay
calls 'the too fair and most frail ladies of London' recur in the many
ballads written about the great freeze. The best of them is *Great
Britain's Wonder: or, London's Admiration*, which was published
underneath a lively engraving of the fair, printed on the ice by
Robert Walton and John Seller, and sold for threepence. 'Behold
the Wonder of this present Age, / A Famous River now become
a Stage' it begins, going on to bring out all the fun and raucous
bawdry of the fair. It warns against gambling dens and brothels
such as the Flying Piss-Pot and the Whip and Eggshell', and
admires 'small Vessels under Sail' on the ice which 'little Guns do
fire' as they pass, a whole Ox roasting, and a fox-hunt with dogs.

Another snide warning to women appeared in a 1684 broad-
sheet, published by William Shad:

Women, beware you come not here at all,
You are most like to slip and catch a fall,
This you may do, tho' in your gallant's hand,
And if you fall, he has no power to stand;
Tis ten to one you tumble in a trice,
For you are apt to fall where there's no ice,
Oft on your back, but seldom on your face,
How can you stand then on such a slippery place?

Two decades after the great frost, John Gay's topographical
poem *Trivia, or the Art of Walking the Streets of London*[6] (1712)
recalled:

               that wondrous year
When winter reigned in bleak Britannia's air;
When hoary Thames, with frosted osiers crowned
Was three long moons in icy fetters bound. ...
Thick-rising tents a canvas city build.
And the loud dice resound through all the field.

With macabre humour, he tells the sad story of the gruesome death of a well-known apple-seller called Doll who was caught out by the sudden thawing of the river.

> The cracking crystal yields: she sinks, she dies, –
> Her head chopt from her lost shoulders, flies;
> Pippins, she cried, but death her voice confounds,
> And pip, pip, pip, along the ice resounds.

Virginia Woolf's *Orlando* undoubtedly has the finest fictional evocation of a frost fair on the Thames. Although set just after the coronation of James I, the intensity and long-lasting freezing that Woolf describes is that of the 1683–4 frost fair rather than the only Jacobean one, a relatively brief affair in 1608.

> While the country people suffered the extremity of want,
> and the trade of the country was at a standstill, London
> enjoyed a carnival of the utmost brilliancy. The Court was
> at Greenwich, and the new King seized the opportunity that
> his coronation gave him to curry favour with the citizens.
> He directed that the river, which was frozen to a depth of
> twenty feet and more for six or seven miles on either side,
> should be swept, decorated and given all the semblance
> of a park or pleasure ground, with arbours, mazes, alleys,
> drinking booths, etc. at his expense. For himself and the
> courtiers, he reserved a certain space immediately opposite
> the Palace gates; which, railed off from the public only by a
> silken rope, became at once the centre of the most brilliant
> society in England. Great statesmen, in their beards and
> ruffs, despatched affairs of state under the crimson awning
> of the Royal Pagoda. Soldiers planned the conquest of
> the Moor and the downfall of the Turk in striped arbours
> surmounted by plumes of ostrich feathers. Admirals strode
> up and down the narrow pathways, glass in hand, sweeping
> the horizon and telling stories of the north-west passage and
> the Spanish Armada. Lovers dallied upon divans spread with
> sables. Frozen roses fell in showers when the Queen and her
> ladies walked abroad. Coloured balloons hovered motionless

in the air. Here and there burnt vast bonfires of cedar and oak wood, lavishly salted, so that the flames were of green, orange, and purple fire. But however fiercely they burnt, the heat was not enough to melt the ice which, though of singular transparency, was yet of the hardness of steel. So clear indeed was it that there could be seen, congealed at a depth of several feet, here a porpoise, there a flounder. Shoals of eels lay motionless in a trance, but whether their state was one of death or merely of suspended animation which the warmth would revive puzzled the philosophers.

Among the ships held by ice in the Port of London is a Muscovite trading ship, and from it descends the dashing Sasha. Orlando falls head over heels in love as they frolic on the ice.

They seemed to be skating in fathomless depths of air, so blue the ice had become; and so glassy smooth was it that they sped quicker and quicker to the city with the white gulls circling about them, and cutting in the air with their wings the very same sweeps that they cut on the ice with their skates.

But on the night Orlando plans to elope with her, Sasha fails to meet him. The thaw has come, and she leaves with her ship. Woolf had clearly researched contemporary accounts, even including a vision of poor Doll, visible among the eels deep down in the lucidly frozen water.

The widened arches of the 1832 London Bridge, and the gradual embankment of the river, ended the era of London frost fairs. Further upstream the Thames in Oxford froze in 1853 and 1891, and an 1895 photograph shows a heavily laden coach and four passing the college barges on the river above Iffley Lock. The river also froze along its length in the legendarily cold winters of 1946–7 and 1962–3, although not in Central London, where effluent and the Battersea and Bankside power stations warmed the water. Little literature of note survives concerning these times, only prosaic newspaper stories and personal memories.

Men – and women – behaving badly on the ice in 1814, depicted by George Cruikshank.

Limiting this chapter to the four historic occasions most rich in literary comment has meant leaving out other occasions which notable writers thought historically significant. In *The Historic Thames* (1907), the Roman Catholic author Hilaire Belloc argues that the Dissolution of the Monasteries in the 1530s profoundly changed the character of the Thames by removing the religious foundations that once clustered all along the river, not only caring for bridges, fords and weirs, but also providing hospitality for travellers. From the Tudors to our own times, waterborne processions have marked coronations, jubilees, triumphs and funerals. Samuel Pepys described the flotilla ordered by Charles II in 1662 to celebrate the arrival of his queen, Catherine of Braganza, as 'the most magnificent triumph that ever floated on the Thames, considering the innumerable boats and vessels dressed and adorned with all imaginable pomp' and the 'music and peals of ordinance from both the vessels and the shore'. In 1806, the body of Admiral Lord Nelson was rowed from Greenwich to Whitehall in a royal barge built for Charles II, covered with black velvet and adorned with plumes of black feathers; C.S. Forester's *Hornblower and the Atropos* has Hornblower organising the occasion, and having to cope with a leak in the barge carrying the body.

The Thames celebration most vivid in our own minds is of course that of Queen Elizabeth II's Diamond Jubilee in 2012. Poet Laureate Carol Ann Duffy rose to the occasion with 'The Thames, London 2012', a splendid poem that paid tribute not just to the Queen's reign, but to the river's long history.

> History as water, I lie back, remember it all.
> You could say I drink to recall; run softly
> till you end your song. I reflect. There was a whale
> in me; a King's daughter livid in a boat.
> A severed head fell from its spike, splashed.
> There was *Fire* – birds flailed in me with burning wings –
> *Ice* – a whole ox roasting where I froze, frost fair –
> *Fog* – four months sunless, moonless, spooked by ships –
> *Flood* – I flowed into Westminster Hall
> where lawyers rowed in wherries, worried –
> *Blitz* – the sky was war; I filmed it. Cut.
> I held the *Marchioness*.
> My salmon fed apprentices
> until I choked on sewage; my foul breath
> shut Parliament.
> There was lament
> at every stroke of every oar
> which dragged the virgin's barge downstream.
> Always bells; their timed sound, somewhen,
> in my tamed tides, deep.
> Caesar named me.
> I taste the drowned.
> A Queen sails now into the sun, flotilla
> a thousand proud;
> my dazzled surface gargling the crown.

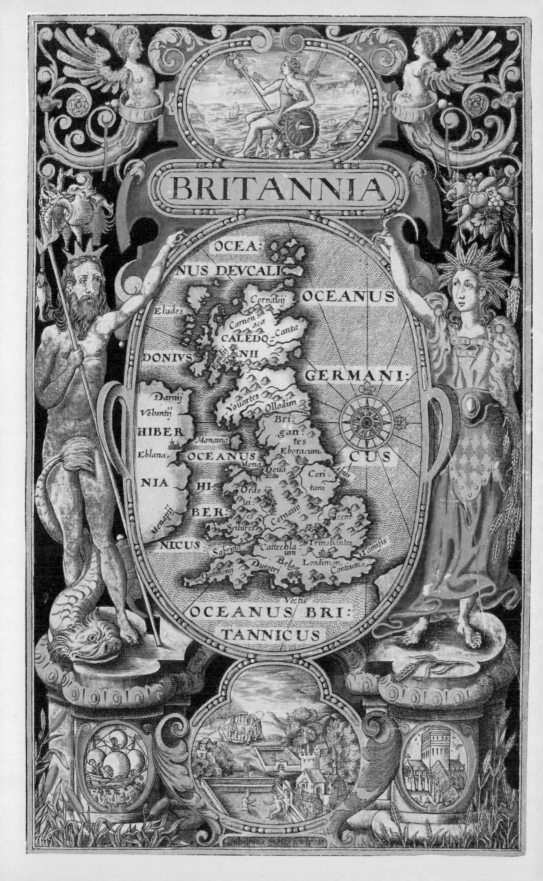

BRITANNIA

OCEA:
NUS DEVCALI

OCEANUS

Eludes

Cornauij

Carnon ace

CALEDO
NII

Canta

DONIVS

Ebudi

GERMANI:

Darnij
Voluntij

Nouartes

Olladim

HIBER

Monanna

Bri:
gan:
tes

CUS

 Eblana

OCEANVS

Eboracum

Mona

NIA

HI

Deua

Cori
tani

BER:

Ordo
ut
ces

Cornauii

Ilbus

Silures

Icent

NICUS

Sabrina

Cattechla
un

Trinobiantes

Tamiis

Belg

Londinum

Danmoni

Durotri

Centium

Vectis

OCEANUS BRI:

TANNICUS

Guilhaus Hollar fecit

TWO

TOPOGRAPHERS
AND TOURISTS

F OR centuries the curious have been exploring the length of
the Thames from its source near Cirencester to the shifting
sands of its amorphous and extensive estuary. Books galore have
been devoted to describing its course in total or in part, both in
prose and in verse. An early summary, short, snappy and in-
accurate, occurs in the 26th book of the Italian Polydore Vergil's
1534 *Anglica Historia*:

> This most attractive river originates a little above the village
> of Winchcombe, Gloucestershire, and having increased its
> flow for the first time at Oxford, from thereon it flows past
> London with remarkable placidity, and issues violently into
> the Bay of Biscay.

Equally small and more perfectly formed are the first three couplets of the Elizabethan poet George Peele's 'Farewell to Sir John
Norris and Sir Francis Drake', written on the eve of their 1589
departure from London to harry the Spanish in Lisbon.

> Farewell; bid stately Troynovant [London] adieu,
> Where pleasant Thames, from Isis' silver head,
> Begins her quiet glide, and runs along
> To that brave bridge, the bar that thwarts her course,
> Near neighbour to that ancient Stony Tower,
> The glorious hold that Julius Cæsar built.

Hand-coloured engraved title page from the 1610 edition of William Camden's
Britannia, a landmark of topographical scholarship. Aquatic motifs abound, and
the Thames, which Camden explored thoroughly, is clearly visible on the map.

The early Thames 'chorographers' were as interested in local history, archaeological antiquities and literary associations as in mapping landscape; they were also fond of metaphorical conceits involving swans and river marriages. In the eighteenth century, artists inspired by William Gilpin's several books on the picturesque set up their easels along its banks. In the first half of the nineteenth century, the river was described in detail and at length by the forerunners of the legion of pleasure-seekers native and foreign who would later record their experiences along its banks. Running as a common thread through everything the first topographers wrote about the river was a deeply felt patriotism, a belief that the history of the river was also the history of England and the Empire.

SWAN SONGS

So many fields and pleasant woods, so many princely Bowres,
And Palaces we saw besides, so many stately towres,
So many gardens trimly dressed by hand with curious care,
That now with Roman Tyberis the Tamis may well compare.

William Camden, *Britannia*, 1586

The swans of the Thames have always been highly prized. Their flesh was fine eating, their quills made excellent, hard-wearing pens (selected according to the writer's handedness from left or right flight feathers), and the majesty of their appearance led to their early association with royalty. They were celebrated in the classical literature rediscovered by the humanists, and it was natural for sixteenth-century writers to find inspiration in these 'snow-white aristocrats of the stream'. England's first topographer John Leland (1503–1552) described the Thames in Latin verse. He was a humanist cleric, a poet, and a protégé of both Cardinal Wolsey and Thomas Cromwell, but retained the favour of Henry VIII after their deaths. In 1533 he was asked to visit monastic libraries, and list books of interest he found there; after the dissolution of the monasteries began in 1536, the books he listed were removed to the libraries of Henry's palaces at Greenwich, Westminster and Hampton Court. Leland's researches in the libraries fed his interest in biography, archaeology and topography, and during the next decade he travelled all over England. His rough notes on his itineraries have numerous mentions of the Thames. In 1544 he described his journeys to Henry VIII:

> I have so travelled in your dominions both by the seacoasts
> and the middle parts, sparing neither labour nor costs, by
> the space of these six years past, that there is almost no cape,
> nor bay, haven, creak or pier, river or confluence of rivers,
> breaks, wastes, lakes, meres, fenny waters, mountains,
> valleys, moors, heaths, forests, woods, cities, boroughs,
> castles, principal manor places, monasteries, and colleges,
> but I have seen them; and noted in so doing a whole world of
> things very memorable.[1]

Leland decided to give up poetry in favour of attempting encyclopaedic books recording his discoveries. Aware of classical Greek and Latin farewell swan songs, he penned his own 'Cygnia Cantio' of 1545, elegantly combining the form of his old craft with the content of his new interest, as he explained in its introduction addressed to the king:

> I thought of the Thames, that foremost of all the rivers which
> water Britain. I once made a most careful survey of it, from
> its very sources, together with its banks, curves, twistings
> and turnings, meanderings and mid-river islands, and
> committed this all to memory. Nobody does not know that
> the Thames is the greatest nourisher and supporter of swans,
> particularly at the islands hard by that city which it embraces
> at the ford of the Isis, well-known even to high heaven for
> its erudition and goodly letters. … So accept this swan,
> swimming downstream from [Oxford] as far as your lofty
> palace at Greenwich, telling many things about the Thames

drawn from the secret storehouses of antiquity, and finally
singing of your achievements.

The poem describes a swan scudding down the Thames with
twelve companions, and tactfully makes much of any palatial location connected with the Tudors and their ancestors. At Hampton
Court he dares a reference to Wolsey's fall: 'scarlet Cardinals'
caps do not shine as once they were wont to do'. At Limehouse,
'burning smoke wafted before my nostrils; ... the white clay
is controlled by constant fire [of potteries], and all the bank
glows white'. After naming the 'goodly number of men o' war'
anchored at Deptford ('Here is the *Primrose*, here the *Swallow*, the
Sweepstake, the barque, the swift galeass'), he reaches Greenwich.

> As if spreading a sail I outstretched my wings. The river
> continued to aid me, and my Zephyr supplied a wind. See
> how the place I was seeking shone forth like the house of a
> celestial cathedral! What multicolored roofs! What windows!
> What turrets reaching toward the stars! And what pleasure
> gardens and ever-flowing fountains! Handsome flowers cover
> the bend in the river, furnishing the delights of a bright
> garden.

'Cygnea Cantio' is an early flowering of the Tudor conceit of
classifying the Thames from its source to Dorchester as the Isis,
and there marrying it to the tributary Thame, so begetting the
Thamisis, or Thames. In fact, historians had called the whole
river the Thames since Roman and Anglo-Saxon times. Leland
probably got the conceit from Ranulph Higden (1280–1364), who
said in his *Polychronicon* that 'Thamesis appears to be composed
from the names of two rivers, the Thama and the Ysa or Usa.'[2]
Both *Tam* (cf. Tamar) and *Isa* (cf. Ouse) are Celtic words for a
river, so locals might well have given passing topographers either
name for what is undoubtedly one river.

Sadly, Leland's ambitious visions of publishing comprehensive
topographies remained unfulfilled. In February 1547 he 'fell beside

William Harrison endorsed the medieval myth of a species of geese hatching from barnacles when he claimed to have plucked one off the keel of a ship in the Thames estuary in which 'the feathers hung out of the tail at least two inches' (*Description of England*, 1577). *MS. Bodl. 764, fol. 58v* (*detail*)

his wits'; he was certified insane in 1550, and died two years later. His notebooks survived to provide copious material for the next generation of topographers. The first of these was William Harrison (1534–1593), whose *Description of England* formed the first part of the Great Chronicle compiled by a group of London stationers, published in 1577, and named for Raphael Holinshed, the longest serving of the contributors. Six chapters of Harrison's work described English rivers and their tributaries, including the Thames, but it is doubtful whether Harrison examined the river himself. He does, however, endorse the popular medieval myth that barnacle geese actually hatched from barnacles. He describes picking one from the keel of a ship in the Thames estuary, in which he saw the proportion of a fowl more perfectly than in all the rest, saving that the head was not yet formed, by cause the fresh water had killed them all, and thereby hindered the perfection ... Certainly the feathers of the tail hung out of the shell at least two inches, the wings (almost perfect touching form) were guarded with two shells or shields proportioned like the self wings, and likewise the breast-bone had the coverture of a shelly substance ... I am now fully persuaded that it is either the barnacle [goose] that is engendered after this manner in these shells, or some other sea-fowl to us as yet unknown.

Next came William Camden (1551–1623), whose magnificent *Britannia* was first published in Latin in 1586. In 1607 it appeared in an English translation by Philémon Holland, embellished with maps of each county.[3] It is full of vivid glimpses of the Thames, such as this description of Canvey Island:

It lieth against the coast of Essex, from Leigh to Hole Haven, five miles in length ... but so low that often times it is quite overflowen, all save hillocks cast up, upon which the sheep have a place of safe refuge. For it keepeth about four hundred sheep, whose flesh is of a most sweet and delicate taste, which I have seen young lads, taking women's function, with stools fastened into their buttocks to milk, yea and to make cheeses of ewes' milk.

Camden regarded the Thames as a national asset, not only tidal remarkably far (up to Kingston, he claimed), but wide enough to admit 'the greatest ships that be daily bringing in great riches from all parts of the East and West'. London was made by it into 'a market where the world's goods can be peacefully exchanged'. As to the Pool of London below London Bridge, 'a man would say that seeth the shipping there, that it is, as it were, a very wood of trees disbranched to make glades and let in light: so shaded it is with masts and sails.' He followed Leland in saying that the Isis, or Ouse, 'which has his head' in Gloucestershire, afterwards entertaineth Tame, and by a compound word is called Tamisis, Sovereign as it were of all rivers in Britain, of which a man may well and truly say, as ancient writers did of Euphrates in the East part of the world, that it doth both sow and water the best part of Britain.

The idea of two rivers uniting gathered an elaborate literature. Revisions of *Britannia* added lines from a poem 'De Connubio Tamae et Isis', which Camden probably wrote himself. 'It skilleth but little', he wrote modestly, but was clearly fond of it, adding more lines in each succeeding edition. Here's a taster of its fanciful description of the source of the Thames:

> a Cave is seen,
> Whereof the entry glistereth with soft stones richly gilt,
> The Hall is seal'd with Ivory, the roof aloft built
> Of Jet, the best that Britain yields. The pillars, very strong,
> With Pumice laid each other course, are raised all along . . . .
> Here painted is the Moon, that rules the sea like Crystal glass,
> As she through rolling Signs above with traverse course doth
> pass. . . .
> All over, and on every side breaks out some water vein.
> In secret wat'rish rooms within, the little fishes plaie,
> And many a silver Swan besides his white wings doth display,
> And flutter round about

Camden may have been influenced by his contemporary Edmund Spenser (1552–1599), who composed but never published a long poem titled *Epithalamion Thamesis*, which imagined all England's rivers appearing at the wedding feast of Thames and Isis, and described their courses. Incomplete versions of both Spenser's and Camden's poems were read in manuscript by the poet and antiquary William Vallans (*fl.* 1578–90), who urged them to finish them. Vallans also wrote a poem of his own. 'The Tale of Two Swans' (1590) tells of two swans gliding down the River Lea from its source to its joining the Thames, 'together with the Antiquities of sundry places and towns seated upon the same'. It is, he tells us, 'pleasant to be read and not altogether unprofitable to be understood'.

When Spenser came to write *The Faerie Queen* (1590) he returned to the theme of river marriage, this time of the marriage of Thames, offspring of Isis and Thame, to Medway. In Canto XI of the fourth book the world's oceans and rivers, including sixty-four English and Irish ones, each celebrated with an apt phrase of adjective, gather to celebrate the marriage of the Thames and the Medway. Isis is described as 'almost blind through eld', helped along by her tributary pages the Churn and the Cherwell. Clearly Spenser is identifying her with the ancient Egyptian goddess, mother of the Sun and oldest of the old, 'from whom all being arose'. An attractive passage celebrates the tributaries of the Thames:

> And round about him many a pretty Page
> Attended duly, ready to obey;
> All little Rivers, which owe vassalage
> To him, as to their Lord, and tribute pay:
> The chalky Kennet, and the Thetis gray,
> The moorish Cole, and the soft sliding Breane,
> The wanton Lee, that oft doth loose his way,
> And the still Darent, in whose waters clean
> Ten thousand fishes play, and deck his pleasant stream.

Perhaps inspired by Vallans, Spenser revisited the river nuptials theme in his 1596 *Prothalamion*, 'a Spousal Verse in Honour of the Double Marriage of Lady Elizabeth and Lady Katherine Somerset, Daughters to the Right Honourable the Earl of Worcester and espoused to the two worthy Gentlemen M. Henry Gilford, and M. William Peter Esquires'. The poem tells of how he sees a 'flock' of green-haired nymphs gathering flowers,

> the violet, pallid blue,
> The little daisy, that at evening closes,
> The virgin lily, and the primrose true,
> With store of vermeil roses

Map from Michael Drayton's *Poly-Olbion* (1612) showing the marriage of 'lovely Isis' and Tame, 'brave as May', where they meet in 'the goodly Vale of Al'sbury' near Dorchester.

beside 'the silver streaming Thames'. He and they suddenly see two magnificent swans 'softly swimming down the Lee' to join the Thames near Greenwich. Recognising them for the two brides ('bred of Somers-heat, they say, In sweetest season', he puns), the nymphs scatter flowers so that the river is 'like a Bride's chamber floor', and put wreaths on the swan's 'snowy foreheads'. Then he follows as the swans, escorted by a flock of nymphs, reach the Thames near Greenwich, then swim upstream to 'merry London' and Essex House, centre of an influential literary circle. There the Earl, 'great England's glory and the wide world's wonder', and their 'bridegrooms, 'two gentle Knights of lovely face and feature / Beseeming well the bower of any queen', are waiting for them. The poem overtly begs Essex for patronage and covertly hints at the romance between him and the Queen. Its chorus line 'Sweet Thames run softly, till I end my song' would be used both by the poet T.S. Eliot, in *The Waste Land* (1922), and by the wood engraver Robert Gibbings (1889–1958) for the titles of his two books about exploring the Thames.

Michael Drayton (1563–1631) wrote a sonnet on English rivers which begins 'Our flood's-queen Thames for ships and swans is crown'd', and goes on to declare that 'Cotswold commends her Isis to the Thame'. He also describes the Marriage of Tame and Isis in the fifteenth 'song' of *Poly-Olbion*, and features the river in his lengthy pastoral 'Song To Beta' (1600). It praises the Queen (Beta) as 'the phoenix of all thy watery brood', and orders all the river's swans to line up on its banks up to salute her as she passes on its 'clearest crystal flood'. He outdoes Spenser in botanical flourish:

> Make her a goodly chaplet of azured columbine,
> And wreath about her coronet with sweetest eglantine;
> Bedeck our Beta all with lilies,
> And the dainty daffodillies,
> With roses damask, white, and red, and fairest flower delice,
> With cowslips of Jerusalem, and cloves of Paradise.[4]

Swans recur in later poems about the Thames, but not as guides to the topography of the river. With the passing of the age of Gloriana, the riverine nuptial poems that had often contained coded hints to the determinedly virgin queen declined to a trickle, 'conceived by minor poets whose gurgling songs are no longer remembered', Jack Oruch cuttingly concludes in his article 'Spenser, Camden, and the Poetic Marriages of Rivers'.[5] In his 1724 *A Tour Thro' the Whole Island of Great Britain*', Daniel Defoe declares that he will 'talk nothing of the marriage of old Isis, the male river, with the beautiful Thame, the female river (a whimsy as simple as the subject was empty)'.

IN SEARCH OF THE PICTURESQUE

I went to Cliveden, that stupendous natural rock, wood,
and prospect, of the Duke of Buckingham's, buildings
of extraordinary expense. The grotto in the chalky rock
is pretty: 'tis a romantic object, and the place altogether
answers the most poetical description that can be made of
solitude, precipice, prospect, or whatever can contribute to a
thing so very like their imaginations.

John Evelyn, *Diary*, 23 July 1679

The next wave of Thames enthusiasts sought a different kind of romance, journeying on or beside the river carrying drawing materials, easels and a Claude glass (a shaded, slightly convex mirror that gave more focus to a feature in the landscape, named for the French landscape painter Claude Lorraine). John Evelyn was before his time in his appreciation of Cliveden's romantic prospect. In the second half of the eighteenth century, cultivated young Englishmen and a few doughty women took the 'Grand Tour' around Europe, enjoying the 'agreeable horror' of the Alps, and the craggy scenery of the Rhine. They were inspired by the ideas of Edmund Burke, whose *Enquiry into the Origins of the Sublime and Beautiful* (1757) argued that 'exaltation, awe and delight' were to be found in Nature's most dramatic manifestations. The outbreak of the French Revolution in 1789, and the wars against Napoleonic France between 1803 and 1815, made Europe a risky destination, and soon, encouraged by the new accessibility of remote parts of Britain as roads and maps improved, the idea of 'Home Tours' became fashionable.

Aesthetic appreciation of landscape was intensified by the paintings and writings of William Gilpin (1724–1804), who emerged in the 1770s as an authority on the 'picturesque', which he defined as 'that kind of beauty which is agreeable in a picture'. From 1755 to 1777 Gilpin taught at Cheam School; he spent his summers touring the British Isles and published eleven books devoted to discerning the picturesque in scenery that ranged from the Scottish Highlands and the mountains, lakes and rivers of Cumberland and Wales to the subtler beauties of the Home Counties. Gilpin was particularly fond of rivers.

> I have often thought, that if a person wished particularly to amuse himself with picturesque scenes, the best method he could take would be to place before him a good map of England, and to settle in his head the course of all the chief rivers of the country.

His very first journey in search of the picturesque was a voyage on the Thames in 1764. He planned to divide this 'magnificent subject' into three parts: Oxford to Windsor, Windsor to London, and London to the sea. 'An imperial river like the Thames must be navigated, at least for its two lower divisions; but inferior rivers are best examined by an excursion along their banks' he later wrote in his first book, *Observations relative chiefly to picturesque beauty, made in the year 1776.* However, he never published the well-filled memorandum book and the sketches he and his brother Sawrey made on their voyage from Windsor to London that summer in a small wherry. Nor, perhaps disappointed by the lack of truly picturesque subjects found on that trip, did he make his planned journeys from Oxford to Windsor, and from London to the sea. Between 1798 and 1802 he did transcribe his notes on the Windsor to London trip in the form of a descriptive catalogue of the sketches that he and Sawrey made. These were sold with other 'books of drawings' in 1802 to raise money for his parish school; he was by then vicar of Boldre, near Lymington.

In 1994 Gilpin's notes and his and Sawrey's sketches were published by the Walpole Society. They make fascinating reading. Gilpin complains that the Thames lacked picturesque beauty except here and there — the timber bridge immortalised by Canaletto at Walton-on-Thames, cows on a spur of the river at Datchet, Pope's house at Twickenham. He thought its suburban reaches

In 1764, William Gilpin made the first of his famous tours in search of 'picturesque beauty' on the Thames with his brother Sawrey Gilpin, who sketched the 1750 timber bridge over the Thames at Walton. It was designed by William Etheridge, whose bridge over the Cam at Queens' College still exists.

lamentably artificial, but conceded that it was often 'agreeable' and 'amusing'. He admired the old-fashioned working boats known as 'west-country barges', but deplored the pretentiousness of the gilt barges of the wealthy. In London, he noted that

> The clouded atmosphere, which hangs over London, has often a very picturesque effect. A morning sun contending with so vast a body of vapour, and struggling between light, and darkness, is as grand, as it is beautiful. The many gradations also which it exhibits of light and shade blending into each other, abound with picturesque ideas. An evening sun often produces similar effects: but as it is not attended with the haziness of a morning sun, it wants one of its most picturesque appendages.

Gilpin thought the swan 'a very picturesque bird', except when in a hurry.

> On the water he appears to most advantage; but not equally so. When he is bent on expedition, with his breast sunk deep in the water – his wings close to his body – and his neck erect; though his motion, as he drives the water before him, is pleasing; his form is the reverse; his neck and body being at right angles. As a loiterer, he makes the best figure; when with an arched neck, and wings raised from his sides, he rests upon his oars on its waves, motionless on the surface.

Gilpin's observations on the picturesque influenced his near contemporary Samuel Ireland, whose lavishly illustrated *Picturesque Views on the River Thames from its Source in Gloucestershire to the Nore; with Observations on the Public Buildings and other Works of Art in its Vicinity* was published in two folio volumes in 1792. Ireland didn't make the mistake of travelling only by water. Instead, he ambled along the banks of the river, often climbing hills to find a 'station', as seekers after the picturesque described viewing points with drama and perspective. He explored much more of the river than Gilpin did, and had absolutely no reservations as to its suitability as a subject, describing the stretch from Maidenhead to Tilbury as

> such a combination of magnificence, both natural and artificial, as is perhaps not to be equalled in this kingdom! Castles and palaces proudly vying with each other in displaying the munificence of their Sovereign; – stately mansions of an ancient and splendid Nobility; – and rich and costly villas, principally raised and supported by that spirit of enterprise and industry in commerce, which is so happily characteristick of the genius of Britain.

Rivers were becoming big literary and artistic business. Ireland went on to produce similar volumes on the Medway, the Avon, the Wye and the Severn. In the early 1790s, John and Josiah

In his *History of the River Thames* (1794) William Combe praised Nuneham Courtenay as 'the place most distinguished for beauty along the course of the river'. Engraving from a painting by Joseph Farington.

Boydell planned a rival project in several volumes: *Picturesque Views and Scenery of the Thames and the Severn, the Forth and the Clyde, from their Sources to the Sea.* They hired the versatile pamphleteer and journalist William Combe (1742–1823) to write the text. A friend of Laurence Sterne, and best known for his satires, Combe began his topographical texts as lucrative hack work that catered to the current rage for the picturesque. In 1794 the Boydells published his handsome two-volume folio *An History of the River Thames*; Combe dedicated it to Horace Walpole, a notable connoisseur of the picturesque. Illustrated with aquatinted engravings from original drawings by Joseph Farington, its scope was ambitious:

> The history of a river is the history of whatever appears on its banks, from metropolitan magnificence to village simplicity; from the habitations of kings to the huts of fishermen; from

the woody brow, which is the pride of the landscape, to the secret plant that is visible only to the eye of the botanist.

Financial difficulties meant that the Boydells could not afford to complete their surveys of British rivers, but Combe continued to provide texts for illustrated guides and histories. The temptation to make fun of William Gilpin's earnest and exact judgements on landscapes soon became irresistible, and between 1809 and 1811 he teamed up with Thomas Rowlandson as illustrator to produce a series in Ackerman's *Poetical Magazine* titled *The Travels of Dr Syntax in Search of The Picturesque*. Written in doggerel verse, it and its sequels *Syntax in Search of a Wife* and *Syntax in Search of Consolation* were a huge success, and were reprinted in book form. Combe also found time to furnish the text for another two-volume book about the Thames published by Ackerman in 1811: *The Thames; or Graphic Illustrations of Seats, Villas, Public Buildings, and Picturesque Scenery on the Banks of that noble River*. This had engravings by W.B. Cooke from lively and dramatically composed drawings by Samuel Owen. Combe praised Nuneham Courtenay, 'the place most distinguished for beauty along the course of the river', Taplow House, where 'from buildings judiciously placed in commanding points, or openings, tastefully made, as inlets to particular objects, the country is seen in various directions', and the church at Twickenham, 'embosomed among lofty trees on the banks of the river'.

In 1845 the Irish poet and humourist John Fisher Murray completed his *A Picturesque Tour of the River Thames in its Western Courses, including particular descriptions of Richmond, Hampton Court and Windsor*. It had 'upwards of a hundred highly-finished wood-engravings by Orrin Smith, Branston, Landells, and other eminent artists', four intricately engraved maps and a fine aerial view of Hampton Court. Its text, derived from Ireland's, is lively, but the day trips described are only between Westminster and Windsor. Murray informs his readers 'of their near approach

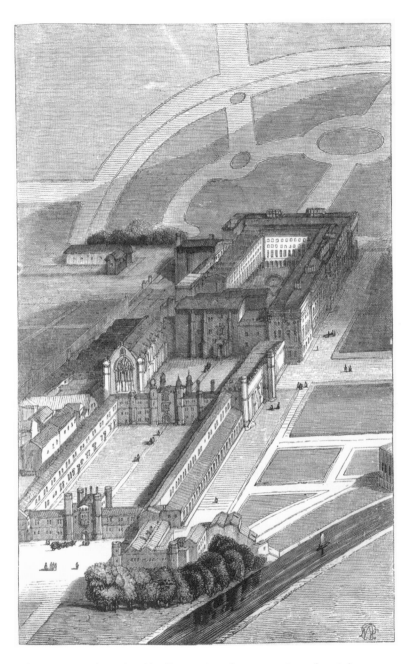

The imaginatively rendered bird's-eye view of Hampton Court from John Murray's *A Picturesque Tour of the River Thames* (1845) shows the Thames flowing past, and a barge under sail.

to places enriched with classical associations', and gives plenty of historical, biographical and cultural detail, devoting several pages to listing every single one of the many paintings which then hung at Hampton Court. At Chertsey Abbey, he muses on the fate of the monks whose many monasteries once bordered the Thames, and quotes a macabre discovery described by the antiquary William Stukeley (1687–1765) in his 1724 *Itinerarium Curiosum*. In the grounds of the house that had replaced the abbey, Stukeley found a fashionably picturesque artificial mount

> entirely made up of the sacred rudera [debris] and rubbish of continual devastations. Human bones of the abbots, monks, and great personages, who were buried in great numbers in the church and cloisters, which lay on the south side of the church, were spread thick all over the garden, which takes up the whole church and cloisters; so that one may pick up handfuls of bits of bones at a time everywhere among the garden-stuff.

Murray suggests a voyage by steamer from Lambeth to Richmond, then taking a local train to Twickenham, and walking the towpath to admire the many riverside villas with famous literary associations. Getting an omnibus all the way from Piccadilly to Hampton Court will 'avoid the unseemly struggling for places in the omnibuses which so often occurs at railway stations'. Finally he suggests riding the Great Western Railway all the way to Slough as the best way to reach Windsor.

In the second half of the century, delight in the picturesque was diluted with personal experiences and practical advice. *The Royal River: The Thames from Source to Sea* (1885) is a hefty folio designed to be shown off on Victorian display tables. Each chapter is written by a knowledgeable local author, and lavishly illustrated with attractive photogravures and engravings. An artist is shown sketching at Streatley Mill. Aaron Watson praises the aesthetic atmosphere of the river below London Bridge:

The island by Shiplake Lock, 'a favourite camping-out spot for boating-men who do not fear the risk of rheumatism' according to W. Senior, describing the river between Streatley and Henley in *The Royal River* (1885).

You will find it stated in most books on the subject that the river ceases to be picturesque when it has passed St. Paul's. A French poet calls it 'an infected sea, rolling its black waters in sinuous detours'... Yet in the eyes of those who have roamed about this section of the river, and have loved it, only at London Bridge does the Thames become really interesting. In the higher reaches it is an idyllic river, swooning along through pleasant landscapes; after St. Paul's it takes on a new and more sombre sort of glory, assumes a mightier interest, and is infinitely more majestic in the lifting of its waters. Above London Bridge, even when the wind is blowing, the waves are small and broken, like those of a mountain lake; in the Pool the water surges and heaves in broad masses, the light seems to deal with it more nobly, and the Thames assumes such majesty as becomes a stream which flows through the grandest city, and bears so great a portion of the commerce, of the world.

There are little maps of each section of the river, showing railway stations. An island near Shiplake Lock 'is a favourite camping-out spot for boating-men who do not fear the risk of rheumatism, and who prefer a night on shore to the cramped and unsatisfactory repose attempted by those who decide to spend the night in their boats'.

Geraldine Mitton's *The Thames* (1906) has some lively anecdotes, but her narrative is mainly a vehicle for sumptuous illustrations by Mortimer Menpes. Mitton (1868–1965) was an adventurous travel writer whose *A Bachelor Girl in Burma* (1907) still makes fascinating reading. Before heading to the East, she wrote a dozen or more books about London; she would later collaborate with her husband, the colonial administrator Sir George Scott, on four novels set in the Far East. The Australian-born painter Menpes (1855–1938) was a pupil of Whistler and an accomplished etcher, who supplemented his income by illustrating travel books. Perhaps seduced by the experience of illustrating *The Thames*, he moved to Pangbourne a year later and spent the rest of his life there, running flower and fruit farms. Although their book only describes the river between Oxford and Windsor, it has over a hundred colour plates and chapter heads of the cottage garden school, many featuring winsome damsels punting or paddling. Mitton's prose is flowery and romantic, and a shade bathetic.

> After rain, when the water comes thundering over the weirs in translucent hoops of vivid green, and the boiling foam below dances like whipped cream, to walk along the sedgy banks is to leave a trail of 'squish-squash' with every step. All the yellow and brown flat-leaved green things that grow thickly near the edges are barely able to keep their heads above the stream, and the long reeds bend with the current like curved swords. Every little tributary gushes gurgling to join in the mad race, and the sounds that tell of water are in our ears like the instruments in an orchestra. There are the rush, the dip, and the tinkle, as well as the deep-throated roar. Watching and listening, we feel a strange sympathy with the new life brought by the increased current; we feel as if it were flooding through our own veins, and as if we, like the squirming, wriggling things that live in the slime

below the flood-curtain, were waking up anew after a long torpor.

The invention of the camera added a new dimension to recording the picturesque quality of the Thames. The most artistic of Thames photographers was the Oxford-born and -bred Henry Taunt (1842–1922). He produced short illustrated guides to villages and towns local to Oxford, as well as a succession of immensely popular maps and pocket guides to the river. All were illustrated with his startlingly crisp and well-framed photographs. He loved the river, and travelled along it in a houseboat which sported a camera on a tripod on its roof. Taunt's photographs are a feature of the last Thames book specifically devoted to the picturesque, John Leyland's *The Thames Illustrated: A Picturesque Journeying from Richmond to Oxford* (1897). To modern eyes, the reproductions seem a little drab, but there are some gems among

Artistic renderings of the Thames and its environs were the speciality of Oxfordshire photographer and mapmaker Henry Taunt (1842–1922), seen here in 1895 on his houseboat, which was topped by a camera on a tripod.

Father Thames sitting to Henry W. Taunt for his Photograph.

Henry W. Taunt's

ARTISTIC PHOTOGRAPHS OF

THAMES ✳ SCENERY

EMBRACE EVERY POINT OF INTEREST,

FROM THAMES HEAD TO THE NORE,

THIS SERIES NOW NUMBERS OVER FOUR THOUSAND VIEWS.

Extract from letter:—

"Your photographs are by far the finest published of our dear Old Father Thames."

CATALOGUES GRATIS AND POST FREE.

SELECTIONS SENT ON APPROVAL.

HENRY W. TAUNT & CO., OXFORD.

Taunt was also the author of numerous local guidebooks; this comic advertisement of his services appeared in *Goring, Streatley and the Neighbourhood* (1894).

its 300 and more photographs. 'Kennington Reach: a Sailing Race' is full of movement, 'Boulter's Lock' predictably chaotic. They are taken by a variety of photographers, including Henry Taunt and Francis Frith. Leyland over-eggs his subject; few paragraphs pass without a 'delightful' this or a 'picturesque' that, but he supplies copious curious facts and literary references. I like the idea of Charles James Fox taking his ease in his house overlooking the river at Chertsey, 'sitting on a haycock, reading novels, and watching the jays stealing his cherries'.

THAMES EXPLORERS

We go as an inoffensive tourist, in search of traditions, in search of antiquities, in search of poetry, in search of fresh breezes, in search of fish.

Charles Mackay, *The Thames and Its Tributaries* (1840)

Concurrently with seekers after the picturesque, early Victorian tourists explored the river in the tradition of the early chorographers, fascinated by the history and literature of the river and its adjacent countryside. They published their experiences in the form of more personally voiced but still proudly patriotic guides to the river. Among the earliest is the short and amusingly opinionated *A Tour on the Banks of the Thames from London to Oxford* by A Pedestrian (1834), which was privately printed 'for distribution among a small circle of friends and acquaintances' by a Mr A. Walton.

On 'a fine autumn morning' in 1829, Walton sets off from Islington for Fulham, crossing the river at Putney, 'a pretty village, having several gentlemen's seats'. On Richmond Hill, 'variety is presented in all the witchery of winning ways: alike the mossy tower, the stately palace, the luxurious villa, and the humble shed'. After revelling in the peaceful countryside between Twickenham and Kingston, and describing Hampton Court, he spends some pages defending the idea that Coway Stakes were indeed a defence against Caesar. He pauses respectfully at Runnymede and climbs Cooper's Hill. A long account of Eton, 'the finest school in all the British dominions', is followed by a brief nod at Windsor and a moonlight walk to Maidenhead, which 'dwells in the memory as a fairy scene'. Admiring Cliveden's 'assemblage of the romantic and the sublime' and cottagey Cookham, he reaches Henley, then peaceful in pre-regatta days. He visits the aviary and the Druid's Temple above Park Place, and admires the view from Shiplake Church. At Sonning, he enjoys 'the sweet ambrosia of a veritable Havana, of which your true pedestrian always carries a store'.

Oxford is described at length, before Walton signs off with praise of 'pedestrianising' over other forms of travel.

Pierce Egan's *The Pilgrims of the Thames, in Search of the National* (1838) is a light-hearted and patriotic account of a series of excursions made by three jolly Londoners called Makemoney, Flourish and Sprightly. Egan (1779–1849) relished popular culture, and was well known for his commentaries on prizefights and horse races. As the plethora of faces on the frontispiece of his book suggests, Egan is more interested in conveying national character through the people that his young heroes encounter than in the river itself, though historical and literary associations are noted. Makemoney concludes proudly that 'The more I visit old Father Thames, the more I am delighted with my native country … The inroads of war can never interrupt its peace and happiness; and the simple peasant sits down contented by his fire-side with the blessings of liberty attendant upon every meal; other countries cannot make such a boast.'[6]

Patriotism is also to the fore in Charles Mackay's *The Thames and Its Tributaries*. 'Rivers are rich in remembrances', he declares. 'To them are attached all the poetry and romance of a nation'. He aims 'to act the part of a gossiping, not prosy, fellow traveller'.

> If thou art an antiquary, we also have some sneaking affection for thy hobby, and will now and then throw thee a tit-bit for it. If thou art an angler, and fishest with a rod, we will show thee all the best places in the river from Vauxhall Bridge to Crick lade; or, if thou preferest to cast thy nets, we will accompany thee from London Bridge to Margate. If thou lovest water-sports, we will discourse to thee on that subject, and tell thee a thing or two worth knowing about river pageants, boat-races, and sailing-matches, and something also about some rare old games of the water, which have now fallen into disuse. …
>
> Sometimes we may travel at railway speed, and at others linger about for days in one spot, sauntering over the hills, sitting under the trees, by the riverside, but conning all the while something for thy edification and amusement.

His first volume proceeds from London to Oxford; the second goes downstream from London to Hever Castle. Since he wanders up tributaries and to interesting places in the Thames Valley, he manages to fill over 800 pages.

As it became easier to explore the river by road and rail, guides to the Thames flourished. In 1849, James Thorne (1815–1872) published a book on the Thames as the last in his series of *Rambles by Rivers*. Thorne's forte was history, and there is little reference to the picturesque in his pages. His writing is marked by frankness. Cricklade is 'dull to live in, dull to look at, and dull to talk about'; Faringdon is 'a wearisome place to spend a wet day'; Cumnor 'has little to reward the visitor'; Abingdon is 'quiet, clean and dull'; the 'peasantry' of the Chiltern Hills 'are among the most uncouth in England'; bottom fishing from punts is 'monstrously monotonous'. From Lechlade, a public path runs along the river almost all the way to London, but the rambler will require 'Odcombian shoes' to walk in, for

> it is not, as he may suppose, a narrow winding path, worn
> out of the soft green grass by the foot of the pensive angler
> or patient pilgrim, with daisies and celandines and other
> field-flowers on either side of it, but, on the contrary, it is
> a broad towing-path for horses, formed of flint-stones and
> flanked by a ditch – at least that is its general character. At
> times the rough flints give place to sand, at others to mud.
> He must make the best of it.[7]

Thorne could, however, be generous in his praise, not just of well-known places but of

> quiet nooks where the angler finds just employment enough
> to give a relish to his meditations, and the rambler is
> tempted to lie down and let the minutes roll away in dreamy
> enjoyment. Willows, alders, and poplars skirt the banks,
> and send their contorted roots into the stream; while their
> reflected forms and colours mingle with the hue imparted to
> the water by the tints of the sky.

Like Murray, Thorne recommends making a series of excursions from different points to explore the river, its tributaries, and nearby places of interest, rather than merely journeying along the length of the river. He thought Goring a particularly fine base.

> The river expands to a great width, so as to enclose a large island, or rather a chain of islands, which occupies the centre of it, and is clothed with goodly trees. On the right of the island is a lock, on the left are the mill and weir, and beyond is the grim old tower of Goring church rising from the light vapoury smoke of the little village. ... A glimpse is caught of the village of Streatley on the opposite bank, and the lofty Berkshire downs close in the distance, while all the nearer objects are repeated in the clear water.

He skips London itself, as its proper treatment 'would require a volume in itself', and takes a sailing skiff from Greenwich to The Nore, signing off with lines from Abraham Cowley's lament for the days 'when all the Riches of the Globe beside / Flow'd in to Thee with every Tide' and 'all the liquid World was one extended Thames'.[8]

Thorne's convenient pocket-sized volume was much thumbed by Samuel Carter Hall (1800–1889) and his wife Anna Maria Fielding (1800–1881), whose rambling and idiosyncratic *The Book of the Thames from its Rise to its Fall* was published in 1859. The Halls gratefully acknowledged their many debts to Thorne, 'a scholar, a gentleman, a close observer, and a lover of nature'. Carter Hall, whose writing has the air of being delivered from the pulpit, was an influential art critic and editor of *The Art Journal*. He was identified by Nathaniel Hawthorne's son Julian as the inspiration for Charles Dickens's hypocritical and sanctimonious Mr Pecksniff. Anna Maria, plain, plump and self-effacing, was the author of novels about her native Ireland, as well as improving books for children; 'She does it all. Hall is an 'umbug', said the critic Thomas Purnell.[9]

The Halls were in their late fifties when they researched and wrote *The Book of the Thames*. Besides noting the picturesque qualities of the 'King of Island Rivers', it records architecture, history, botany and natural history, and is well-laced with literary allusion. A succession of artists travelled with them on their many expeditions, and the book is a cornucopia of intriguing details of Thames life, with over 300 illustrations. Carter Hall contributed grandiloquent comments on the river's picturesque qualities and arcane historical and architectural information. He was also a keen fishermen, and provided both advice to fellow 'brethren of the angle' and the names of local experts. Anna Maria specialised in nature notes and dramatic anecdotes often only loosely connected to the river.

At Castle Eaton, Carter mourned the replacement of the old village schools hung with creepers and surrounded by flowers, and once 'nearest in picturesque effect to the village church', by raw redbrick or cold white stone National Schools. Anna told the story of a wronged wife who became a dame at an old-style village school not far from the river. At Bablockhythe they meet Tom Hirsell, an owl-finder who had 'imbibed some of the owl nature', and had a sleepy look, moving his head 'in a sort of half circle as he spoke'. Nearing Oxford, Binsey church 'has a heart-broken look', but the University's paper mill at Wolvercote is deemed to have 'a picturesque character' and duly appears in an engraving. So, too, do the many towers and spires of 'ancient and venerable Oxford' then visible from Port Meadow. 'Nowhere do we obtain a more striking view' say the Halls; today the view is ruined by a line of eight hideous student blocks erected by the University in 2012.

Oxford itself is passed over, since 'the visitor will readily lay his hand on one of the many books in which it is ... described fully', but the Halls wax lyrical on the variety of river craft encountered downstream of Folly Bridge: the two-oared 'skimmers', the little pleasure yachts, the massive barges used as clubhouses by college rowers, and the houseboats. Henley's regattas are described, and much is made of the mansions ancient and modern that fringe the river's banks. The 'sense of solitude' higher upstream is now lost, and the river 'takes on a more busy and active character'. They were writing just as the freight trains that ran on Brunel's new Great Western Railway were spelling the decline of working boats, and such Thameside stations as Goring and Maidenhead were allowing the invasion of London holidaymakers in their thousands.

Rowing beneath the thick woods of Taplow and Cliveden, where 'taste, in association with wealth, [renders] every part delightful', Thames tourists 'will have no difficulty in imagining themselves in one of the grandest and richest, in picturesque attractions, of our English lakes'. After devoting some forty pages to Eton and Windsor, they praise the 'solitude and fine fishing' at Penton Hook. As they arrive at Chertsey, its traditional curfew is tolling (once for each day of the month), and they admire the staircase up a gigantic oak tree outside the Golden Grove. They provide a useful plan of the maze at Hampton Court, and describe the 'Seething Wells' waterworks at Walton in detail. The Halls excelled in explaining how things worked, and offered intricate drawings of the weir paddles, winches and towing posts that helped boats navigate the often tricky waters of the river. They show a steam-powered dredger in action off Millbank. Charles Barry's rebuilt Westminster 'starts up like a glorious giant from the hovels near it', and hay boats with 'brilliantly-coloured hulls' unload near Isambard Kingdom Brunel's elegant Hungerford Suspension Bridge.[10]

Below London Bridge they board a steamship, from which they admire Greenwich, then the home of thousands of veterans and also source of whitebait dinners, 'a treat peculiar to the metropolis'. They note the mouth of the Lea 'made famous by Isaak Walton', see Shooter's Hill from a distance, and admire the many 'picturesque hulks, reminding one of olden times and fights long past'. Erith is voted 'one of the most charming spots on the

Carter and Anna Hall were especially interested in the new technology that was making the Thames more easily navigable: their *The Book of the Thames* (1859) explained the workings of this steam-powered dredger off Millbank.

river'. They glimpse Gad's Hill, Cliffe, and the entrance to the Medway. The last pages of the book describe the lightship at The Nore, and the Reculvers, the twin peaks of the ruined church that was once Reculver Abbey. 'The voyager is now on the open sea, but still, so to speak, on the territory of England', for 'the ocean waves that roll around our coast are the fortifications that protect us.' They close the book with patriotic fervour and a quotation from Thomas Campbell's 'Ye Mariners of England' (1800):

> Britannia needs no bulwarks,
> No towers along the steep;
> Her march is o'er the mountain-waves,
> Her home is on the deep.

For the early explorers, the Thames was more than just a beautiful and historic waterway. It was the symbolic heart of England, and to praise it enhanced the nation's sense of self-worth. Fred Thacker, who devoted his life to the river, deserves special mention in this context. His approach to writing its history combined pragmatism and romance. His first book, an account of his own journey from Osney to the river's source, reads like a love

Reculver Church on the Isle of Thanet (now far more ruinous than when it was painted by James Ward in 1818) is the 'last prominent object on the Kentish coast that will attract the attention of the voyager down the river before he reaches the open sea' (*The Book of the Thames*, 1859).

letter. He called the plump green volume *The Stripling Thames* and published it in 1909 at his own expense. The title page sets the tone with two lines from Horace and a frontispiece showing his chosen conveyance, a skiff called *Phasellus Ille* ('That Boat', a name taken from a poem by Catullus). He burrowed in libraries (especially the Bodleian) and quizzed local people to uncover a phenomenal amount of history, folklore and literary association to enrich the reader's understanding not just of the Thames but of the villages north and south of the river.

In the introduction Thacker nails his colours to the mast. 'I write for no maker and breaker of records, for none who delights in engines of locomotion, whether on land or water'. Travelling without mechanical assistance is crucial. 'You must traverse its roads upon your feet, and pull and steer your craft along its winding reaches with your own arms'. Thacker's prose is both informed and arresting. The breadth of knowledge he displays both of the river itself, its fords, weirs, locks, bridges and inns past and present, and of the towns and villages within 5 miles of it, made me realise how superficial my own excursions had been. He was not averse to risk.

> The one real adventure of river life still survives at Hart's Weir; and for many years may it flourish with its white rymers and paddles, and fresh tumbling water filling the air all day long with the murmurous sound ... Your lightened boat is pulled over with a rope, going upstream; and shoots through all aboard going down, guided by a pole from the bank, with an exhilarating swirl that sweeps you far away before you can get your sculls out.

The Stripling Thames is my own favourite book about the river, but Thacker's greatest achievement was *The Thames Highway: A History of the Inland Navigation* (1914), which cites a formidable number of obscure chronicles and legal records. The first volume tells the frequently dramatic story of how the competing interests of millers, fisheries and barge-masters were gradually regulated first by local commissions and finally by the Thames Conservancy. The second volume details the history of all the locks and weirs that had ever existed on the river above Teddington, from a 'primordial water pen' of 1066 to the improved 'pound locks' of his own time.

Thacker was exceptional in his scholarly rigour and his respect for the men and women who worked the river's locks, weirs and commercial boats. As the Victorian Thames became thronged with pleasure-seekers of all classes, interest in the picturesque and the patriotic was replaced by snobbery and concern for personal comforts. It was also the golden age of fictional accounts of the river. But before turning to the glorious days of Jerome K. Jerome and Max Beerbohm, we will break away from river journeys and consider the writers who loved the Thames so much that they elected to live beside it.

THREE

WRITERS'
RETREATS

L IVING beside the Thames has been popular with writers
for centuries. Anonymous and solitary retreats of one sort
or another are dotted along its course; some are humble shacks
at the end of riverside gardens, some boats discreetly moored in
quiet reaches. There is something about the river's sureness of
itself, its purposeful motion, sometimes fast, sometimes slow, that
propels one's own thoughts and words onwards. Although all
writers need peace, not all demand solitude. Like-minded spirits
gathered together in a variety of locations along the Thames. The
Thames at Chelsea, an easy boat ride or even walk from the city,
has been home to a host of distinguished scribblers for centuries.
The stylish literary colony that grew up around Alexander Pope's
and Horace Walpole's villas at Twickenham was a briefer phenomenon; its members travelled in elegant barouches and barges
to visit each other, and to reach London when they wished to.

As London became unhealthy, squalid and fogged with smoke,
writers drifted further afield, using the improved roads and the
railways to reach such distant retreats as the pretty riverside
village of Marlow, which offered Thomas Love Peacock, Percy
Bysshe and Mary Shelley, and James Leigh Hunt not only charming and inexpensive lodgings but stimulating companionship.

Horace Walpole in his library at Strawberry Hill, posing pensively beside a
window through which the Thames can be seen. Stipple and line engraving
made in 1858 by William Greatbach, after a painting by Johann Heinrich Muntz,
'resident artist' at the house 1755–59.

Even further afield is Oxford, home of a legion of more or less successful writers, many of whom have found special solace in the distractions of its web of waterways, and featured them in their writing.

The ultimate enthusiast for living and working by the Thames, and the owner of its most delightful literary retreat, was William Morris, who swam, fished, rowed and sailed on the river all his life. He printed stunningly beautiful books at his house by the river in Hammersmith, and revelled in the peace of Kelmscott Manor near Lechlade. His fantasy of the future, *News from Nowhere*, was in part a stirring call for a return to simple community life, in part a love letter to the river that was such a centre point of his life.

HAUNT OF SAGE AND SEAGULL

I sit here with my big south window open to the River, open wide, and a sort of healing balm of sunshine flooding the place. Truly I feel I did well for myself in perching – even thus modestly for a 'real home' – just on this spot.

Henry James to Mrs William James, March 1913

The village of Chelsea's first famous literary resident was the humanist scholar Sir Thomas More (1478–1535). He built his riverside house there in 1524–5; it was convenient for both Richmond and Greenwich, Henry VIII's favourite palaces. Described by More's friend the painter Hans Holbein as 'dignified without being ostentatious', the house had acres of gardens and orchards; a 1591 copy of Holbein's portrait of the More family shows these and the river beyond. More built a library with a chapel attached to it in the garden. In his *Dialogue of Comfort against Tribulation* (1553), he suggested that a man should

choose himself some secret solitary place in his own house as far from noise and company as he conveniently can. And

Sir Thomas More's Thameside garden can be seen through the window of Rowland Lockey's 1593 watercolour-on-vellum version of the famous portrait by Hans Holbein the Younger of Sir Thomas More and his family.

> thither let him some time secretly resort alone, imagining himself as one going out of the world even straight unto the giving up his reckoning unto God of his sinful living.

More would also spend his last hours looking over the Thames, from the Bell Tower, in the Tower of London.

A century and a half after More's death, Chelsea was still thought of as attractively distant from the hubbub of the city. It was praised for 'the sweetness of its air and pleasant situation' by John Bowack, who lived there while he was writing his *The Antiquities of Middlesex* (1705–6). It could boast the well-maintained

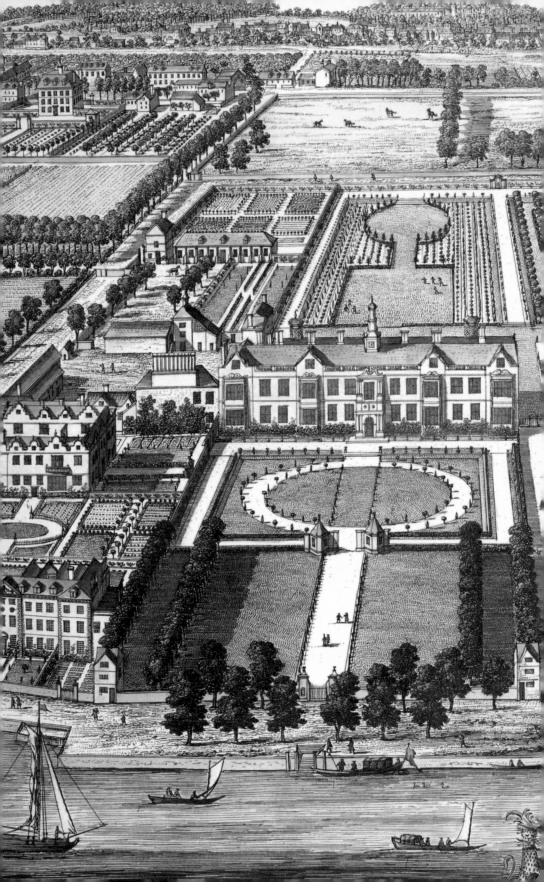

King's Road, and such fine buildings as Christopher Wren's handsome Royal Hospital for retired and disabled servicemen, which opened in the 1680s. Jonathan Swift lived in Chelsea for a year or so, arriving in the summer of 1711. 'I design, if possible, to go to lodge in Chelsea for the air' he wrote to Stella, as he called his protegée Esther Johnson, adding that he planned to walk into the city, fortified by one of the famous Chelsea Buns ('a zephyr in taste, fragrant as honey') that were the speciality of the Bun House, a local bakery.[1]

By the nineteenth century, Chelsea was thronged with writers, poets and artists. Cheyne Row, which led to the river, and Cheyne Walk, which had gardens fronting on it, were especially popular. The poet, critic and campaigning journalist James Leigh Hunt (1784–1859) settled in 1833 at 4 Upper Cheyne Row, where he remained until 1840. In 1834, he helped Thomas and Jane Carlyle find a property at nearby 5 (now 24). Carlyle wrote to Ruskin in 1874 to praise the Embankment designed by Joseph Bazalgette which opened that year:

> Miles of the noblest Promenade. The Thames pushing grandly past you, & even at low-water leaving a foot or two of *pure* gravel; a labyrinthic [sic] flower-garden, subsidiary walks, & grand pavements; Cheyne Walk looking altogether royal on you through the old umbrage & the new … To me it will be a great resource for the rest of my appointed days here. In another 50 years, were the shrubs & saplings all grown, I think it would be admitted universally that there is no other such pretty region in all London and its environs.

Chelsea's most eccentric resident was the artist and poet Dante Gabriel Rossetti (1828–1882), who lived with his family and many other animals at Tudor House (now 16 Cheyne Walk) between

PREVIOUS SPREAD Chelsea's busy waterfront and extensive gardens can be seen in this bird's-eye view of Beaufort House, once owned by Sir Thomas More, but renamed by the Dukes of Beaufort, who lived there between 1682 and 1738. Coloured engraving by Johannes Kip after a painting by Jacob Knyff (c.1720).

1862 and 1882. The menagerie he kept in their garden included at various times a bull, a kangaroo, monkeys, a salamander, an owl, an armadillo and a wombat; the last was brought to the table to amuse guests and is said to have inspired the Dormouse in *Alice's Adventures in Wonderland* (1865). Charles Dodgson visited in 1863 and photographed Rossetti with his second wife Elizabeth Siddall, his mother and his sister, the poet Christina Rossetti, in the garden.

After his marriage to Florence Balcombe in 1878, the theatre manager and novelist Bram Stoker (1847–1912) lived at 27 Cheyne Walk. He pulled a would-be suicide out of the Thames, and carried him into the house, but the man died on his kitchen table. A few years later, Stoker moved a block or two away from the river to Durham Place (now St Leonard's Terrace), which is where he wrote *Dracula*. His next novel *Miss Betty* was a romance set in eighteenth-century Cheyne Walk; the story centres around Rafe Otwell, an up-and-coming waterman, who first sees Miss Betty during the preparations for the famous race among the watermen known as Doggett's Coat and Badge. She is jolted into the water when a clumsy barge collides with her boat. Rafe leaps after her, but finds that they are both in peril from the press of craft around. He promptly dives under water with her in his arms and swims clear, surfacing near his own boat, and handing her to his oarsmen, gasping 'Take the lady'.

> Four strong hands raised her and lifted her into the barge
> whilst he himself clung to the gunwale, panting. Instantly
> all those around began to cheer in true British fashion; even
> those in the mass of boats up and down and across the stream
> who had not seen what had happened but knew from the
> struggling and the pressing together of the boats and by the
> cheers that something unusual had taken place, took up the
> shout.

As a young man, Arthur Ransome lived in Chelsea when he was working on his *Bohemia in London* (1907), a lively autobiographical account of the writers and artists he met when he was an aspiring literary critic. Among them was Hilaire Belloc, who wrote *The River of London* (1912) while living at 104 Cheyne Walk. Ransome also wrote a literary critique of Oscar Wilde, whose fine poems about the river, written when he lived in Tite Street, Chelsea, appear in Chapter VII. Ransome returned to London's riverside in 1950, when he acquired a handsome mansion flat overlooking the Thames in Hurlingham Court, Fulham, and kept a sailing dinghy at the nearby London Corinthian Sailing Club.

Built in 1886 on the site of the Three Cricketers Inn and the Thames Coffee House and named for Thomas Carlyle, Carlyle Mansions is an imposing riverside block of apartments that offer the comfort and convenience of a flat inside the elegant proportions of a great house. 'This Chelsea perch, this haunt of sage and seagull, proved, even after a brief experiment, just the thing for me' declared Henry James, who took a four-year lease on number 21 in 1912 as a winter alternative to his Sussex home in Rye, Lamb House. His fondness for the river was established during a visit to London forty years earlier; watching the Boat Race in 1876, he admired 'the great, white, water-skimming birds with eight-feathered wings'; he also visited the 'great and strange and more or less sinister D G Rossetti', and was struck by 'the really interesting and delightful old Thames-side Chelsea' with its 'admirable water-view'. James's most vivid picturing of the Thames comes in his *English Hours* (1906). He recommends an excursion down the river to Greenwich 'where there is a charming old park, on a summit of one of whose grassy undulations the famous observatory is perched'.

> To do the thing completely you must take passage upon one of the little grimy sixpenny steamers that ply upon the Thames, perform the journey by water, and then, disembarking, take a stroll in the park to get up an appetite for dinner. I find an irresistible charm in any sort of river-navigation, but I scarce know how to speak of the little voyage from Westminster Bridge to Greenwich. It is in truth the most prosaic possible

form of being afloat, and to be recommended rather to the enquiring than to the fastidious mind. It initiates you into the duskiness, the blackness, the crowdedness, the intensely commercial character of London. Few European cities have a finer river than the Thames, but none certainly has expended more ingenuity in producing a sordid river-front.

James also knew the upper Thames, visiting Cliveden on several occasions. It may have inspired the setting of *Portrait of a Lady* (1881), which opens on the lawn of Gardencourt, an ancient country house on the banks of 'the reedy, silvery Thames' 40 miles from London. Isabel, Ralph and Henrietta spend long afternoons rowing on the river. James died in his Chelsea perch in February 1916.

William Somerset Maugham penned *The Merry-Go-Round*, a collection of sharp little stories about Londoners, while living at 27 Carlyle Mansions in 1904. Erskine Childers lived with his family first at number 20, where he wrote *The Riddle of the Sands* (1903), and later at number 16. T.S. Eliot lived at number 19 from 1946 to 1957, and found the name of the main protagonist in *The Cocktail Party* (1949) on a gravestone to Edward Chamberlayne in Chelsea Old Church. Ian Fleming wrote his first Bond book, *Casino Royale*, at number 24 in 1952. Unsurprisingly Carlyle Mansions has gained the nickname the 'Writer's Block'.

Virginia Woolf set her 1919 novel *Night and Day* in Chelsea, where Mrs Hilbery has a Cheyne Walk home. The river, especially at night, recurs as a motif, a symbol of the dark depths of the subconscious, throughout the book. Fascinated by Katherine, Ralph follows her along the Strand.

Very far off up the river a steamer hooted with its hollow voice of unspeakable melancholy, as if from the heart of lonely mist-shrouded voyagings.

As their acquaintanceship deepens into love, they visit Kew, where Katherine watches as Ralph stopped … and began inquiring of an old boatman as to the tides and the ships. In thus talking he seemed different, and even looked different, she thought, against the river, with the steeples and towers for background. His strangeness, his romance, his power to leave her side and take part in the affairs of men, the possibility that they should together hire a boat and cross the river, the speed and wildness of this enterprise filled her mind and inspired her with … rapture, half of love and half of adventure.

In the last paragraph, as she and Ralph walk back to the Hilberys' house, their love at last resolved, they look 'down into the river which bore its dark tide of waters, endlessly moving, beneath them'.

TWIT'NAM'S BOWERS

At the name of this village, the imagination glows! Learning, wit and poetical genius have rendered the neighbourhood classic ground.

Ernest Brayley, 1810

Far removed from the bustle of the city, yet linked to it by water and road, the peaceful banks of the river at Twickenham were immediately attractive to those inclined to literature. Among the earliest eminent writers to settle there was the philosopher and statesman Sir Francis Bacon (1561–1626), Viscount St Albans. From 1580 to 1608 he lived at Twickenham Park, which fronted the river opposite Richmond on the western border of Isleworth. 'One day draweth on another, and I am well pleased in my being here, for methinks solitariness collecteth the mind as shutting the eyes doth the sight', he wrote in a letter of October 1594 to his brother Anthony.[2] It was at Twickenham that he wrote his *The Advancement of Learning* (1605) and many of his *Essays*; he also laid out an elaborate garden, of which a 1609 plan survives, probably drawn by Robert Smythson. Debts forced Bacon to sell

Alexander Pope believed in the 'genius of the place': his Twickenham villa had an exquisite setting on the banks of the Thames. He lived there with his elderly mother, his childhood nurse Mary Beach and a hound named Bounce.

the house in 1608; when his fortunes improved and he was made Lord Chancellor in 1618, he tried to buy it back in order to set up an institute for the study of mineralogy, 'since I experimentally found the situation of that place much convenient for the trial of philosophical conclusions', he wrote in a memorandum to his servant.

The house retained its literary importance under its next occupant, the independently minded Lucy Harrington, Countess of Bedford and Lady of the Bedchamber to Queen Anne. Herself a poet, she made Twickenham Park a meeting place for poets, writers and wits. Among them was John Donne, who lived nearby, valued her friendship greatly, and wrote elegies for members of her family; she in return paid his debts just before his ordination in 1614. At some point he wrote 'Twickenham Garden' an elegant metaphysical tribute from a forlorn lover to the 'true paradise' of her renowned garden.

Alexander Pope (1688–1744) spent his childhood close to the Thames at Binfield, in Windsor Forest, after his linen-draper father acquired the small estate he called Popeswood in 1700, and the river runs through his work like the lifeline on a hand. His long poem 'Windsor Forest' (1713) guaranteed him a place among London's literati, and he became a leading member of the Scriblerus Club, which was dedicated to satirising the pretentious. Pope was widely admired for his barbed wit; he was reputed to have 'the voice of a nightingale matched to the tongue of a wasp'. In 1714 his *The Rape of the Lock* was published to general acclaim. It is a satire on high society, in which the beautiful Belinda is 'launched upon the bosom of the silver Thames', and voyages down the river to Hampton Court, where a wicked Baron snips off one of her two glorious ringlets, occasioning a tantrum: 'then flash'd the living lightning from her eyes, / And screams of horror rend th' affrighted skies'.

In 1716 Pope joined his parents in their new house close to the Thames in Chiswick (now the Mawson Arms), where he completed his translation of Homer's *Iliad*, which he had undertaken to print by subscription, publishing a volume annually between 1715 and 1720. The six-volume work – sold to 525 subscribers, some of whom wanted two sets – was a huge success, netting Pope over £5,000. This enabled him to finance an annuity income and to buy the riverside property at Twickenham on which he commissioned the little mansion that became legendary as Pope's Villa. Pope thought the setting around a house ('the genius of the place') was just as important as the house itself, and was then advising Lord Bathurst on the laying out of the grounds of his great house at Cirencester, close to the source of the Thames.[3] At Twickenham, he let his imagination run riot. In a 1725 letter to his friend Edmund Blount, he wrote:

Pope sitting in his shell- and mirror-glass-encrusted grotto, which was the central feature of a tunnel that ran from the cellars of the house under the road behind it to extensive gardens, and had views both to the river and to the gardens. Pen and ink drawing by William Kent (c.1725).

I have put the last hand to my works, finishing the subterraneous way and grotto. I there found a spring of the clearest water, which falls in a perpetual rill, that echoes through the Cavern day and night. From the river Thames, you see through my arch up a walk of the wilderness to a kind of open temple wholly composed of shells in the rustic manner; and from that distance under the temple, you look down through a sloping arcade of trees, and see the sails on the river passing suddenly and vanishing as through a perspective glass. When you shut the doors of this grotto it becomes on the instant, from a luminous room, a *Camera Obscura*, on the walls of which all the objects of the river, hills, woods and boats are forming a moving picture in their visible radiations; and when you have a mind to light it up, it affords you a very different scene.

It is finished with shells interspersed with pieces of looking-glass in angular forms; and in the ceiling is a star of the same material, at which when a lamp, of an orbicular figure of thin alabaster, is hung in the middle, a thousand pointed rays glitter, and are reflected over the place. There are connected to this grotto by a narrower passage two porches with niches and seats – one towards the river, of smooth stones, full of light and open; the other towards the arch of trees, rough with shells, flints and iron-ore. The bottom is painted with simple pebble, and the adjoining walk up the wilderness to the temple is to be cockle-shells, in the natural taste, agreeing not ill with the little dripping murmur, and the aquatic idea of the whole place.

Scriblerus Club friends often came by river to visit Pope. Jonathan Swift, Henry Fielding and Voltaire, an exile in England between 1726 and 1729, stayed frequently. John Gay wrote *The Beggar's Opera* in a summerhouse on the river at Petersham.

In 1747, Henry Fielding 'laid out all my money at present in purchasing a little Estate at Twickenham'; discretion was demanded when, after his first wife's death, he married her maid Mary Daniel with what some thought was indecent haste. Mary gave birth to their son there, while Henry worked on *Tom Jones*, which was published in 1749.

'Barges as solemn as Barons of the Exchequer move under my window; Richmond Hill and Ham Walks bound my prospect ... and Pope's ghost is just now skimming under the window in a most poetical moonlight' wrote Horace Walpole of Chopped Straw Hall, the 'little plaything-house' that he acquired as a summer retreat on the Thames between Twickenham and Teddington in 1747. 'A small Euphrates through the piece is rolled', he joked in a letter to his cousin Henry Conway; it was a borrowed line from Pope's *Epistle to Mr Addison*.[4] When he discovered that one of the fields attached to the property was called Strawberry Hill Shot, he rechristened the house, and began to remodel it in the Gothic style, a highly innovative undertaking at a time when the Palladian neoclassicism of Marble Hill and Chiswick House was the general rule. He wrote a *Description of the Villa*, and printed it in 1774 in the printing house he had built in his garden. Passing Strawberry Hill on his tour of the Thames in 1795, William Combe wrote that its arched and ogee windows, pinnacles, turrets, castellations and decorated chimneys 'compose a very pleasing and picturesque object as we approach and glide by it'.

Walpole quickly settled down to write and print books to match his creation. *The Castle of Otranto* (1764), inspired by the menacing suit of armour halfway up the house's crepuscular staircase, began a fashion for Gothic fiction that survives to this day. His essay *The History of the Modern Taste in Gardening* (1771) suggested creating landscapes that related to literature and art, and introduced the idea of the ha-ha, a 'sunk fence' that drew a line 'between the near and the rude'. Gardens, he wrote, 'focus the art of place-making or landscape architecture in the way that poetry can focus the art of writing'. Walpole's greatest literary achievements were his voluminous memoirs and his letters, by turn intimate, satirical, outrageous and amusing, and full of the gossip of the age. Thomas Gray, who was at Eton with Walpole,

Strawberry Hill after Walpole's improvements, by the Swiss painter and architect Johann Muntz (1727–1798). Sailing wherries scud along the Thames; and the town of Twickenham in the distance, looks, wrote Walpole, 'exactly like a seaport in miniature'.

was a frequent visitor. 'I do not know a more laughing scene than about Twickenham and Richmond', he wrote in a letter to Thomas Warton.

The fame of first Pope and then Walpole meant that wealthy groupies flocked to build, buy or rent properties in the muse-haunted environs of Twickenham. 'Dowagers as plenty as flounders inhabit all around', wrote Walpole soon after he acquired Strawberry Hill. He likened Twickenham to Tivoli, and the many waterside mansions between Hampton and Kew to the Palladian villas that lined the Brenta between Padua and Venice. 'At the name of this village, the imagination glows!' wrote Edward Brayley in 1810. 'Learning, wit and poetical genius have rendered the neighbourhood classic ground.'

Walpole gave the renowned comic actress Kitty Clive a little villa next door to Strawberry Hill to live in after her retirement; it was jokingly nicknamed Clive's Den in her honour. After her death in 1785, he gave the villa to sisters Agnes and Mary Berry, whom he met in his seventies and adored ever after. The villa was renamed Little Strawberry Hill, and the sisters were soon known as the Strawberries. Mary, author of several social histories, was largely responsible for editing the handsome five-volume collected works of Walpole published in 1798, a year after his death. The Berry sisters remained life tenants of Little Strawberry Hill. Strawberry Hill itself was inherited by Walpole's former ward, the sculptor Anne Damer (1749–1828). She had been brought up on the Thames at Park Place, near Remenham. Her career flourished after her divorce; Walpole furthered it with enthusiastic reviews of her work, which he likened to that of Bernini. Damer admired the Thames as much as Walpole did, and was responsible for the bas-relief keystones of Thames and Isis on Henley Bridge. 'We went on the Thames to see the new bridge at Henley, and Mrs. Damer's colossal masks', wrote Walpole in August, 1786. 'There is not a sight in the island more worthy of being visited. She and the Berry sisters became firm friends, co-hostessing musical, theatrical and literary events. In 1816, her cousin Mary Georgiana Seymour bought Richmond House, which was actually in Twickenham, and in 1818 Anne Damer bought nearby York House, which had its own theatre.

A little downstream of York House was Marble Hill House, built for George II's mistress Henrietta Howard, Countess of Suffolk, in the 1720s. Pope and his friends were frequent visitors, not least because the countess had an excellent wine cellar. Swift declared that 'Mr Pope was the contriver of the gardens, Lord Herbert the architect, and the Dean of St Patrick's [Swift himself] chief butler and keeper of the ice-house'.[5] Pope thought Lady Howard 'that rare being: a reasonable woman, handsome, witty, yet a friend'. Later Horace Walpole enjoyed gossiping with her over strawberries and cream.

James Thomson (1700–1748), author of the hugely popular poem series *The Seasons* (1725–30), moved to a house on Richmond Green in 1736. In 'Summer', he praises 'the matchless Vale of Thames, / Fair-winding up to where the Muses haunt, / In Twit'nam's bowers'. His other enduring claim to fame was 'Rule Britannia', originally a song in a masque titled *Alfred*, which was set to music by Thomas Arne and sung for the first time in 1740 at Cliveden, then the home of Frederick, Prince of Wales. Thomson's fondness for the river was the death of him. According to Dr Johnson, 'by taking cold on the water between London and Kew, he caught a disorder, which, with some careless exasperation, ended in a fever that put an end to his life'. He was buried in Richmond.

In 1783 Fanny Burney described a visit to Richard Cambridge, poet and editor of *The Scribleriad*, who lived at a villa on the Thames called Twickenham Meadows (later Cambridge Park). 'We had an exceeding pleasant excursion. We went up the river beyond the Duke of Montagu's, and the water was smooth and delightful. Methinks I should like much to sail from the very source to the mouth of the Thames.' Cambridge told her that Edward Gibbon had recently visited, but 'in stepping too lightly from, or to, a boat of Mr Cambridge's, had slipt into the Thames; whence, however, he was intrepidly and immediately rescued, with no other mischief than a wet jacket, by one of that fearless, water-proof race, denominated, by Mr Gibbon, the amphibious family of the Cambridges.'

In 1851 Alfred Lord Tennyson (1809–1892) moved to Chapel (now Holyrood) House, one of the handsome residences in Montpelier Row, which runs along the western boundary of Marble Hill Park down to the Thames. His visitors included Coventry

Patmore, the photographer Julia Cameron, Thomas and Jane Carlyle, John Everett Millais, W.M. Thackeray, Edward Fitzgerald, the sculptor Thomas Woolner and Robert Browning. William Allingham, best known for his poem 'Fairies' ('Up the airy mountain, / Down the rushy glen'), recorded an 1851 visit to Chapel House in his diary. Tennyson read aloud from Allingham's 'Aeolian Harp'; 'the rich, slow solemn chant of his voice glorified the little poem'. It was an appropriate choice for the setting.

> What saith the river to the rushes grey,
> Rushes sadly bending,
> River slowly wending?
> Who can tell the whisper'd things they say?
> Youth, and prime, and life, and time,
> For ever, ever fled away!
> Drop your wither'd garlands in the stream,
> Low autumnal branches,
> Round the skiff that launches
> Wavering downward through the lands of dream.

However, the recently opened railway line from London to Windsor meant that Tennyson, now hugely popular, had too many unwelcome visits from admirers; he also complained that he found the countryside too tame. In 1853 he decamped to the seclusion of the Isle of Wight.

Last in Montpelier Row is Southend House, which fronts on the Thames. Between 1940 and 1956 the poet Walter de la Mare rented it, welcoming such friends as Joyce Grenfell, Richard Church and the glass engraver Laurence Whistler, who inscribed a window looking on to the Thames with four lines from 'Farewell', one of the finest of de la Mare's poems:

> Look thy last on all things lovely
> Every hour. Let no night
> Seal thy sense in deathly slumber
> Till to delight thou hast paid thy utmost blessing.

THE HERMITS OF MARLOW

Waterfalls leap among wild islands green,
Which framed for my lone boat a lone retreat
Of moss-grown trees and weeds

Percy Bysshe Shelley, *The Revolt of Islam*, 1818

It is clear from stray details in Thomas Love Peacock's *The Genius of the Thames* (of which more in Chapter VII) that his happiest days were spent on and beside the river. His idea of bliss was living 'in some hermit-vale … by the lone river's shore'. He mentions sailing on summer evenings at Richmond

> … I have roamed, at evening hours,
> Near beauteous Richmond's courtly bowers,
> When, mild and pale, the moon-beams fell
> On hill and islet, grove and dell;
> And many a skiff, with fleecy sail
> Expanded to the western gale.

In 1812 Peacock was introduced to Percy Bysshe Shelley and his wife Harriet, and they became firm friends. Shelley invited him to stay in Bracknell, and to go with them on a tour of the Lakes and then Edinburgh. Peacock stood by Shelley when he eloped with Mary Godwin, and Shelley provided him with an annuity of £120, which enabled him to settle with his mother close to his beloved river in West Street, Marlow. After Harriet's suicide in 1816, Shelley married Mary Godwin, and they moved into Albion House, also in West Street. It was large and damp, with plenty of bedrooms, attics, spacious reception rooms, a well-stocked library and an acre of garden. Mary finished *Frankenstein* there, and Shelley completed and dedicated to her his long poem *The Revolt of Islam*, working on it while he lay in his boat, 'where the woods to frame a bower / With interlaced branches mix and meet'. He also published two political tracts under the pseudonym 'The Hermit of Marlow'.

In 1817 Shelley sketched the poplars and willows under which he used to dawdle in a boat on a page of the manuscript of his *Laon and Cythna*, a poem he eventually called *The Revolt of Islam*; the manuscript is held in the Bodleian Library.

In September 1815 Peacock, Shelley, Mary Clairmont and her stepbrother Charles set off on an expedition up the river to the source. At Inglesham, Shelley suggested they continue along the Thames and Severn Canal, row up the Severn to North Wales, and then tour the Lakes, the Tweed and Durham, but as they didn't have enough money for the canal toll they returned to Lechlade. They spent a few days staying at the Swan Inn, still a fine place for waterborne explorers to moor up and enjoy the home-made steak pies. The voyage inspired Shelley's melancholy and atmospheric poem 'A Summer Evening Churchyard, Lechlade', and Peacock's humorous satirical novel *Crotchet Castle* (1831). Crotchet's son, a caricature of Shelley, proposes the fitting out of

> a flotilla of pleasure boats, with spacious cabins and a good cellar to carry a choice philosophical party up the Thames and Severn, into the Ellesmere Canal, where we shall be among the mountains of North Wales; which we may climb or not, as we think proper; but we will, at any rate, keep our floating hotel well provisioned and we will try to settle all the questions over which a shadow of doubt yet hangs in the world of philosophy.

The poet and essayist James Leigh Hunt and his wife often visited Peacock and the Shelleys at Marlow, enjoying walks, picnicking, and boating on the Thames. They shared Shelley's house, and erected an altar to Pan in the woods, a happy contrast to the two years Hunt spent in prison between 1812 and 1814 for calling the Prince of Wales 'a fat adonis of forty'. Leigh Hunt, who mentions the Thames several times in his book about London, has a splendid anecdote about Lord Byron swimming in the river:

> The first time I saw Lord Byron, he was rehearsing the part of Leander, under the auspices of Mr. Jackson, the prize-fighter. It was in the river Thames, before his first visit to Greece. There used to be a bathing-machine stationed on the eastern side of Westminster Bridge; and I had been bathing, and was standing on this machine adjusting my clothes, when I noticed a respectable-looking manly person, who was eying something at a distance. This was Mr. Jackson waiting for his pupil. The latter was swimming for somebody for a wager. I forgot what his tutor said of him; but he spoke in terms of praise. I saw nothing in Lord Byron at that time, but a young man who, like myself, had written a bad volume of poems; and though I had a sympathy with him on this account, and

Marlow was much favoured by eighteenth-century writers in search of both peace and affordable lodgings. *View of Great Marlow* by Joseph Farington, from William Combe's *An History of the River Thames* (1794).

more respect for his rank than I was willing to suppose, my sympathy was not an agreeable one; so, contenting myself with seeing his lordship's head bop up and down in the water, like a buoy, I came away.

Vaulting from the sublime to the cosy, the last Marlow author to be celebrated is Enid Blyton (1897–1968), who lived in a house called Old Thatch on Coldmoorholme Lane in Bourne End for a decade between 1929 and 1938. The first of the twenty-eight books in her Old Thatch series, *The Talking Teapot and Other Tales*, was published in 1934. While at Bourne End, Blyton began to write full-length stories, beginning with *The Adventures of the Wishing Chair* and *The Enchanted Wood*, the first book in the

Enid Blyton was living close to the Thames in Bourne End in a house called Old Thatch when she began her series of 'Tales of Old Thatch'; the river banks and nearby woods provided inspiration for her books about the 'Five-Findouters' and the 'Faraway Tree'.

Faraway Tree series. According to Blyton's daughter Gillian, her mother's inspiration for the magic tree came from 'thinking up a story one day and suddenly she was walking in the enchanted wood and found the tree'. Books about the magic 'Faraway Tree', Silky the Fairy, Moonface, Mr Watzisname, Dame Washalot, Saucepan Man and the other curious folk who live in it and feast on Google Buns and Pop Biscuits, and the extraordinary lands that arrive at the top of it, are still hugely popular.

Marlow, Maidenhead and Sheepridge (the name of the road opposite Coldmoorholme Lane) appear in Blyton's 'Mystery' books, as does Burnham Beeches. The Thames is often mentioned: Fatty jogs along the towpath to Marlow in *The Mystery of the Missing Man*; the Five Find-Outers cross the river by ferry in *The Mystery of the Pantomime Cat*, and investigate a house on the river bank from a little boat in *The Mystery of Tally-Ho Cottage*.

CITY OF LEARNING

Where the Cherwell flows along with the Isis, and meets it;
and where their divided streams make several little sweet and
pleasant Islands; is seated on a rising Vale the most famous
University of Oxford ... our most noble Athens, the seat of
our English Muses, the Prop and the Pillar, nay the Sun, the
Eye, the very Soul, of the Nation.

William Camden, *Britannia*, 1610

Since scholars first gravitated to Oxford in the tenth century, it
has been a place of learning and literature. Many of its writers
have been struck by the way it is threaded by waterways great and
small. The city is 'sweetly hugged in the pleasant arms of those
two pure rivers, the Thames and Cherwell' wrote Thomas Bask-
erville in his *Account of Oxford* (1686). Although Max Beerbohm
argued in *Zuleika Dobson* that its 'mild miasmal air ... saps the
will-power, the power of action', he added that it also 'clarifies
the mind, makes larger the vision'.

The city was reputedly founded in the early eighth century by
the learned Princess Frideswide, who established a convent on the
site of the present cathedral after the miraculous blinding of the
Mercian Prince Algar, her would-be ravisher, and her restoration
of his sight with water from a spring at Binsey, which Frideswide's
protector St Margaret of Antioch magicked out of the ground.
The well at Binsey church was for centuries a popular pilgrimage
destination, flanked on the east by the Thames and on the west
by the Seacourt Stream, a medieval cut that allowed boats swift
passage round the city via Wytham and Hinksey. King Alfred,
a great patron of learning, endowed St Frideswide's generously,
and soon Oxford became noted for its 'learned clerks'.

The thirteenth century boasted Roger Bacon, a 'brave Nigromancer', who lived in a tower overlooking the river near Folly
Bridge, from the roof of which he made observations of the stars,
and imagined constructing a telescope:

'Bold Nigromancer' Roger Bacon's tower on Folly Bridge, as it appeared in Carter and Anna Hall's *The Book of The Thames* (1859).

For we can so shape transparent bodies, and arrange them in such a way with respect to our sight and objects of vision, that the rays will be reflected and bent in any direction we desire, and under any angle we wish, we may see the object near or at a distance ... So we might also cause the Sun, Moon and stars in appearance to descend here below.

John Wycliffe (1330–1384), first translator of the Bible into English, taught in the University until he was expelled for heresy. He missed it acutely. 'Not unworthily is it called the vineyard of the Lord', he wrote longingly to a follower. 'It was founded by the holy fathers and situated in a splendid site, watered by rills and fountains, surrounded by meadows, pastures, plains and glades ... I will sum up in one word. Oxford is place gladsome and fertile so suitable for the habitation of the gods that it has been rightly called the house of God and the gate of heaven.'

The city became a centre of humanism in the late fifteenth century. Richard Hakluyt (1553–1616) taught geography at Christ

Church, where he held a studentship until 1583, He used Oxford libraries to inform his *Principal Navigations, Traffiques and Discoveries of the English Nation* (1589–1600); perhaps he occasionally took time off to explore the river. Robert Burton was working on his *The Anatomy of Melancholy* (1621) in his Christ Church study when he wrote:

> So that as a river runs sometimes precipitate and swift, then dull and slow; now direct, then *per ambages*, now deep, then shallow; now muddy, then clear; now broad, then narrow; doth my style flow: now serious, then light; now comical, then satirical.

Oxford's backwater character changed during the Civil War after Charles I made the city his capital in 1642. But by 1681, when Charles II opened the Oxford Playhouse, John Dryden could boast, in the lines he composed for the occasion, that it was a retreat for scholars once again:

> This place, the seat of peace, the quiet cell
> Where arts remov'd from noisy business dwell,
> Should calm your wills, unite the jarring parts,
> And with a kind contagion seize your hearts:
> O may its genius like soft music move
> And tune you all to concord and to love!
> Our ark that has in tempests long been toss'd
> Could never land on so secure a coast.

For the next century or so, Oxford's ivory towers became somewhat begrimed. Edward Gibbon (1737–1794) complained that the six terms he spent at Magdalen College were 'the most idle and unprofitable of my whole life'. Pope, Addison and Steele were uniformly dismissive of their alma mater, though Magdalen has named a quiet walk from the cloisters to the Cherwell after Addison. Thomas Warton (1728–1790) was equally critical, though he spent his whole life at Oxford researching and writing poetry; he also enjoying duck-shooting, drinking with Thames bargees and swapping witticisms with Samuel Johnson, who was made an Oxford Master of Arts on the publication in 1755 of his *Dictionary*.

Since the nineteenth century, countless historians, literary critics, scientists, poets, novelists, diarists and essayists have found Oxford a congenial place to write in and about. Excellent books have been devoted to praising such famous men and women, notably John Dougill's *Oxford in English Literature* (1998), and all the colleges can boast literary figures, many of whom loved the city's waterways. Shelley, who was sent down from University College in 1811 for publishing a pamphlet titled *The Necessity of Atheism*, revelled in exploring watery nooks and walking the banks of the Thames during the single summer he spent there; he also wrote political squibs, folded them into paper boats, and sent them downstream. Keats worked on his 'Endymion' while he was in Oxford and wrote to his sister Fanny (10 September 1817):

> This Oxford I have no doubt is the finest City in the
> world – it is full of old Gothic buildings – Spires – Towers
> – Quadrangles – Cloisters – Groves etc. and is surrounded
> with more clear streams than ever I saw together. I take a
> Walk by the Side of one of them every Evening.

Just over a week later he wrote to John Hamilton Reynolds (21 September 1817):

> For these last five or six days, we have had regularly a Boat
> on the Isis and explored all the streams about, which are
> more in number than your eye-lashes. We sometimes skim
> into a Bed of rushes.

As all the world knows, Charles Dodgson, a mathematics don at Christ Church, made up his 'Adventures of Alice' as he rowed the three daughters of the head of the college, Dean Liddell, up the Thames to Binsey. The poem he put at the start of the book he published under the pseudonym Lewis Carroll describes how the girls rowed while he told them stories.

All in the golden afternoon
Full leisurely we glide;
For both our oars, with little skill,
By little arms are plied,
While little hands make vain pretence
Our wanderings to guide.

Apart from the book's many satirical references to Oxford figures, Carroll used Binsey's holy well in his story about a Treacle Well in which lived 'Elsie, Lacie and Tilly' (the Liddell sisters themselves). 'Treacle' is Middle English from Old French *triacle*, and means an antidote against venom; and treacle wells were those which, like Binsey, boasted miraculous powers.

In Thomas Hardy's *Jude the Obscure* (1895), Jude approaches 'Christminster' from the south-west; he pauses at the top of 'a crooked and gentle declivity' and looks at the city.

Grey-stoned and dun-roofed, it stood within hail of the Wessex border, and almost with the tip of one small toe within it, at the northernmost point of the crinkled line along which the leisurely Thames strokes the fields of that ancient kingdom. The buildings now lay quiet in the sunset, a vane here and there on their many spires and domes giving sparkle to a picture of sober secondary and tertiary hues. Reaching the bottom he moved along the level way between pollard willows growing indistinct in the twilight.

He lodges near the canal in 'Beersheba', a thinly disguised Jericho, but Oxford fails him, hampered as he is by his incautious marriage to the shallow and venal Arabella. With savage irony, Jude's death takes place offstage, while Arabella, who has deserted him in his dying hour, is enjoying herself flirting at the Bumps races.

On the opposite side of the river, on the crowded barges, were gorgeous nosegays of feminine beauty, fashionably arrayed in green, pink, blue, and white. The blue flag of the boat club denoted the centre of interest, beneath which a band in red uniform gave out the notes she had already heard in the death-chamber. Collegians of all sorts, in canoes with ladies, watching keenly for 'our' boat, darted up and down. While she regarded the lively scene somebody touched Arabella in the ribs, and looking round she saw Vilbert.

'That philtre is operating, you know!' he said with a leer. 'Shame on 'ee to wreck a heart so!'

'I shan't talk of love to-day.'

'Why not? It is a general holiday.'

She did not reply. Vilbert's arm stole round her waist, which act could be performed unobserved in the crowd. An arch expression overspread Arabella's face at the feel of the arm, but she kept her eyes on the river as if she did not know of the embrace.

Oxford has inspired more nostalgic novels of youth than any-where else in the world, and most have scenes set on its rivers. The most famous is Evelyn Waugh's *Brideshead Revisited* (1945), which opens with Charles Ryder's reminiscences of Oxford in Eights Week, and of a walk along the river from Godstow into the city with the fey and charming Sebastian Flyte, but is otherwise little concerned with the Thames.

Today Oxford's most famous author is Philip Pullman, who taught in the city for several years before writing his best-selling fantasy trilogy *His Dark Materials*. Oxford's waterways feature largely in *Northern Lights*, in which Pullman relates how his heroine Lyra finds refuge with the 'Gyptians', the barge-dwellers who arrive in Oxford for their spring and autumn fairs. She also swims in the Cherwell with her friend Roger, the kitchen-boy. Pullman adopts the name Isis for the Thames both upstream and downstream of the city.

> East along the great highway of the River Isis, thronged
> with slow-moving brick-barges and asphalt boats and
> corn-tankers, way down past Henley and Maidenhead to
> Teddington, where the tide from the German Ocean reaches,
> and further down still to Mortlake, past the house of the great

magician Dr Dee, past Falkeshall, where the pleasure-gardens spread out bright with fountains and banners by day, with tree-lamps and fireworks by night; past White Hall Palace, where the King holds his weekly Council of State, past the Shot Tower dropping its endless drizzle of molten lead into vats of murky water, further down still, to where the river, wide and filthy now, swings in a great curve to the south.

This is Limehouse and here is the child who is going to disappear.

Pullman has retreated from Oxford itself, finding peace to write in a village very close to it. His research into canal history and Jericho have made him an eminent advocate for preserving the traditions of the old waterway that 'comes into town quietly almost surreptitiously without many people being aware of it; not a thundering highway but a secretive back street'.[6]

TOPSY AND THE THAMES

Hove to on right bank just above Bray Lock. W.M. set to cooking in seclusion of cabin, and in due time filled the whole party with delight and with provisions of a most satisfactory kind (very thick soup, rice, vegetables, meat, etc., results showing both knowledge and skill).

Janey Morris, 'Log of the Ark', 1880

The Thames ran through William Morris's life in an unbroken thread from 1834, when he was born in Walthamstow, close to its tributary Lea, to his death in 1896 at Kelmscott Manor, the 'heaven on earth' on the Thames near Lechlade, which he discovered in 1871. When he was six, his father's City brokerage firm had become so successful that the family moved to Woodford Hall, a Georgian mansion with fifty acres of park and its own farm, which ran down to the Roding, another Thames tributary. From its windows the river itself could be seen 'winding through the marshes, with white and ruddy-brown sails moving among cornfields and pastures'. The boys rode Shetland ponies in Epping Forest and along the Lea, and Morris was thinking of his childhood when he wrote in *News from Nowhere*:

> It does not make a bad holiday to get a quiet pony and ride about there on a sunny afternoon of autumn, and look over the river and the craft passing up and down, and on to Shooter's Hill and the Kentish uplands, and then turn round to the wide green sea of the Essex marshland, with the great domed line of the sky, and the sun shining down in one flood of peaceful light over the long distance.

When William was 13 his father died, and in 1848 his mother moved to Water House, a smaller but still very substantial Georgian house in Walthamstow, named because its grounds included a 40-foot-wide moat around a thickly wooded island. There the children bathed, boated, fished for pike and chased the swans in summer, and skated in winter.

William was by now at boarding school at Marlborough, in Wiltshire. Yet another Thames tributary, the Kennet, ran through its grounds, and before long he had exchanged some baby rabbits for a fishing rod. After Marlborough, he went to Exeter College, Oxford, where as well as pursuing his deepening interest in medieval art and architecture he enjoyed messing about on the river. 'Just as in after years, in the thick of his work it was noticeable how he never seemed to be particularly busy', wrote his closest Oxford friend, Edward Burne-Jones.

> He had plenty of leisure for expeditions, for fishing, for amusement, if it amused him; he never seemed to read much, but always knew, and accurately; and he had a great instinct at all times for knowing what would not amuse him, and what not to read.

They spent long afternoons on the river, rowing and sailing upstream to Godstow and beyond, and downstream to Dorchester.

One of the first poems Morris wrote was 'The Willow and the Red Cliff', which told of a love affair that began by the river's edge:

> Dost thou know my misery?
> Dost thou know the willow tree
> Underneath whose branches he
> Plighted well his troth to me?
> O! the happy willow tree
> With the river by it sighing,
> And the swallow by it flying,
> And the thrush singing to it from the thorn-bush.

After leaving Oxford, Morris became apprenticed in 1856 to the architect George Street. While painting frescos in the new neo-Gothic Oxford Union building, he met and fell in love with Janey Burden, and within months they were engaged to be married, though not before another river adventure, this time on the Seine. He and Philip Webb rowed from Paris to Rouen in a boat sent over from Bossoms Boatyard on Oxford's Port Meadow. By this time Morris was working under Webb in Street's London office. As they travelled, he and Webb planned a medievally inspired house for William and Janey.

The site eventually chosen for the Red House was at Upton, near Bexley, surrounded by orchards and meadows, close to the Darent, which flows into the Thames at Dartford. It suggests that Morris hoped to re-create for his children his own idyllic childhood in Walthamstow in what would be a Tennysonian 'Palace of Art' all his own. He and Janey were married in April 1859, and moved into the Red House in 1861. The experience of designing and building the house inspired Morris to establish an interior design company with fellow artists, including Burne-Jones, in Red Lion Square, Bloomsbury. However, after only five years the difficulties of living in the country and commuting to Red Lion Square forced William to move both home and workplace into one large house in Queen's Square, Bloomsbury.

The Morris family spent the summer of 1867 in Oxford, enjoying frequent excursions on the river. Morris was now working on his *The Earthly Paradise*, and in it he celebrated a day spent on the peaceful waters above Eynsham.

> What better place than this then could we find
> By this sweet stream that knows not of the sea,
> That guesses not the city's misery,
> This little stream whose hamlets scarce have names,
> This far-off, lonely mother of the Thames?

Four years later, Morris found his own earthly paradise 25 miles by road and rather more by river upstream from Oxford. In 1871 he wrote to his friend Charles Faulkner:

> I have been looking about for a house for the wife and kids, and whither do you guess my eye is turned now? Kelmscott, a little village about two miles above Radcot Bridge – A heaven on earth; an old stone Elizabethan house like Water Eaton, and such a garden! Close down on the river, a boat house and all things handy.

Rossetti was less enamoured of it, dismissing it as 'the doziest dump of old grey beehives'. When Morris lived at Kelmscott, a creek ran up to the house, and going fishing, or just reading, in a punt on the river was the work of a moment. Floods sometimes came right up to the house itself; in a letter to Janey in 1876, Morris sent his love to his daughter May, adding, 'wouldn't she have liked to have been out on the flooded river with me, the wind right in one's teeth and the eddies going like a Japanese tea-tray?'

By this time, he had also acquired new quarters in London, settling his family first into a house near Turnham Green in 1873, then, in 1879, to The Retreat, which was directly on the Thames in Upper Mall, Hammersmith. He had visited it and admired its large garden when the novelist George MacDonald was living there, and was very taken with the idea that the water flowing past it had passed the grey gables of Kelmscott Manor 130 miles

Dante Gabriel Charles Rossetti's *Water Willow* (1871) was a portrait of William Morris's wife Janey. The Thames and Kelmscott Manor can be seen in the background.

upstream, and that he could travel between the two houses by boat. He renamed it Kelmscott House, and in the summer of 1880 set off upriver.

Morris took William de Morgan, Cornell Price and Richard Grosvenor, as well as Janey, their daughters May and Jenny and their friend Elizabeth Macleod, and Eliza, a housemaid. They travelled in a Salter's boat called the *Ark*, which was sent up from Oxford.

> Jenny and I went out before breakfast to see the craft. She is odd but delightful: imagine a biggish company boat with a small omnibus on board, fitted up luxuriously inside with two shelves and a glass-rack, and a sort of boot behind this: room for two rowers in front, and I must say for not many more except in the cabin or omnibus. Still what joy (to a little mind) to see the landscape out of a square pane of glass, and to sleep a-nights with the stream rushing two inches past one's ear. Then after all, there is the romance of the bank, and outside the boat the world is wide: item, we can always hire a skiff for some of the party to row in and stretch their muscles.

They did hire a skiff, *Alfred*, from Biffen's, a local boatyard. The ladies travelled in the *Ark*, and the skiff was rowed by Morris and de Morgan. Morris related their adventures in letters, and Janey recorded the voyage in a twelve-page 'Log of The Expedition of the *Ark*', which survives among the Morris papers held in the British Museum. This was later transcribed by William, and passed round for the other members of the party to annotate; their lively interjections appear on the backs of its pages, which are full of colourful incident, including groundings, perils at weirs, and an unexpected sighting of the Northern Lights at Marlow. Morris, who loved cooking, was in charge of the galley, 'appearing like the high-priest at the critical moment pot in hand'.[7]

The portly *Ark* was either rowed by hired men, or towed, sometimes by men or horses, occasionally by obliging 'tin-kettles', as Janey called the steam launches by then popular on the river. The ladies spent the nights at inns in Sunbury, Windsor, Marlow, Wallingford and Oxford, and Morris and de Morgan slept in the *Ark*. At Oxford, *Ark* and *Alfred* were returned to their respective boatyards. Janey went ahead by road to get Kelmscott ready, and the others piled their possessions into two Bossoms boats hired on Port Meadow.

> Night fell on us long before we got to Radcot, and we fastened a lantern to the prow of our boat ... Charlie was waiting for us with a lantern at our bridge by the corner at 10 p.m., and presently the ancient house had me in her arms again; J had lighted up all brilliantly.

The voyage was repeated with a slightly different crew and equal success the next summer. 'We none of us stopped laughing all the way', de Morgan told Morris's biographer, John Mackail.

Morris united his concern for the common man and his love of the Thames when he wrote a fantasy version of the journey from London to Kelmscott in his futuristic novel *News from Nowhere* (1890). Its hero William Guest wakes one morning to find that the industrial city he had walked home through from a meeting of the Socialist League has vanished; instead the Thames is 'a crystal river', and fishermen are winding in salmon nets on its banks. The soap and lead works that once polluted its waters are gone, and instead of ugly iron suspension bridges, a many-arched medieval stone bridge spans the river: 'I fairly felt as if I were alive in the fourteenth century.' He meets Dick and Clara, and after bathing in the river, journeys up it with them to go haymaking at Kelmscott, gradually realising that England is now an agrarian society, in which people delight to work in the fields, and children learn from nature rather than in schools. The great houses on the banks of the river are museums or communal homes; 'the banks of the forest that we passed through had lost their gamekeeperish trimness, and were as wild and beautiful as need be.' The 'cockney

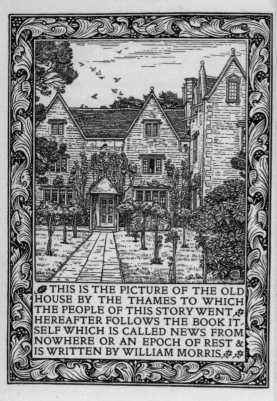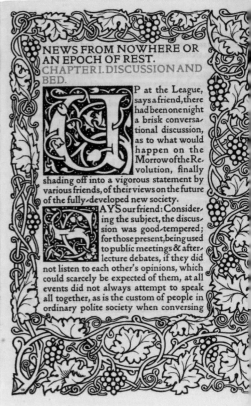

Kelmscott Manor was drawn by William Morris as the frontispiece for his fantasy of a reborn Thames, *News from Nowhere* (1892).

villas' built by riparian stockbrokers have gone, 'and the damned flunkies sent packing'. As their boat reaches the 'baby Thames' near Kelmscott, Ellen, a sun-tanned embodiment of nature and freedom who joined them in Oxford, says, 'I had no idea of the charm of a very small river like this. The smallness of the scale of everything, the short reaches, and speedy change of the banks, give one the feeling of going somewhere.'

Morris wrote a final hymn to Kelmscott in the magazine *The Quest* in November 1895, a year before his death. Titled 'Gossip about an Old House on the Upper Thames', it describes Kelmscott Manor in loving detail, likening the great parlour at the heart of the house to 'a particularly pleasant cabin at sea, were it not for the elms and the rooks on the west, and the green garden shrugs and the blackbirds on the east', and explaining how its grey slates 'are "sized down"; the smaller ones to the top and the bigger towards the eaves, which gives one the same sort of pleasure in their orderly beauty as a fish's scales or a bird's feathers.'

FOUR

MESSING ABOUT
IN BOATS

ALTHOUGH there were adventurous pioneers who braved the undisciplined waters of the Thames in fragile craft before the nineteenth century, the real heyday of pleasure-boating came after commercial water traffic was removed from waterways by the railways, and before two world wars and the Depression of the 1930s transformed the social landscape, a window of about eighty years. All manner of new craft were developed to suit both the active and the lazy: punts for pleasure and for racing, racing skiffs and cumbersome camping craft, dangerously over-canvassed yachts and tiny cockleshells with pocket handkerchief sails, birchbark and Rob Roy canoes, houseboats small enough to be towed and large enough for parties, private steam launches and public steamships.

A lively literature devoted to describing adventures afloat and excursions both on and beside the water soon developed. In the second half of the century, there were many Americans among such authors, because fast transatlantic steamships brought thousands of tourists from the United States. Exploring the Thames was hugely popular, offering as it did a passport into the heart of an elusively private England. The new wave of books were marked by much personal reminiscing, and a depressing number

Spring on the River Thames (1935) by Charles Pears, a poster for London Transport, shows the elaborately decorated houseboats fringing the banks of the Thames that were rented out to holidaymakers; in J.M. Barrie's play *Walker London*, a punt was provided with the boat.

of uncharitable remarks about 'cockney' river-users. The literature of sporting events, especially rowing, on the Victorian river was equally tainted with snobbery, but satirists got their own back by ridiculing those who took themselves too seriously. Finally, this golden age of watery high jinks produced two enduring classics, Jerome K. Jerome's *Three Men in a Boat*, and Kenneth Grahame's *The Wind in the Willows*.

EARLY AQUATIC EXCURSIONS

We had now got past The Nore
And lost the sight of Shepey's shore,
The ebbing tide of Thames we met
The wind against it fiercely set;
This made a short and tumbling sea,
And finely toss'd indeed were we…
Troubles crowd upon us thick;
Our hero Scott grows very sick;
Poor Hogarth makes wry faces too
(Worse faces than he ever drew)

William Gostling,
Five Days' Peregrinations (1781)

Among the first writers to celebrate amusements on the Thames was John Taylor (1577–c.1653), a London waterman, who rose to fame at court as 'the King's Acqua-Muse'. He had a quaint way with words (Chertsey Bridge 'sure was made all by left-handed men'), and ended his lengthy rhyming report on an exploratory journey along the river commissioned by Charles I in 1632 with

… I have described the way we went,
Commixing truth with honest merriment,
My threadbare wit with a mad wool-gathering goes,
To show the things in verse I saw in prose.

Taylor published over 150 poems about the river, organised pageants, and took bets on his completion of such unlikely rowing feats as sculling from London to the Isle of Sheppey in a boat made of hempseed paper, using bamboo cane oars with blades made of the stiff dried cod known as stockfish.

> The water to the paper being got,
> In one half hour our boat began to rot.
> In which extremity I thought it fit
> To put in use a stratagem of wit,
> Which was, eight bullocks bladders we had bought
> Puffed stiffly full with wind, bound fast and taut,
> Which on our boat within the tide we tied
> One each side four upon the outward side.
> The water still rose higher by degrees,
> In three miles going, almost to our knees.
> Our rotten bottom all to tatters fell,
> And left our boat as bottomless as hell.

Robert Herrick (1591–1674), who lived at Westminster when he was young, loved outings along the 'silver-footed' river to Hampton Court. In 'His Tears to Thamasis', probably written while he was vicar of Dean Prior in Devonshire, he recalled traditional May Days on the river in boats decked with young leaves and blossoms.

> No more shall I reiterate thy strand.
> Whereon so many stately structures stand;
> Nor in the summer's sweeter evenings go,
> To bath in thee, as thousand others do;
> No more shall I along thy christall glide
> In barge with boughes and rushes beautifi'd,
> With soft smooth virgins for our chast disport
> To Richmond, Kingstone, and to Hampton-Court.

John Evelyn's diary records his participation in a sailing race between Charles II and his brother James:

1st October 1665: I sailed this morning with his Majesty
in one of his yachts (or pleasure boats), vessels not known
among us till the Dutch East India Company presented
that curious piece to the King; being very excellent sailing
vessels. It was on a wager between his other new pleasure
boat, built frigate-like, and one of the Duke of York's; the
wager £100; the race from Greenwich to Gravesend and
back. The King lost it going, the wind being contrary, but
saved stakes in returning. There were divers noble persons
and lords on board, his Majesty sometimes steering himself.

One of the earliest accounts of fun on the river and the riverbank was Ebenezer Forrest's burlesque journal of the *Five Days'*
Peregrination by Land and Water made by William Hogarth and
four inebriated friends in May 1732. They set out from the Bedford
Tavern in Covent Garden at one in the morning, and hired a
sailing hoy bound for Gravesend. 'Straw was our bed and a tilt [a
hooped awning] our covering ... we had much rain and no sleep
for three hours'. They ate 'hung beef' and biscuits, washed down
with gin, and admired the anchored men-of-war. After a night at
Gravesend, they summoned a barber to shave them and powder
their wigs, then drank coffee and buttered toast before setting off
on foot for Rochester Castle. There they consumed 'a Dish of
Soles & Flounders with Crab Sauce, a Calves heart Stuff'd and
Roasted, the Liver Fry'd and the other appurtenances Minc'd, a
Leg of Mutton Roasted, and Some Green pease, all Very Good
and well Dress'd, with Good Small beer and excellent Port'.

Over the next three days, they visited the warships in the
Medway, and explored the Isle of Grain, then took a boat to
Sheerness. Pickled in liquor, they walk to Queenborough, behaving remarkably badly along the way. They chucked 'sticks,
pebbles and Hog's Dung' at each other, and at Hoo, Hogarth
'untruss'd upon a Grave Rail in an unseemly Manner', and was
duly punished by being thrashed with nettles 'on the part offend-
ing'. At five in the morning next day they hired a small sailing

Literary and artistic members of the Beefsteak Club aboard the *Phoenix* wherry, emulating Hogarth's 1732 *Peregrination by Land and Water*. (John Nixon, 1801)

boat known as a bumboat [from the Dutch *boomschuit*] to take them back to Gravesend. It was pouring with rain, and they got thoroughly seasick, alleviated a little with milk punch and the sight of porpoises. Briefly stranded on Blye Sands, they eventually arrived at Gravesend at ten o'clock at night. Next morning, they embarked for Billingsgate in their tilt-boat 'with a truss of clean straw, a bottle of good wine, pipes, tobacco and a match'. The weather was at last fine, and they made merry on the four hour journey, topping the trip off by taking a wherry to Somerset Gate, and spending the last evening of the trip as they had begun it, in the Bedford Tavern. Ten years later, the journal, illustrated in part by Hogarth, was reprinted with an additional account 'in hudibrastic verse' by William Gostling. Similar excursions became a regular tradition of the Bedford Tavern-based Beefsteak Club, which they founded in 1735.

The building of such canals as the Wey Navigation (1653), the Thames Severn (1789), the Oxford to Birmingham (1790) and the Kennet and Avon (1804) led to improved locks and weirs on the Thames. Messing about on the river, especially at Oxford and between London and Hampton Court, became more and more popular. In 1818 John Hassell recommended 'an aquatic excursion to Richmond'. It was best to leave on a morning tide for a long day's amusement.

> On these occasions, it is customary to carry with the company all that will supply the wants of a rural festival, even to their knives and forks; and a cold collation, which, on a warm summer's day, must always be considered a treat.[1]

In the 1830s, when Charles Dickens penned his magazine series of 'Sketches by Boz', the river was even busier. In his chapter 'The River', Dickens makes fun of amateur excursionists:

> Something has always gone wrong. Either the cork of the salad-dressing has come out, or the most anxiously expected member of the party has not come out, or the most disagreeable man in company would come out, or a child or two have fallen into the water, ... or the gentlemen who volunteered to row have been 'out of practice,' and performed very alarming evolutions, putting their oars down into the water and not being able to get them up again, or taking terrific pulls without putting them in at all; in either case, pitching over on the backs of their heads with startling violence, and exhibiting the soles of their pumps to the 'sitters' in the boat, in a very humiliating manner.

By the second half of the century, the railways had removed most commercial traffic from the non-tidal Thames. The numbers of boats, and of eager amateur authors, grew exponentially.

A VARIETY OF CRAFTS

The river is so inconveniently crowded with steam launches, houseboats, skiffs, gigs, punts, dinghies, canoes and every other conceivable and inconceivable variety of crafts, that the racing boats have sometimes great difficulty in threading a way through the crowd.

Charles Dickens Jr, *Dictionary of the Thames*, 1890

The literature of the river mentions leisure craft of all kinds. I will start with my own favourite, the punt. It was also that of George Dunlop Leslie, who expands at length on its virtues in *Our River* (1881), a hymn in part to the Thames, especially his favoured stretches between Wallingford and Henley, but primarily to the punt. Leslie's punt had a mast so that he could sail it when occasion arose. He favoured walking its length to pole it along. and emphasised the importance of handling the pole lightly.

Hold the pole like a billiard cue, lightly in the hand; avoid carrying it bodily up the boat after a shove, as this tires you quite unnecessarily. The proper way is merely to carry the pole back, with the fingers of one hand loosely holding the thin end, allowing the other to trail in the water, which will bear the main weight.

Women were as dexterous at punting as men. 'To Isis, by Argol', a gently satirical anonymous poem of the 1890s, recalls the author's 'vernal heyday' at Oxford, where 'How oft in summer's languorous days, / With some fair creature at the pole, / I Have thrid the Cherwell's murmurous ways'.

In Dorothy Sayers's *Gaudy Night* (1935), Lord Peter Wimsey invites Harriet Vane to go punting, and she appears in 'a dazzling display of white linen and pipe-clay'. Wimsey was 'a pretty punter to watch, easy in action and quite remarkably quick'. When they start going down the wider stream of the Thames itself, 'he bent his knees to the stroke, making the punt curtsey and the water

Friends at Yewden (1882–85), by Henry Tamworth Wells: George Dunlop Leslie
lolls on his punt pole on the left of this group portrait of the painters and river
lovers who gathered at Yewden Manor, near Henley, the Thames-side home
of the painter Gustav Schwabe. The white house opposite is Greenlands, then
owned by W.H. Smith.

run chuckling under the bows'. They double-punt to Iffley, and
Harriet in the bow, 'conscious of Wimsey of Balliol's critical eye
upon her handling of the heavy pole', reflects that 'either you look
graceful or you look ghastly; there is no middle way in punting'.
After dining at Iffley, they sit together on the stern cushion, and
paddle back to Oxford.

In his semi-autobiographical novel *A Girl in Winter* (1946),
which is set in the late 1930s, Philip Larkin sends his heroine

Katherine and her prickly friend Jane out in a punt with Robin, an accomplished punter, though his pole is oddly short.

> After each stroke, Robin threw the twelve-foot pole
> carelessly upwards before negligently slipping it back into
> the water. It whistled through his hands. He stood easily, but
> quite still, not seeming to shift his stance in the slightest.

Katherine has a go, feeling 'as insecure as if she was carrying a long plank along a high scaffolding'. She loses the pole, but wisely abandons it and stays aboard; after much exertion, she finds it much easier, and she is soon driving them along 'in an ungainly but decided way'. Larkin uses the scene as a symbol of Katherine's fading love for Robin: she no longer needs him.

Most amateur boaters preferred a rowing boat of some kind. They were to be had in all shapes and sizes. *The Stream of Pleasure* (1891), written by the American novelist and travel writer Elizabeth Robins Pennell and illustrated by her artist husband Joseph, is an account of the couple's experiences when they hired a stubby pair-oared skiff from Salter's of Oxford, planning to camp in it during a three-week cruise downstream to Richmond.

> It had a green waterproof cover which stretched over
> three iron hoops and converted it for all practical purposes
> into a small, a very small, houseboat. By a complicated
> arrangement of strings, the canvas could be so rolled up
> and fastened on top as – theoretically – not to interfere with
> our view of the river banks on bright days; or it could be
> let down to cover the entire boat from stern to bow – an
> umbrella by day, a hotel by night. ... We should go to
> bed with the swans and rise up with the larks, and cook
> our breakfast under the willows, and wash our dishes and
> ourselves in quiet, clear pools.

The most heart-stirring craft on the Thames are its sailing boats. 'Sail to Sandford', a lovely description of learning to manage a sailing boat by John Skinner (1772–1839), was written in 1793, while he was an undergraduate of Trinity College.

> At Folly Bridge we hoist the sail
> And briskly scud before the gale
> To Iffley where our course awhile
> Detain its locks and Saxon pile
> Affording pause to recommend
> The *Hobby-horse* unto my friend,
> Our light-built galley: ours, I say,
> Since Warren bears an equal sway
> In her command; as first, in cost
> The half he shared; himself a host,
> Whether he plies the limber oar

Or tows the vessel from the shore,
Or strains the main sheet tight astern
Close to the wind. Of him I learn
Patient to wait the time exact
When jib and foresail should be backed
To bring her round; or mark the strain
The boat on gunwale can sustain,
Without aught danger of upsetting
Or giving both her mates a wetting.[2]

In his 1890 *Summer Days on the Thames*, Alfred Church admires the 'white canvas wings' of sailing boats 'as they fly to and fro in the broad reach above Binsey' as 'a picturesque feature in the landscape'. Their 'wild career used to be a terror in former days to the throngs of rowers on the lower river', and they 'have been banished or removed by common consent'.

'There is no more thrilling sensation I know of than sailing. It comes as near to flying as man has got to yet' wrote Jerome K. Jerome. He soon discovers that sails make skiffs perilously unstable.

Fishermen recovering from a collision with the 'Three Men'. Illustration by
A. Frederics for Jerome K. Jerome's *Three Men in a Boat* (1889).

As the river grew more crowded, collisions with sailing boats
increased. The Pennells pull up at Hampton at the sight of a
fleet of sailing boats tacking from side to side – 'as dangerous,
it seemed to us, as the much hated steam launches'. Jerome K.
Jerome's three men hoist a sail, and the narrator glories in the
experience of sailing – until disaster strikes.

> There is no more thrilling sensation I know of than sailing. It
> comes as near to flying as man has got to yet ... The wings
> of the rushing wind seem to be bearing you onward, you
> know not where ... you are a part of Nature! Your heart is
> throbbing against hers! ... We seemed like knights of some
> old legend, sailing across some mystic lake into the unknown
> realm of twilight, unto the great land of the sunset.
>
> We did not go into the realm of twilight; we went slap
> into [a] punt, where three old men were fishing.

In the first half of the twentieth century, dinghy sailing on the
Thames blossomed. A charming book on the subject is Clifton
Reynolds's *Sailing Small Waters* (1946), written while he was living
in a house on the Thames near Bourne End. He records his experi-
ences of learning to sail International 14-foot dinghies at the Upper
Thames Sailing Club with the freshness of a beginner's mind:

Such boats sail well in the lightest airs. In stronger breezes they are as sensitive as race-horses. Their grace I think is derived from harmony and balance. The area of snow-white sail they carry is immense in proportion to the size of the boats.

At the other end of the scale of sailing beauty are Thames barges. In 1918 Cyril Ionides published *A Floating Home*, with atmospheric illustrations by Arnold Bennett. The story of his family's life on the waters of the Estuary, it was offered partly as a solution for those who were finding it difficult after the war to afford both a house and a public-school education for children, but also as a tribute to the life and work of barge skippers. Bargees also enjoyed themselves: A.P. Herbert gets over all the excitement of a barge race in the estuary in his novel *The Singing Swan* (1968):

> The *Singing Swan* was lying over, white water came on deck
> by the leeboard, and slipped away through the scuppers,
> the main-sheet block strained and creaked at the end of the
> horse. Almost for the first time that day there was the sense
> of urge and power which meant that we were truly sailing.

The river was opened up to leisure in a quite different way by the advent of steam-driven boats. By 1820 regular passenger services were set up between London and Gravesend, which could offer the allurements of Rosherville Gardens, as the Kent Zoological and Botanical Gardens Institute was known. Laid out in 1837, it boasted Greek temples, a baronial hall and an archery lawn. Writers as varied as Thackeray, George Gissing, E. Nesbit and P.G. Wodehouse mention trips to Rosherville.

Steamer services were soon extended down the estuary to Southend, Margate and Whitstable. The problem of shallow water near the banks was solved by embanking the river in London and building wharfs and piers that transformed quiet retreats into hectic holiday resorts. In *Martin Chuzzlewit* (1844), Charles Dickens describes the steam packets at London Bridge Steam Wharf:

Shoals of passengers, and heaps of luggage, were proceeding hurriedly on board. … In the midst of all this turmoil there was an incessant roar from every packet's funnel, which quite expressed and carried out the uppermost emotion of the scene. They all appeared to be perspiring and bothering themselves, exactly as their passengers did; they never left off fretting and chafing, in their own hoarse manner, once; but were always panting out, without any stops, 'Come along do make haste I'm very nervous come along oh good gracious we shall never get there how late you are do make haste I'm off directly come along!'

As steamers grew in size, piers were extended, in Southend's case to 1.3 miles, making it the longest in the world. In 1890 an electric railway replaced the horse-pulled tram that used to carry passengers to and from the boat. A pavilion at the pierhead offered entertainments, refreshments and penny-in-the-slot amusements. 'The Pier is Southend', said Sir John Betjeman, calling for its preservation. 'Southend is the Pier.'

Once locks and weirs were improved, and the Thames was better dredged, steamer services upstream of Richmond increased. Slim steam launches with propeller-driven engines could navigate the whole river; by 1898 the SL *Nuneham*, built by Clark of Brimscombe, was taking passengers along not only the Thames but also the Thames and Severn canal: too late for Captain Hornblower, however, who helps a drink-sodden bargee 'foot' the boat through the canal's 3,817-yard-long Sapperton Tunnel in C.S. Forester's *Hornblower and The Antropus*, which is set in 1806. Hornblower continues to skipper the barge for much of his journey down the Thames all the way to London, where he takes charge of the boats required for Nelson's funeral.

Small steam launches soon developed, but were regarded by many writers, especially those in unpowered boats, as a positive menace. In *Our River*, G.D. Leslie fulminates against them.

Steam launches grew to be a great nuisance on the river: Frederick Walker's cartoon for *Punch* magazine, Captain Jinks of the 'Selfish' and His Friends Enjoying Themselves on the River, shows Walker himself fishing (21 August 1869).

The river from the 'Roebuck' to Maple Durham is of perfect beauty; overhung with wide spreading trees, its banks decorated with flowers of every sort, the water as clear as could be wished … There is only one thing to wish for when passing this lovely spot; that in it you may not meet a hateful steam launch, fouling the water with its screw, scaring the rooks with its discordant whistle, blackening the air with its dirty smoke, and robbing the view of all its calm sentiment and beauty.

In the 1890s, first naptha and then electric launches appeared, and by the 1920s petrol-driven boats were introduced. However, steamers were preferred for passenger services until diesel engines were introduced in the 1950s.

THE STREAM OF PLEASURE

> I know of no other classic stream that is so splashed about
> for the mere fun of it. There is something droll and almost
> touching in the way that on the smallest pretext of a holiday
> or fine weather, the mighty population takes to boats.
>
> Henry James, *English Hours*, 1905

Besides removing commercial traffic from the Thames, trains
provided holidaymakers with easy access to the river. Inns that
once catered for the rough bargee trade changed into luxurious
hostelries for gentry afloat. Regattas, pageants and aqua-fêtes
were held in most Thameside towns, and the river's banks and
islands were fringed with houseboats with elaborate roof gardens
and gaily striped awnings.

Poems and songs about the river abounded; before the invention of the gramophone, everyone made their own music. Passenger steamers typically had a small dance band, and private or
chartered steam launches often had a piano. An advertisement for
Frank Attwell of Reading's piano and organ store at the end of
Taunt's 1894 guide *Goring, Streatley and the Neighbourhood* offered
'Quadrille Bands and Artistes'. On smaller boats, accordions,
fiddles and penny whistles accompanied more or less talented
singers, or, after their introduction in the 1900s, portable wind-up
gramophones. A typical cabin library might include G.R. Leslie's
Our River, the Halls' *The Book of the Thames*, J. Ashby-Sterry's
The Lazy Minstrel, the latest Taunt map of the Thames, and the
invaluable *Dictionary of the Thames: An Unconventional Handbook*
by Charles Dickens (son of the novelist). Updated every year
between 1880 and 1896, this last was an alphabetical cornucopia
of fascinating information about places on and events connected
with the Thames, as well as providing details of train and steamer
times, special excursions, facilities for anglers, boat hire and inns
along the river. Charley, of whose 'indescribable lassitude' his
father often complained, may have got his affection for the river at

A colourful variety of craft, including houseboats, skiffs and steam launches, wait to enter Boulters Lock, near Maidenhead, one of the busiest locks on the Thames. Picture painted in 1906 by Mortimer Menpes, RA.

Eton; he boasts of 'a practical Thames experience of over twenty years'. He gives several pages of recipes for 'Cups, Cocktails and Grogs', all of which 'have successfully passed the ordeal of personal experience', and the text often verges on the personal, as in this entry under B for Bathing:

> Few things are pleasanter on a hot day than a plunge into one of the deep, quiet, shady pools in which the Thames abounds. Few things are more exhilarating than to rise after a scientific header in the rushing waters below some such weir as that at Marlow.

People recorded their adventures in both words and sketches: this was a golden age for Thames art as well as its literature. Some books are personal accounts, some are practical guides, some are novels that feature the river as a source of recreation comic and romantic (the darker ones will feature in a later chapter).

The American novelist Nathaniel Hawthorne describes an expedition on the Thames near Oxford in *Our Old Home*, his affectionate account of time spent in England in 1863. He was rowed down the Thames from Stanton Harcourt to Oxford, and then took possession of 'a spacious barge, with a house in it, and a comfortable dining-room or drawing-room within the house, and a level roof, on which we could sit at ease, or dance if so inclined'. And eat:

> A table had been laid in the interior of our barge, and spread with cold ham, cold fowl, cold pigeon-pie, cold beef, and other substantial cheer, such as the English love, and Yankees too – besides tarts, and cakes, and pears, and plums, – not forgetting, of course, a goodly provision of port, sherry, and champagne, and bitter ale, which is like mother's milk to an Englishman, and soon grows equally acceptable to his American cousin.

Hawthorne goes on to explain that such barges were common in Oxford, and, drawn by horses, 'slipped through the water ... with a gentle and pleasant motion'. Their destination was Nuneham Courtenay, and they feasted as they travelled.

> It was life without the trouble of living; nothing was ever more quietly agreeable. In this happy state of mind and body we gazed at Christ Church meadows, as we passed, and at the receding spires and towers of Oxford, and on a good deal of pleasant variety along the banks: young men rowing or fishing; troops of naked boys bathing, as if this were Arcadia. … We were a large party now … poets, novelists, scholars, sculptors, painters, architects, men and women of renown, dear friends, genial, outspoken, open-hearted Englishmen, – all voyaging onward together, like the wise ones of Gotham in a bowl.

One particularly resourceful cruise was made by Howard Williams, a city clerk who took the train to Oxford with four friends and a double-sculled skiff on a flatbed truck. Sending boats by train to save upstream work was by then common practice, but Williams had no intention of taking things easy. His *Diary of a Rowing Tour from Oxford to London in 1875*, which he decorated with lively sketches, describes how the stalwart lads rowed, towed and paddled up the Oxford Canal to Warwick, where they carried the boat across to the Avon. From there, they rowed via Stratford-upon-Avon to Tewkesbury, where they joined the Severn. This took them to Gloucester, where they turned west into the Hereford–Gloucester canal. In Hereford they had their boat taken across town to launch it in the River Wye, down whose perilously rapid and shallow waters they careered to Ross, then proceeded more sedately to Monmouth and Chepstow, where they were towed across 9 miles of rough Severn water down to the mouth of the Avon. There they took the Avon and the Kennet and Avon canal to Reading, where they at last joined the Thames, enjoying its luxuries the more for their formidable journey. 'It was quite a change getting into civilized places again, where we were not stared at, and where we saw other pleasure boats.' The

434-mile trip took three weeks, and passed through 231 locks and four tunnels.

My favourite explorer of the river is James S. Whitman of Illinois. He travelled in a birchbark canoe which he had brought all the way from the backwoods of Nova Scotia, where it had been made by the Mi'kmaq people from 'some stately birch in the Acadian forest'. His account of his voyage, which began the tradition of recording personal tribulations as well as fine sights, was published in 1881 in the January edition of the popular magazine *Harper's Monthly*. Pictures of a moose and a fish were scraped on each side of the canoe's stern, and it caused vociferous comment.

'It's an alligator skin!'
'Look at the Chinese junk!'
'That's made of leather!'

Whitman boiled resin with soap 'to the consistency of molasses candy, daubing the mixture over likely leaking spots'. Then, with a friend to help as far as Abingdon, he set off from Oxford, finding 'a fascination about everything'. At Nuneham, he admired the 'princely home of the Harcourts … where the sheep pant beneath a shady elm, or swans "row their state with oary feet"' (a quotation from *Paradise Lost*). After Abingdon, Whitman continued alone, battling against contrary winds, and using an umbrella to take advantage of fair ones until 'it finally succumbed to its natural fate under the circumstances'. At Wallingford, jeering youths watching him struggle were persuaded to tow him for a penny each for a couple of miles. Despite the worsening leaks in the canoe, he persevered to Pangbourne ('captivating loveliness') and Mapledurham ('a very painter's paradise'). After passing Bisham Abbey, 'where lie the mortal parts of Richard Neville "the Kingmaker"', and noting the woods where Shelley worked on *The Revolt of Islam*, Whitman dozed off, 'lulled by the canoe's motion', until 'a noisy steam launch brought me to my senses',

James S. Whitman enjoys a tranquil stretch of the river in a birchbark canoe from Nova Scotia: he wrote up his adventures for *Harpers Monthly* in 1881.

and he found himself under Marlow's elegant little suspension bridge. By then it was raining, and he was relieved to arrive at Cookham, where 'the good landlord supplied me with a change of clothes and supplied every possible comfort'.

Whitman passed the 'massive pile' of Windsor Castle, and followed 'the sinuous course of the stream' to Runnymede and Chertsey, the home, he noted, of the poet Abraham Cowley. At Coway Stakes, Whitman got out not just to see the reputed site of Caesar's crossing, but to smear the last of his soap, 'the only expedient to hand', into the leaky stern of the canoe. He admired Walton Bridge, but began, like Gilpin, to feel that the river was losing 'those charms that gave such peculiar loveliness to the scenery of the Upper Thames'. But he persevered past Garrick's Villa to Hampton Court, which he found thronged by 'hundreds of men, women and children', brought there by a

London steamboat. There the article ends rather abruptly, and I can find no further mention of Whitman's adventures. What became of the canoe? Sunk perhaps.

Joseph Ashby-Sterry (1835–1917), a popular novelist and poet, wrote several volumes of doggerel, some comic, some maudlin, but all of it hugely popular with Victorian boaters, who declaimed it over tankards of beer or sang it to the strumming of ukuleles and thumping of piano keys. His delightful novel *A Tale of the Thames* (1896) starts at Trewsbury Mead on foot, then by canoe, skiff, steamer and steam yacht down the river, with much romantic interplay between upright young men and feisty girls. Knowing the wicked wanderings of the tiny river between Cricklade and Inglesham, I was astonished to read that 'after passing beneath Eisey Footbridge' in their canoe, Sterry's intrepid crew

> stepped the tiny mast and hoisted an enormous sail … The stream gurgled musically as the light craft flew over the waters. Occasionally the haymakers looked at them with open-mouthed surprise, and fancied that they had seen a daylight ghost.

Ashby-Sterry may have been using excess imagination. 'Not one boatman knows Eynsham or Lechlade for a thousand who are well acquainted with Medmenham or Marlow', wrote Paul Blake in a four-part article for *The Boy's Own Paper* in 1883. His own account of three young sportsmen venturing upriver in a skiff might have been calculated to deter other explorers. Having rowed and towed for several days, snapping off their towing mast under a bridge arch, and negotiating 'cantankerous rush beds' in a stream that wriggled 'like an eel in convulsions', they collapse with relief at Cricklade. 'That's over at last. I never did such a piece of river in my life', says one of the lads. 'And what a pace we went. A mile an hour at least.' That's more like it. I remember my own punt being overtaken upstream of Castle Eaton by two dear old ladies on zimmer frames promenading on the Thames Path.

Holiday reading was provided by *The Lock to Lock Times*, which began publication in 1887. By 1893 it had amalgamated with *River Views*, and was avidly read by the prosperous middle classes. 'Cygnetta' wrote a column titled 'Our Waterwomen', which specialised in current boating fashions, and 'Sportfolio' gave news of racing fixtures, regattas and fishing competitions. There was society tittle-tattle about who would be staying beside or on the river, and sale notices for steam launches, canoes, skiffs and houseboats ('four bedrooms, two e.c.s [earth closets] awning and frame, saloon, kitchen'). The 23 March 1893 edition complained that naptha and electric launches were making a nuisance of themselves in the peaceful Cookham backwaters, but that ''Arry and 'Arriet' (as vulgar cockney merrymakers had been christened in a *Punch* magazine series) were happily still 'conspicuous by their absence'.

J.M. Barrie's 1892 play *Walker, London*[3] is set on a Thames houseboat. Barrie loved the river, and lived in a London flat that overlooked it. In 1887 he rented a houseboat moored at Tagg's Island with a fellow journalist. He was soon singing *Arcadia*'s praises in the July edition of *British Weekly*:

> One of the charms of a houseboat is that it makes a
> backwoodsman of you for the time. ... All communication
> with the land is by small boat. You have a punt or dinghy for
> this purpose. ... For obvious reasons it is well to lie within
> easy distance of a village. Telegrams are brought to you
> (or rather to the opposite side of the river, where you must
> cross in your dinghy for them), and the shopkeepers, being
> largely dependent on houseboats, also send purchases up the
> towpath. ...
>   The life is quiet but not monotonous, for no day is quite
> like another. Hundreds of boats pass by every hour, from
> shrieking steam-launches to Canadian canoes, and on
> Sundays there is a wonderful procession to church that blocks
> the landing stage and brings craft together that were built on
> many waters.

In the play, derision is poked at 'swells' and cockneys alike, and at a Girton bluestocking who reasons logically that she should marry one man, but ends up following her heart and accepting an unreconstructed bully. Barrie's future wife Mary Ansell was given the leading part, that of a thoroughly sensible girl called Nanny. Much use is made of the punt rented with the boat, including the bluestocking getting her pole stuck in the mud and falling into the river.

Elizabeth and Joseph Pennell soon discovered that riverside inns were much more comfortable than sleeping on board their skiff. Elizabeth had a sense of humour, and *The Stream of Pleasure* is amusingly frank about the pouring rain, the perils of negotiating bridges, weirs and locks in a strong current, the unlovely aspects of houseboats on which 'buckets, brooms and life-preservers were the only ornaments', and 'those river fiends, the steam launches'. They made one attempt to make tea on the spirit stove, but 'the trouble was great, and the tea was bad'. After that, 'it rested from its labours in the box in which Salter had packed it, and for the privilege of carrying it with us we afterwards paid in our bill.'

Henry Wellington Wack's *In Thamesland, Being a Gossiping Record of Rambles through England from the Source of the Thames to the Sea, with Casual Studies of the English People, their Historic, Literary, and Romantic Shrines* (1906) is a mix of exuberant Yankee descriptions of the 'sylvan beauty' of 'the great little river' and disapproval of the enfeebling 'national *penchant* for small play and pastoral pastime'. A bellicose young democrat, Wack was baffled by the English approach to life. How could a nation that spent so much time in idle amusement have garnered the greatest empire known to man? Used as he was to the wilder shores of the Missouri and the rough rapids of the St Lawrence, the Thames seemed to him at first 'a well-groomed, quaintly-banked park rivulet, an aqueous dwarf', for all its 'picturesque swagger and a pride typically British'. Although won over by the combination of history and beauty of the 'sinuous little creek' that had been 'the inspiration of more lettered lore than any other stream in the world', he still concluded that the nation as a whole had had it.

> City cancer, town typhus, and village vagabondia are
> denuding the land of the sturdy sower and the bronzed
> reaper, and producing anaemic, clock-eyed clerks, tip-taking
> parvenus, and a legion of petty players of 'the winner'.

He and his tubby companion Russell (who had 'a wild spirit for petty adventure' and was a dab hand at mixing cocktails) travelled in the *Fuzzy-Wuzzy*.

> She was a light, tippy, fifteen-foot canoe, prettily-ribbed
> with ash and cedar, and decked-in fourteen inches from stern
> to bow. She was a rakish little craft, promising sport and
> mishap. How she came by her silly name, her owner said he
> never knew. A sturdy boy could lug her over a portage of
> five hundred yards, She could, and did, spill out her cargo
> on so slight a favour as the shifting of my pipe from the
> windward to the leeward side. She was fleet, and a capricious
> delight of fine lines and many graces.

Not a little shocked by the 'love dalliance afloat, lispings and kissings and woodland spooning' in backwaters by picknicking 'swains of Teddington', Wack and Russell arrive at Richmond, from where they travel by steamer through London to the Nore. 'Thamesland is a region of delight', Wack concludes. 'Foreigners flock to it in great numbers, Whatever else they fail to visit, they always travel through Thamesland on a natural tide of transit and summer pleasure.'

The upstream Thames equivalent of the Estuary's pleasure resorts were its islands. One of the most popular was Eel Pie Island at Twickenham. In his 1839 novel *Nicholas Nickleby*, Charles Dickens relates how

> It had come to pass, that afternoon, that Miss Morleena
> Kenwigs had received an invitation to repair next day, per

steamer from Westminster Bridge, unto the Eel-pie Island at Twickenham: there to make merry upon a cold collation, bottled beer, shrub, and shrimps, and to dance in the open air to the music of a locomotive band.

Monkey Island, near Bray, was originally known as Monk's Eyot, popularised to Monkey Island; hence the elegantly clad little apes in the ceiling paintings in the pavilion. This was built in 1738 by Charles Spencer, 3rd Duke of Marlborough, who used the island as a fishing lodge. By 1840, the lodge had become a riverside inn. During his affair with Rebecca West, H.G. Wells used to row up from the Royal Oak, his uncle's Windsor pub, to meet her there, and West makes it the place where Chris, the hero of her novel *The Return of the Soldier* (1918), meets Margaret, the love of his life. She is the daughter of the island's innkeeper, and manages the punt that brings visitors to the island.

> One sounded the bell that hung on a post, and presently Margaret in a white dress would come out of the porch and would walk to the stone steps down to the river. ... As she came near the steps she would shade her eyes and peer across the water ... A sudden serene gravity would show that she had seen one, and she would get into the four-foot punt that was used as a ferry and bring it over very slowly, with rather stiff movements of her long arms, to exactly the right place. When she had got the punt up on the gravel her serious brow would relax, and she would smile at one and shake hands and say something friendly, like, 'Father thought you'd be over this afternoon, it being so fine; so he's saved some duck's eggs for tea.'

The descriptions of the island and the lovers' meetings gain resonance knowing of West's experiences; although Margaret and Chris are deliberately made different in appearance from her and Wells, Margaret's straight, strongly marked eyebrows are Rebecca's own, as is her short-sightedness, and Chris has all Wells's energy and fire.

Meeting at Monkey Island was probably Wells's idea. The Thames recurs in his novels: Mr Polly finds great contentment with the plump landlady of a pub on an island in the Thames, and makes a fool of himself punting its ferry. Wells re-examined his relationship with Rebecca in *The Secret Places of the Heart* (1922), in which she appears as 'Martin Leeds … a young woman of considerable genius'. It too had an episode on the river. 'I know my Maidenhead fairly well', says Sir Richmond. 'Aquatic activities, such as rowing, punting, messing about with a boat-hook, tying up, buzzing about in motor launches, fouling other people's boats, are merely the stage business of the drama. The ruling interests of this place are love – largely illicit – and persistent drinking.' *The Time Machine* is set in the Thames Valley, and Martians blast the Shepperton to Weybridge ferry queue in *The War of the Worlds*.

THIS SPORTING LIFE

Oh shall I see the Thames again?
The prow-promoted gems again,
As beefy ATS
Without their hats
Come shooting through the bridge?
And 'cheerioh' and 'cheeri-bye'
Across the waste of waters die,
And low the mists of evening lie
And lightly skims the midge.

John Betjeman, 'Henley-on-Thames',
from *New Bats in Old Belfries*, 1945

Writers often watch racing on the Thames with a sardonic eye. My favourite summary of rowing eights is Iain Sinclair's 'Out on the river eight giants – heads in laps – were tongue-lashed by a squeaking midget' (*Radon's Daughters*, 1994). But Nathaniel

Hawthorne had only admiration for a barge race that he watched from a steamer taking him from Greenwich to London.

> A regatta of wherries raced past us, and at once involved every soul on board our steamer in the tremendous excitement of the struggle. The spectacle was but a moment within our view, and presented nothing more than a few light skiffs, in each of which sat a single rower, bare-armed, and with little apparel, save a shirt and drawers, pale, anxious, with every muscle on the stretch, and plying his oars in such fashion that the boat skimmed along with the aerial celerity of a swallow. ... it stirs one's sympathy immensely, and is even awful, to behold the rare sight of a man thoroughly in earnest, doing his best, putting forth all there is in him, and staking his very soul (as these rowers appeared willing to do) on the issue of the contest.

The outstanding locations for racing on the upper Thames are Oxford and Henley. Richard Hippisley Domenichetti's poem *The Thames* (1885) has a dramatic description of the Bumps.

> Once more he scans the crowded banks, once more
> He hears the shouting storm along the shore,
> Crowded with eager faces; round the bend
> The tense oars sweep along, and flashing send
> The boats, like lines of light, towards the goal.
> The old familiar frenzy stirs his soul.
> Again he grips the oar; the swift prow flies:
> One long, strong stroke, one bound, and then the prize!

Cuthbert Bede was the pen name of the novelist Edward Bradley (1827–1889). He spent a year at Oxford after taking his degree at Durham. His *The Adventures of Mr Verdant Green* (1853), which he illustrated himself, satirised such hearties. Fired by hero worship of 'Billy Blades', stroke of the college boat, 'who was fashioned somewhat after the model of the torso of Hercules', Verdant Green decides to try his hand at rowing.

To the river he next day went, and ... made his first essay in a 'tub' from Hall's. Being a complete novice with the oars, our hero had no sooner pulled off his coat and given a pull, than he succeeded in catching a tremendous 'crab', the effect of which was to throw him backwards, and almost to upset the boat. Fortunately, however, 'tubs' recover their equilibrium almost as easily as tombolas, and the *Sylph* did not belie its character; so the freshman again assumed a proper position, and was shoved off with a boat-hook.

Just as he feels he is getting the hang of things, disaster strikes:

He had left the Christ Church meadows far behind, and was beginning to feel slightly exhausted by his unwonted exertions, when he reached that bewildering part of the river termed 'the Gut'. So confusing were the intestine commotions of this gut, that, after passing a chequered existence as an aquatic shuttlecock, and being assailed with a slang-dictionary-full of opprobrious epithets, Mr Verdant Green caught another tremendous crab, and before he could recover himself, the 'tub' received a shock, and, with a loud cry of 'Boat ahead!' ringing in his ears, the University Eight passed over the place where he and the *Sylph* had so lately disported themselves.

Saved by a chum, and comforted with blankets and a brandy-and-soda, Verdant 'renounced the sweets of the Isis, and contented himself by becoming a 'Cherwell water-lily', as loungers in punts were known.[4]

Sandford of Merton (1903) is in all probability the source of the notoriously impossible claim that 'all rowed fast, but none so fast as stroke'. It was a spoof written by 'Belinda Blinders', the pen-name of the soldier and novelist Desmond Coke (1879–1931), and is a send-up both of undergraduate life and of Thomas Day's moral tract *Sandford and Merton* (1789). This is its version of the mythic incident:

The word sounded clear from the mouth of the 'Varsity captain of boats, and at once Ralph exerted the full force of Herculean arms. His blade struck the water a full second before any other; the lad had started well. Nor did he flag as the race wore on. ... As the boats began to near the winning-post, his oar was dipping into the water nearly twice as often as any other.

Zuleika Dobson, Max Beerbohm's affectionate 1911 satire on Oxford life, features a femme fatale who comes up for Eights Week. The novel's climax is the mass suicide by drowning of all its male undergraduates for love of her. It happens just as the Judas College boat is struggling to bump Magdalen. The suicides are led by the Duke of Dorset, who drowns in the full regalia of a Knight of the Garter, conveniently startling the cox of the Magdalen boat so much that Judas wins. But, instead of the usual cheers,

> Victory and defeat alike forgotten, the crews staggered erect and flung themselves into the river, the slender boats capsizing and spinning futile around in a melée of oars.
> From the towing-path – no more din there now, but great single cries of 'Zuleika!' – leapt figures innumerable through rain to river. The arrested boats of the other crews drifted zigzag hither and thither. The dropped oars rocked and clashed, sank and rebounded, as the men plunged across them into the swirling stream.

Most Oxford novels took rowing more seriously. In Thomas Hughes's *Tom Brown at Oxford* (1861), the sequel to *Tom Brown's Schooldays*, Tom goes up to St Ambrose College, and tries his hand with an oar, almost losing his life in the ferocious currents of the Sandford Lasher. He survives to be considered for the college boat. Miller, the cox, 'looked Tom and a few other would-be rowers in the St Ambrose boat over 'as the colonel of a crack regiment might look over horses at Horncastle-fair, with a single eye to their bone and muscle, and how much

'The whole pent-up life and energy which has been held in leash, as it were, for the last six minutes, is let loose, and breaks away': start of the bumps, illustrated by Sydney Prior Hall for Tom Hughes's *Tom Brown at Oxford* (1861).

work might be got out of them'. Hughes, who rowed for Oriel College when he was up at Oxford, describes Tom's race with passionate nostalgia.

> There it comes, at last – the flash of the starting gun. Long before the sound of the report can roll up the river, the whole pent-up life and energy which has been held in leash, as it were, for the last six minutes, is let loose, and breaks away with a bound and a dash which he who has felt it will remember for his life, but the like of which, will he ever feel again? The starting-ropes drop from the coxswains' hands,

the oars flash into the water, and gleam on the feather, the spray flies from them, and the boats leap forward. ... Isn't he grand, the Captain, as he comes forward like lightning, stroke after stroke, his back flat, his teeth set, his whole frame working from the hips with the regularity of a machine?

George Leslie was more interested in stylish spectators than the racing in his 1881 account of a regatta at Henley.

Directly the racing boats have passed, the course is rapidly covered again by boats of every description. There are gigs, skiffs, wherries, stout oak sailing-boats, canoes and punts; there are boats manned or 'girled' by fancy crews; some-times consisting of four pretty little girls in blue sailor dresses, or a set of boys, double-banked, in man-of-war costume.

The most famous rowing event on the Thames is undoubt-edly the Oxford and Cambridge Boat Race. Its inventor had a distinguished literary connection, and was himself both a keen sportsman and a witty wordsmith. The first race, held in 1829 at Henley, was the brainchild of William Wordsworth's nephew Charles, of Christ Church, Oxford and Charles Merivale, of St John's, Cambridge. In the course of their correspondence setting up the match, Wordsworth boasted 'in saucy style' of the prowess of the Oxford crew:

8. Staniforth (Christ Church Boat): 4 feet across the shoulders and as many through the chest ($\delta\iota\alpha\mu\pi\acute{\alpha}\xi$).
7. Moore (Christ Church Boat): 6 feet 1 inch; in all probability a relation of the giant whom the 'three rosy-cheeked schoolboys built up on the top of Helm Crag', so renowned for length and strength of limb.
6. Garnier (Worcester boat): splendid oar.
5. Toogood (Balliol Boat) – [Toogood] for you: but just the man for us.

4. Wordsworth (new oar): has neither words nor worth, action or utterance, etc. I only (row) right on; I tell you that that you yourselves do know.
3. Croft (Balliol Boat): no recommendation necessary.
2. Arbuthnot (Balliol Boat): strong as Bliss's Best [a famous Harrow beer].
1. Carter (St John's four-oar): *'potentior ictu fulmineo'*.

Theodore Hook's edition of Joseph Hewlett's *Peter Priggins, the College Scout* (1841) described a Henley race between the universities, which closely resembled the 1829 race.

> Just before the start, every inch of ground that could command a view of the river on either side was occupied by gazers of all sorts and sizes – lords and ladies, Jans and Jinnies, saints and sinners, cockneys and country bumpkins – it was an universal holiday in that part of the world. ... [I] could hear the steady cry of the steersman, 'Go it, my blues – beautifully pulled! – three minutes more, and your work's done – they lose ground (water he meant) every moment – steady! – no hurry – keep the old stroke! – backs down on the thwarts,' from the Oxford boat; and the 'By George, we're beaten! – quicken your stroke – don't you go back so, you No. 3 – pull for heaven's sake!' of the Cambridge. ... A tremendous shout, and the striking up of the church bells, proclaimed the victory was won by the Oxford men, with one hundred yards to spare!!!

MONTMORENCY AND TOAD

We put the kettle on to boil, up in the nose of the boat, and went down to the stern and pretended to take no notice of it, but set to work to get the other things out. That is the only way to get a kettle to boil up the river. If it sees that you are waiting for it and are anxious, it will never even sing. You have to go away and begin your meal, as if you were not going to have any tea at all. You must not even look round at it. Then you will soon hear it sputtering away, mad to be made into tea.

Jerome K. Jerome, *Three Men in a Boat*, 1889

The two most famous fictions set on the Thames are of course Jerome K. Jerome's *Three Men in a Boat* (1889) and Kenneth Grahame's *The Wind in the Willows* (1908). Jerome Klapka Jerome (1859–1947) was a well-known London journalist, editor of *The Idler*, and a regular contributor to *Home Chimes* magazine. He loved the Thames, and often made excursions on it with his friends George Wingrave (who shared his lodgings until Jerome married) and Carl Hentschel, an expert in photo-etching, whom he met outside the stage door of a theatre (both had a passion for play-going, and Jerome also wrote plays). Carl's and George's respectively extrovert and reticent characters were, according to R.R. Bolland's engaging *In the Wake of 'Three Men in a Boat'* (1995), generally true to life, though Harris's fondness for liquor was a typical Jerome tease: Carl was a teetotaller. The book first appeared in monthly instalments in *Home Chimes* between 1888 and 1889. *Three Men in a Boat (to say Nothing of the Dog)* describes how 'J' and his friends George and Harris hire a boat at Kingston, and row to Oxford, aided and impeded by J's dog Montmorency. The latter was, Jerome admitted in his memoir *My Life and Times*, pure invention. Otherwise the book stays remarkably faithful to truth, not least because it was originally intended to be a travel guide.

I did not intend to write a funny book, at first. I did not know I was a humorist. I never have been sure about it. In the Middle Ages, I should probably have gone about preaching and got myself burnt or hanged. There was to be 'humorous relief'; but the book was to have been 'The Story of the Thames', its scenery and history. Somehow it would not come … I decided to write the 'humorous relief' first – get it off my chest, so to speak. After which, in sober frame of mind, I could tackle the scenery and history. I never got there. It seemed to be all 'humorous relief'. By grim determination I succeeded, before the end, in writing a dozen or so slabs of history and working them in, one to each chapter, and F.W. Robinson, who was publishing the book serially, in *Home Chimes*, promptly slung them out, the most of them. From the beginning he had objected to the title and had insisted upon my thinking of another. And half-way through I hit upon 'Three Men in a Boat', because nothing else seemed right.

Jerome married Georgina Elizabeth Henrietta Stanley Marris ('Ettie') in June 1888, and would have had their honeymoon month of camping on the Thames in a little boat very fresh in his mind when he started the serial. Hence both its effervescent happiness and its occasional romantic transports.

Then we run our little boat into some quiet nook, and the tent is pitched, and the frugal supper cooked and eaten. Then the big pipes are filled and lighted, and the pleasant chat goes round in musical undertone; while, in the pauses of our talk, the river, playing round the boat, prattles strange old tales and secrets… And we sit there, by its margin, while the moon, who loves it too, stoops down to kiss it with a sister's kiss, and throws her silver arms around it clingingly; and we watch it as it flows, ever singing, ever whispering, out to meet its king, the sea – till our voices die away in silence, and the pipes go out – till we, common-place, everyday young men enough, feel strangely full of thoughts, half sad, half sweet, and do not care or want to speak – till we laugh, and, rising, knock the ashes from our burnt-out pipes, and say 'Good-night', and, lulled by the lapping water and the rustling trees, we fall asleep beneath the great, still stars, and dream that the world is young again.

It is also noticeable that Jerome spends much more time describing quiet places than substantial towns. 'Like the true river man he was, Jerome preferred to dwell on the little secret and deserted spots.'[5]

Jerome and Georgina's first home was at 104 Chelsea Gardens, a top-floor flat which had a circular window topped by a turret in one of its rooms. There Jerome wrote his masterpiece, looking down 'upon the river, and over Battersea Park to the Surrey hills beyond, with the garden of old Chelsea Hospital just opposite'. The book is still so funny that it is invariably included in lists of great comic novels, and to open it at random is still to chuckle. Legend has it that registrations of pleasure vessels on the river doubled within two years of its publication.

The other great celebration of the Victorians' love affair with boating on the Thames is of course *The Wind in the Willows*. 'Believe me, my young friend', says the Water Rat to Mole,

'there is NOTHING — absolute nothing — half so much worth doing as simply messing about in boats. Simply messing,' he went on dreamily: 'messing — about — in — boats. ... In or out of 'em, it doesn't matter. Nothing seems really to matter, that's the charm of it. Whether you get away, or whether you don't; whether you arrive at your destination or whether you reach somewhere else, or whether you never get anywhere at all, you're always busy, and you never do anything in particular; and when you've done it there's always something else to do, and you can do it if you like, but you'd much better not.'

The book had its origins in the bedtime stories, continued in letters, that Kenneth Grahame (1859–1932) invented for his only child, Alistair. They evoked the Elysium of the two childhood a shirt, you very silly old woman!" Then the toad lost his temper, + quite forgot himself, + said "Don't you dare to speak to your betters like that! And don't call me a silly old woman! I'm no more an old woman than you are yourself, you common, low, vulgar bargee!" Then the bargee looked closely at him, + cried out "Why, no, I can see you're not really a washerwoman at all! You're nothing but an old toad!" Then he grabbed the toad by one hind-leg + one fore-leg, + swung him round + sent him flying through the air ...... Like that. — Splosh!! He found himself head-over-ears in the water!

When the toad came to the surface he wiped the water out of his eyes + struck out for the shore; but the woman's dress he was wearing got round his legs, + made it very hard work. When at last he was safely on the tow-path again, he saw the barge disappearing in the distance, + the man looking back + laughing at him. This made Mr Toad mad with rage. He tucked the wet skirt up well under his arms, + ran as hard as he could along the path,

+ passed the barge, + ran on till he overtook the horse that was towing it, and unfastened the tow-rope, + jumped on the horse's back, + dug his heels into its sides. — off they went at a gallop! He took one look back as they went, + he saw that the barge had run into the opposite bank of the canal, + stuck, + the bargee was shaking his fist at him + calling out "Stop, stop, stop!!" But the toad never stopped, but only laughed + galloped on + on + on, across country, over fields + hedges, until he had left the canal, + the barge, + the bargee, miles + miles behind him.

I am afraid the Gipsy will have to wait till the next letter.

Your affectionate

Daddy

I am so glad to hear you have been out in a motor boat

'Splosh! He found himself … in the water!' Kenneth Grahame wrote a series of letters about the adventures of Mr Toad to his seven-year-old son Alistair from Cornwall, where he was holidaying with his wife. This one, dated Fowey, 1907, describes a bargee hurling Toad into the river; the brawny bargewoman of *The Wind in the Willows* was a later addition. The letter is now preserved in the Bodleian Library.

years that Kenneth spent near the Thames in Cookham Dene between 1864 and 1865, and that he was at that time trying to re-create for Alistair by moving to Cookham from the city. The book was a call for his contemporaries to appreciate the simple pleasures of the Thames rather than being distracted by the hectic pace of modern life. It shows the river in varied seasonal moods, peopled with animals who are both affectionate portraits of himself and his friends, and types regularly observed on the river. Grahame had all Badger's dignity, but shared Mole's penchant for domesticity and water worship; the Water Rat's rivercraft and wanderlust belonged to the energetic and scholarly Frederick Furnivall, founding editor of the *Oxford English Dictionary* and founder of the Hammersmith Sculling Club for Girls. The Cornish-based seafaring rat was the literary critic Arthur Quiller-Couch, who kept a yacht in Fowey. Toad's bumptious self-importance, fleeting enthusiasms and mania for speed were Grahame's way of criticising the new age of self-made men and rapid change.

> 'Once, it was nothing but sailing,' said the Rat, 'Then he tired of that and took to punting. Nothing would please him but to punt all day and every day, and a nice mess he made of it. Last year it was house-boating, and we all had to go and stay with him in his house-boat, and pretend we liked it. He was going to spend the rest of his life in a house-boat. It's all the same, whatever he takes up; he gets tired of it, and starts on something fresh.'
> 'Such a good fellow, too,' remarked the Otter reflectively: 'But no stability – especially in a boat!'

It was not immediately successful. Reviewing it for *The Bookman*, Arthur Ransome declared it 'like a speech to Hottentots made in Chinese' – going it rather strong considering his own distinctly fey story *Hoofmarks of the Faun* which was published a year later. But someone sent a copy to Theodore Roosevelt, whose praise for it made it an American bestseller. English enthusiasm grew, especially after A.A. Milne's 1930 adaptation of it for the theatre, *Toad of Toad Hall*. Grahame, forlorn after the suicide of his son in 1920, was by then living a reclusive life in Pangbourne, close to his beloved river. E.H. Shepard described coming to see him in 1931 to discuss the drawings he was doing for a new edition of the book.

Not sure about his new illustrator ... he listened patiently while I told him what I hoped to do. Then he said, 'I love these little people, be kind to them.' Just that, but sitting forward on his chair, resting upon its arms, his fine handsome head turned aside, looking like some ancient Viking, warming, he told me of the river nearby, of the meadows where Mole broke ground that spring morning, of the banks where Rat had his house, of the pool where Otter hid, and of Wild Wood way up on the hill above the river. ... He would like, he said, to go with me to show me the river bank that he knew so well, 'but now I cannot walk so far and you must find your way alone.'[6]

Sʳ John   Tradescant Senʳ

NATURALISTS
ON THE THAMES

T HE leisurely motion of a river encourages observation, and some of the most attractive words about the Thames have been written by naturalists. They reveal both how the river's flora and fauna have changed through the centuries, and how attitudes to nature have altered. The first Thames-side botanists were interested in the practical uses of plants, then shifted to a pre-occupation with classification. Their carefully organised gardens clustered along or near to the banks of the river in London. It was a source of irrigation as well as a convenient means of transport, and the city provided customers. Once exotic new specimens began to be imported from the far corners of the world, it also became apparent that London offered a benign microclimate that enabled non-native plants and trees to survive all but the most harsh British winters.

As travelling along and spending time beside the Thames became easier, naturalists explored both upstream and down-stream, and began to make detailed records of the plants, birds, insects and fish they found beside it. Some, like Dr Plot and Gilbert White, interested themselves in geological and natural curiosities; some, like Anna Hall, found it an opportunity for illustrating Divine design. Richard Jefferies warned against the danger of ruining the ecology of the Thames Valley. George

John Tradescant the elder was one of many distinguished plantsmen whose gardens bordered on the Thames. Portrait, probably posthumous, attributed to Emanuel de Critz (1608–1665).

Leslie was opposed to the 'dry nomenclature and everlasting classification' of the trained botanist: his approach was that of the artist. C.J. Cornish, author of *The Naturalist on the Thames* (1902), had a remarkably modern vision of the river as an organic whole. Special mention must be made of Robert Gibbings. who offered a joyful and hedonistic approach to the river in his two famous books *Sweet Thames Run Softly* and *Till I End My Song*. Finally, fishermen as different as Isaak Walton and Arthur Ransome wrote affectionately about the river when experienced with rod in hand.

THAMES-SIDE PARADISES

Delighted Thames through tropic umbrage glides,
And flowers antarctic, bending o'er his tides;
Drinks the new tints, the sweets unknown inhales,
And calls the sons of science to his vales.

Erasmus Darwin, *The Botanic Garden*, 1791

Sixteenth- and seventeenth-century herbalists such as John Gerard and John Parkinson established splendid specimen gardens close to the river in London, notably that of Robert Cecil at Cecil (later Salisbury) House in the Strand, where first Gerard and then John Tradescant were gardeners. Tradescant established his own botanical garden at Lambeth, introducing new species which he and his son found on their travels; it boasted the first English cultivars of Michaelmas daisies, phlox, cos lettuce, lilac, Virginia creeper and the tulip tree. In 1656 John Tradescant the Younger published *Musaeum Tradescantianum*, an account of the Tradescant collection in their Lambeth house 'The Ark'. In addition to plants, there were, he explained,

divers sorts of Birds, four-footed Beasts and Fishes, to whom I have given usual English names. Others are less familiar, and as yet unfitted with apt English terms, as the shell-Creatures, Insects, Minerals, Outlandish-Fruits, and the like.

The novelist Philippa Gregory has published two enthralling novels about them. The first, *Earthly Joys*, opens with Tradescant travelling on the Thames with Robert Cecil; it also describes his voyage from Deptford to Russia. *Virgin Earth* describes his son's plant-hunting in North America.

John Evelyn's *Sylva, or A Discourse of Forest-Trees and the Propagation of Timber* (1664) was informed by the splendid gardens of his home at Sayes Court beside the river at Deptford; they were especially rich in trees of all kinds, including 300 fruit trees. He also visited the remarkable collection of plants and trees established in the Thames-side grounds of Fulham Palace by Bishop Henry Compton. He notes in his Diary on 11 October 1681: 'To Fulham to visit the Bishop of London, in whose garden I first saw the Sedum arborescens in flower, which was exceedingly beautiful.'[1] 'He joined to his taste in gardening a real and scientific knowledge of plants', wrote the botanist Richard Pulteney. Specimens from America, Africa and India were brought back by church missionaries, among them the first magnolia, the tea tree, the cork oak, several maples and the black walnut.

The Chelsea Physic Garden was founded on the banks of the Thames in 1673 by the Society of Apothecaries. In 1712 Sir Hans Sloane (1660–1753), royal physician and eminent naturalist, acquired the manor of Chelsea, but leased the 4-acre site of the garden to the Apothecaries in perpetuity for a £5-a-year rent on condition that 'it be for ever kept up and maintained as a physic garden'; the rent is still solemnly paid. He appointed Philip Miller as gardener in 1722. Miller described his work there in his enormously successful *Gardeners Dictionary; Containing the Methods of Cultivating and Improving the Kitchen, Fruit and Flower Garden, as also, the Physick Garden, Wilderness, Conservatory and Vineyard* (1731). He remarks in it that 'the best and most natural water [for plants] is that of a fine soft river', and that sometimes non-native plants like the American cacalia (part of the aster family) have propagated 'from roots thrown out of the Physic-garden, which

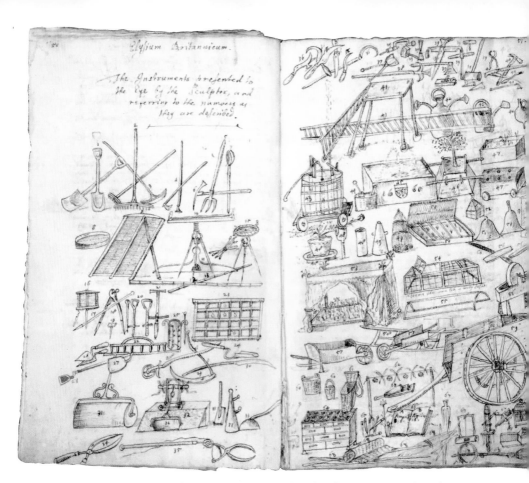

John Evelyn's Deptford garden was watered by the Thames. Pen sketches of garden tools from his unpublished gardening encyclopaedia *Elysium Britannicum*.

have been carried by the tide of the river to a great distance [and] have fastened to the banks, where they grow and spread'.

Hans Sloane spent 18 months in the Caribbean, bringing back over 800 new plants, which he described in a two-volume folio *A Voyage to the Islands* (1707–1725). In 1741 he moved to Chelsea himself, with his vast collection of carefully catalogued plants, stuffed animals, antiquities, coins and curios. He was a collector of other men's collections as well as making his own acquisitions. He bequeathed everything to the nation, inspiring the establishment of the British Museum in 1753.

In 1678 John Evelyn recorded a visit to Kew Park, home of his friend Sir Thomas Capel, brother to the Earl of Essex. 'It is an old timber house, but his garden has the choicest fruit of any plantation in England, as he is the most industrious and understanding in it.' In 1728 Kew Park was substantially rebuilt for Prince Frederick and his wife Princess Augusta, who was the driving force in the extension of its gardens from 7 to over 100 acres. George III grew up there, and after he became king he invited the great naturalist and explorer Sir Joseph Banks, then living across the river in Isleworth, to advise on and furnish its botanical collections by financing the travels of other naturalists. The physician and naturalist Erasmus Darwin emphasised the advantages of Kew's position on the Thames in the opening lines of his epic poem on the natural world, *The Botanic Garden* (1791).

> So sits enthron'd in vegetable pride
> Imperial KEW by Thames's glittering side;
> Obedient sails from realms unfurrow'd bring
> For her the unnam'd progeny of spring;
> Attendant Nymphs her dulcet mandates hear,
> And nurse in fostering arms the tender year,
> Plant the young bulb, inhume the living seed,
> Prop the weak stem, the erring tendril lead;
> Or fan in glass-built fanes the stranger flowers
> With milder gales, and steep with warmer showers.

CLOSELY OBSERVING THE RIVER

> Winding in and out like an Indian in his canoe, perhaps traces of an otter might be found...
>
> Richard Jefferies, *The Modern Thames*, 1884

The earliest book to offer substantial detailed information on the ecology of the Thames Valley was Dr Robert Plot's *Natural History of Oxfordshire* (1677). Rich in engravings of plants and fossils, many from the gravel beds adjoining the Thames, it includes the first known illustration of a dinosaur bone, which Plot thought belonged to a giant. Plot's learning inspired Elias Ashmole to offer his collection to Oxford University, and Plot became first keeper of the Ashmolean Museum. Plot was deeply interested in the healing properties of plants and indeed rocks; he noted a medicinal spring on the banks of the river near Goring as 'celebrated for its efficacy in the cure of cutaneous disorders, and also for ulcers and sore eyes'; it was soon being bottled and sold.

Gilbert White's *The Natural History of Selborne* (1789) combines a naturalist's observation with an engagingly personal style. In the 1750s he visited his friend John Mulso, a Sunbury curate. His diary recalls the bats he saw on the river Thames:

> Pretty late, in a boat from Richmond to Sunbury, on a warm summer's evening, I think I saw myriads of bats between the two places: the air swarmed with them all along the Thames, so that hundreds were in sight at a time ... Bats drink on the wing, like swallows, by sipping the surface, as they play over pools and streams. They love to frequent waters, not only for the sake of drinking, but on account of insects, which are found over them in the greatest plenty.

White also recorded the behaviour of swallows on the river at Sunbury, wondering if it was evidence for the then much-mooted idea that they hibernated underwater for the winter:

> About ten years ago I used to spend some weeks yearly at Sunbury, which is one of those pleasant villages lying on the Thames, near Hampton-court. In the autumn, I could not help being much amused with those myriads of the swallow kind which assemble in those parts. But what struck me most was, that, from the time they began to congregate, forsaking the chimnies and houses, they roosted every night in the osier-beds of the eyots of that river. Now this resorting towards that element, at that season of the year, seems to give some countenance to the northern opinion (strange as it is) of their retiring under water. A Swedish naturalist is so

Anna Hall described this 'curiously constructed' reed warbler's nest, 'lined with a little wool, fine grass, and long hairs', and 'rocked by every breeze' in *The Book of the Thames* (1859).

much persuaded of that fact, that he talks, in his calendar of Flora, as familiarly of the swallows going under water in the beginning of September, as he would of his poultry going to roost a little before sunset.

Mention has already been made of Samuel and Anna Hall's *The Book of the Thames* (1859). Its detailed descriptions of the river's plants, birds, fishes and animals, as well as the moods of both water and weather, were the contribution of Anna Hall, who had already written *Daddy Dacre's School* (1844), a fictionalised child's guide to nature in Dorset. The text of *The Book of the Thames* is embellished with exquisite engravings of crowsfoot and kingfishers, water lilies and tortoise beetles, ancient trees and river fish, and much more. Each is described at length, often with poetic reference. Her passage on the reed warbler includes two quotations from Cowper's *The Task*.

The chorus of lively chirpings that greets our ear from the neighbouring reed-beds, proceeds from those little aquatic songsters, the sedge-warbler (*Salicaria phragmites*), and the reed-warbler (*Salicaria arundinacea*), two birds closely related in appearance and habits, and generally to be found in company in reedy spots by the water-side, uttering their varied chant, the programme of which comprises imitations of the notes of the swallow, lark, sparrow, and linnet, with some original bits of their own ...

Those who row up or down the Thames, or walk along its ever-pleasant banks, have, therefore, a source of enjoyment which inland dells and woods do not afford, for the notes of these birds, even if 'Sounds inharmonious in themselves and harsh', give exceeding pleasure when in keeping with the character of the scene.

Henry Robert Robertson's *Life on the Upper Thames* (1875) is a cornucopia of information about the men and women who at that time made their living on and beside the Thames using the trees, plants, animals, fish and birds of the river. It is packed with his own woodcuts and generously laced with literary reference and dry wit. A plate showing the fun had by the children of a fisherman playing in a wrecked punt has an exquisitely observed landscape behind it; another showing a hunter crouching behind a horse-shaped barrier with a long-barrelled birding gun is accompanied by mentions of stalking horses in Shakespeare, and a description of how to make one in Gervase Markham. He does, however, put in a plea for sparing the graceful and intelligent otter, by then almost exterminated from the river. The wealth of detail in Robertson's observations is impressive. A chapter on polling willows warms up with references to the Book of Job, the Psalms, and *Othello* before describing the best ways of planting and polling, and detailing dozens of uses for the wood, from fences, baskets and the blades of paddle-steamer wheels to fine charcoal for rough sketching. The medical uses of its bark recommended in Gerard's *Herbal* are noted, then two chapters are devoted to growing the willow rods known as osier, and preparing them for making baskets in all shapes and sizes.

'No one English writer before had such a wide knowledge of labourers, farmers, gamekeepers, poachers, of the fields, and woods, and waters, and the sky above them, by day and night' wrote Edward Thomas of Richard Jefferies (1848–1887). Renowned for such accurate and informative but intensely poetic books about country life as *The Gamekeeper at Home* and *The Amateur Poacher*, Jefferies was descended from generations of Wiltshire farmers who lived near the hamlet of Coate, near Swindon, Wiltshire. He first worked for a local newspaper, but soon realised that London offered more opportunities for an aspiring writer. He and his wife moved to Tolworth in 1877, and *Nature Near London* (1883) was the fruit of his rambles in the countryside on the outskirts of the capital. It has a chapter describing the reach above Teddington Lock, 'the portal through which a thousand boats at holiday time convey men and women to breathe pure air'. He rhapsodises about larks there 'singing as they soar', whitening barley interspersed with exuberantly dense poppies and 'the large blue rays of wild succory'.

> In the evening, the rosy or golden hues of the sunset will be reflected on the surface from the clouds; then the bats wheel to and fro, and once now and then a nighthawk will throw himself through the air with uncertain flight, his motions scarcely to be followed, as darkness falls.

A year later, when Jefferies wrote his essay *The Modern Thames* for the *Pall Mall Gazette*, he has become disillusioned. It begins with a haunting sentence: 'The wild red deer can never again come down to drink at the Thames in the dusk of the evening as once they did.'

> The moorhens are shot, the kingfishers have been nearly exterminated or driven away from some parts, the once common black-headed bunting is comparatively scarce in the

more frequented reaches, and if there is nothing else to shoot at, then the swallows are slaughtered.

He must have welcomed new legislation that came into force a year later outlawing shooting on the river. The second half of the essay is a light-hearted description of his decision to take a holiday rowing 'from Teddington Lock upwards to Windsor, to Oxford, on to quiet Lechlade, or even farther deep into the meadows by Cricklade'.

> From its banks I should gather many a flower and notice many a plant, there would be, too, the beautiful water-lily. Or I should row on up the great stream by meadows full of golden buttercups, past fields crimson with trifolium or green with young wheat. Handsome sailing craft would come down spanking before the breeze, laden with bright girls – laughter on board, and love the golden fleece of their argosy.

But he finds rowing upstream much harder work than he thought it would be. Struggling to negotiate his clumsy hired boat through the dense throng of more competent boaters, barges and steam-tugs, he realises that

> There was no place on the great river for an indolent, dreamy particle like myself, apt to drift up into nooks, and to spend much time absorbing those pleasures which enter by the exquisite sensitiveness of the eye – colour, and shade, and form, and the cadence of glittering ripple and moving leaf.

As he watches athletic young men in striped flannels energetically towing boats laden with pretty girls upstream, he has a brainwave worthy of Jerome K. Jerome.

> I began to discern the true and only manner in which the modern Thames is to be enjoyed. Above all things – nothing heroic. Don't scull – don't row – don't haul at tow-ropes – don't swim – don't flourish a fishing-rod. Set

your mind at ease. Make friends with two or more athletes, thorough good fellows, good-natured, delighting in their thews and sinews. Explain to them that somehow, don't you see, nature did not bless you with such superabundant muscularity, although there is nothing under the sun you admire so much. Forthwith these good fellows will pet you, and your Thames fortune is made. You take your place in the stern-sheets, happily protected on either side by feminine human nature, and the parasols meeting above shield you from the sun. The tow-rope is adjusted, and the tugs start. The gliding motion soothes the soul. Feminine boating nature has no antipathy to the cigarette. A delicious odour, soft as new-mown hay, a hint of spices and distant flowers – sunshine dried and preserved, sunshine you can handle – rises from the smouldering fibres. This is smoking summer itself. Yonder in the fore part of the craft I espy certain vessels of glass on which is the label of Epernay. And of such is peace.

Jefferies, who moved to Eltham, near Greenwich, in 1884, had by this time developed the deep hatred of London that is at the heart of his post-apocalyptic fantasy *After London* (1885). Sinking sea levels have led to the blocking of the estuaries of both the Severn and the Thames. Now a vast lake 200 miles wide stretches from the red rocks of the Severn eastwards, divided into two unequal portions by the Vale of the White Horse:

The low-lying parts of the mighty city of London became swamps, and the higher grounds were clad with bushes. The very largest of the buildings fell in, and there was nothing visible but trees and hawthorns on the upper lands, and willows, flags, reeds, and rushes on the lower. These crumbling ruins still more choked the stream, and almost, if not quite, turned it back. If any water ooze past, it is not perceptible, and there is no channel through to the salt ocean. It is a vast stagnant swamp, which no man dare enter, since death would be his inevitable fate.

Almost all William Morris's designs were derived from nature. 'How I love the earth, and the seasons, and weather and all things that deal with it, and all that grows out of it as this has done!', he wrote of Kelmscott Manor. These extracts from letters written while he was there show how keen his observation was:

April: It has just been raining May butter, as Izaak Walton says: looked for an hour as if it would never stop raining again; then it got a little lighter, and then of a sudden was the bright sun and a rainbow. ... I saw a leash of plovers yesterday squawking away, and making believe that they had no nest close at hand. The garden is full of bullfinches, which are fat pretty dears, and sing a little short song very sweetly.

September: In the twilight the stint or summer snipe was crying about us and flitting from under the bank and across the stream: such a clean-made, neat-feathered, light grey little chap he is, with a wild musical little note like all the moor-haunting birds.

Many passages in George Leslie's *Our River* (1888) reflect his interest in ecology, and he declares himself better pleased by the flowers, birds and animals along its banks than the 'noblemen's seats and well-known objects of interest'. Chapter IX is headed 'Notes on the Natural History of the River'. In it he describes his own home near Henley:

In the garden of my cottage at Remenham a great variety of birds can be seen in their different seasons, robins, wag-tails, chaffinches, thrushes and blackbirds, nightingales, and many others. A pair of swallows commenced a nest under the eaves of the stable, but being turned out of it by the sparrows, they took apartments in the hay-loft, which they have continued to occupy for three years; they fly in at one open door and out at another. I am never tired of watching them; the bold way they dart down and scream at the cat is very amusing, altogether disgusting the cat. They occasionally settle on the gutter edge and sing for a considerable time; their song or twitter is excessively pretty and cheerful. There are whole families of sparrows and bats in the roofs.

His *Letters to Marco* (1893) and its sequel *Riverside Letters* (1896) are even more focused on his own observations of natural history. Like Gilbert White's letters, they were written to a friend, Leslie's fellow painter Henry Stacy Marks, who specialised in painting birds. Marks drew the parallel in a bookplate he made for Leslie showing Gilbert White contemplating his famous tortoise. The books were written after the Leslies had moved to Riverside, a house with gardens down to the Thames just upstream of Wallingford Bridge. He looked at nature with an artist's eye, remarking on 'the colourlessness of sunshine during a north-east wind'.

> Sky, trees, and grass all looking washed out and drabby.
> I have been particularly struck with this colourless aspect
> lately; there is always a white haze or glare round the sun,
> which seems to bleach its rays, and when a few thin beggarly
> clouds pass over, it appears, as the Professor [Ruskin] so
> happily expresses it, exactly 'like a bad half-crown at the
> bottom of a basin of soap-suds'. (Letter XXXI)

Many of Leslie's illustrations are exquisite: the bole of the sycamore he sees from his bedroom window, a novel 'bird's-eye view' of a swallow, hungry young swallows peeping out from a corner of the roof of the loggia beside the boathouse, a toad emerging from a hole, a rookery in a gale, seedpods of a hellebore 'looking rather like sucking pigs at their meals'.

Charles John Cornish (1858–1906) was brought up not far from the Thames at Childrey, in Berkshire. After Oxford, he became a Classics master at St Paul's School, and began to write regular nature articles for *The Spectator* and *Country Life*. He and his wife Edith Thornycroft lived at Orford House, one of a pair of semi-detached houses overlooking the Thames on Chiswick Mall which were built for his father-in-law Sir John Thornycroft FRS, a renowned engineer who designed and built steam launches for the river and torpedo boats for the navy at his Chiswick works. The combination of teaching boys and writing for popular magazines rather than scientific journals made Charles Cornish's writing exceptionally approachable; his classical education added elegance and literary depth.

His *Naturalist on the Thames* is in fact a collection of his published articles, with some added material. It begins with a dramatic description of the geology of the river.

> It has ever been a masterful stream holding its own against the inner forces of the earth; for where the chalk hills rose, silently, invisibly, in the long line from the vale of White Horse to the Chilterns the river seems to have worn them down as they rose at the crossing point at Pangbourne, and kept them under, so that there was no barring of the Thames, and no subsequent splitting of the barrier with gorges, cliffs, and falls. Its clear waters pass from the oolite of the Cotswolds, by the blue lias and its fossils, the sandstone rock at Clifton Hampden, the gravels of Wittenham, the great chalk range of the downs, the greensand, the Reading Beds, to the geological pie of the London Basin, and the beds of drifts and brick earth in which lie bedded the frames and fragments of its prehistoric beasts. In and beside its valley are great woods, parks, downs, springs, ancient mills and fortresses, palaces and villages, and such homes of prehistoric man as Sinodun Hill and the hut remains at Northfield. It has 151 miles of fresh water and 77 of tideway, and is almost the only river in England in which there are islands, the famous eyots, the lowest and largest of which at Chiswick touches the London boundary.

Cornish explains that he lives on the Thames at Chiswick, and has also spent 'weeks and months' staying in and around Wittenham, 'at all times of the year', using it as a base from which to explore the Thames Valley. 'There is no better and more representative part of the river than this', he declares.

Fish, fowl and foxes, rare Thames flowers and shy Thames chub, butterflies, eel-traps, fountains and springs, river shells and water insects, are all parts of the 'natural commodities' of the district.

Chapters follow on shells, the antiquity of river plants, chub, crayfish and trout, butterflies and insects, natural springs and London fossils, and much more. Striking images abound: 'A fox has no nerves,' he explains. 'He keeps his head with the coolness of a Red Indian, and a "slimness" all his own.' He discovers neretina shells 'like Venetian beads', limpets 'no larger than a yew berry, and shaped like a Phrygian cap', a great migration of swallows which 'drifted above, in clouds, twisting round like soot in a smoke-wreath'; 'a monster chub rises like a dark salamander out of the depths'. Insects fascinate him. At night, he observes,

> The great carnivorous water-beetle, the dytiscus, after catching and eating other creatures all day, with two-minute intervals to come up, poke the tips of its wings out of the water and jam some air against its spiracles, before descending once more to its subaqueous hunting-grounds, will rise by night from the surface of the Thames, lift again those horny wing-cases, unfold a broad and beautiful pair of gauzy wings, and whirl off on a visit of love and adventure to some distant pond, on to which it descends like a bullet from the air above.

The last chapter echoes the vision of the river as an 'organic whole' in the first one by voicing a plea for the Thames to be made a 'National Trust', and so prevent the dumping of sewage and refuse, ugly developments on its banks, and limitations put on access to it. Cornish would have been delighted to know how much has since been done to protect and restore the river, especially the foundation of the Earth Trust to preserve his beloved Wittenham Clumps and their environs.

RUNNING SOFTLY

I want to disguise myself as a willow, and drift down the
river, seeing, recording and drawing whatever comes my way.

Richard Gibbings to John Hadfield, 1936[2]

The Irish-born writer and artist Robert Gibbings (1889–1958) grew
up on the banks of the River Lee, which gave him a deep love
of nature and an especial affection for rivers. Between 1924 and
1933 he ran the Golden Cockerel Press at Waltham St Lawrence,
not far from the Thames at Wargrave. In 1936, after writing and
illustrating a series of travel books for Penguin, he began teaching
typography at Reading University. As the shadow of war deepened,
and travelling became fraught, 'there arose in me a great desire to
find peace beside a river'. Inspired by natural history trips to the
Thames organised by the University, he proposed a book to John
Hadfield. He designed a purpose-built boat, which was built by
the University's woodwork department. It had a flat bottom for
shallow parts of the river and to give plenty of room to sleep, but
was sculled rather than punted. It sported a prow in the shape of a
ram's horn carved by Gibbings, roomy lockers to hold microscopes
and other apparatus, and hoops to support an awning. *Willow* was
built in two weeks, and proved to be an ideal craft.

Gibbings was towed upstream to Lechlade on 29 July 1939.
Before heading downriver, he drove to the source at Trewsbury
Mead, then walked the 20 miles to Lechlade. After Somerford,
he found 'a wooded fairyland'.

> Here the great water dock, the teasel, the willow-herb, and
> purple loosestrife struggle for supremacy on the banks,
> turquoise dragon flies flit from lily leaf to lily leaf, and
> the pond skater and those small mercurial beetles, the
> whirlygigs, gyrate and skim above the surface of the stream.

Quoting Walton on insects and Pliny on eels bred of dew,
recalling Ovid's Ariadne at the sight of spider's webs and hearing

Robert Gibbings was a river man through and through, exploring waterways all over Britain as well as in France. He pictured himself in this wood engraving (published in *The Wood Engravings of Robert Gibbings*, 1959).

local lore from a self-styled lord of the river called the Viking, he arrives in Lechlade, and sets off for six weeks in *Willow*. Using a glass-bottomed box, he looks under some water lilies:

> No twirl of a ballerina's skirts could be more graceful than the folding and unfolding of those convoluted leaves ... sticklebacks dart here and there, and solemn perch pursue their dignified excursions. Beetles too, some of them burrowing into the mud, others charging about with self-important urgency.

And so downstream he goes, talking to locals, watching water snails as he swims, feeding fish with a crumbled hard-boiled egg. Loaches and leeches are weather prophets, he explains, pike can disguise themselves as old sticks, and a little owl's plumage makes it merge into the bark of a tree.

In succeeding chapters, Gibbings encounters a naked nymph (damsels embellish the narrative at regular intervals), hobnobs with Basil Blackwell in Oxford, calls at numerous hostelries, digresses with memories of the South Seas, and near Reading watches the wild frolics of four boys who execute handstands on the towpath and behave 'with all the effrontery of merry-andrews at a carnival'. On 3 September war with Germany was declared, and his journey had to stop. Too old for active service, he joined the River Patrol, and worked on the book. The rest of the journey had to be made piecemeal: an autumn walk along the Colne, a wander in the woods near Henley, 'marvelling at the lemon and gold of the beech leaves suspended over the dark evergreen undergrowth of box trees and red-berried yews', a digression on the ways of spiders.

May finds him back on the river in *Willow* at Shiplake, chatting as usual to locals; he has a wonderful knack of imparting interesting lore in a conversation. He has a ghostly glimpse of yet another river nymph near the old Hell-Fire Club at Medmenham. At Quarry Woods, below Marlow, he decides that the tutelary deity of its graceful beeches must be female, 'their leaves bearing a delicate downy growth comparable only to what is sometimes found in the small of the back of the "fairer sex"'. Cliveden woods have a pleasing uncaredforness: 'Nature is given her last chance beside the river for many miles, and she makes the most of it.' At Windsor, Gibbings recalls Malory (whose *Morte d'Arthur* he illustrated in 1936), and boards a river steamer to Kingston, tartly remarking that 'the aesthetic note of the bungalows between Datchett and Sunbury wails up and down like an air-raid warning', though he concedes that 'these musical comedy properties represent the attitude of mind of the people who want to relax'.

The war brought restrictions to travel on the river, and Gibbings continues his journey on foot from Kingston, enjoying the exotics at Kew and watching children swimming at Strand-on-the-Green.

Talk about the sacred Ganges. It is nothing to the Thames
at Chiswick. And there were children bathing, swimming in
water the colour of beer, with a sediment on its surface thick
enough to be the beginning of a new continent.

He quotes Whistler's lovely word-picture of Chelsea, then
continues to Blackfriars Bridge, where he visits *Discovery*, the ship
on which Scott and Shackleton travelled to the Antarctic, an epic
voyage 'which makes my fiddling about on the Thames seem very
small'. The book's postscript is heartfelt, and perfectly tuned, as
is the entire narrative, to the mood of the age. Gibbings confesses
to frequent disappointment at the tameness of the Thames, but
admits that 'I came to love the quiet stream which plods its way
obedient to every lock and weir'. What his encounters on his
journeys have taught him is that 'there is cruelty and illness and
poverty, but there is also abundance of kindheartedness, good
health and richness of spirit.' *Sweet Thames Run Softly* (1941)
was an instant success. 'A war-worn Britain responded to it as
soldiers respond to the song of a thrush under gunfire', recalled
John Hadfield. By 1953, it had sold 134,000 copies in a variety
of editions, including a special one for 'The Fighting Forces of
the Allied Nations'.

The companion volume, *Till I End My Song* (1957), was written after Gibbings and Patience Empson moved to Footbridge
Cottage, close to a backwater of the Thames at Long Wittenham,
'a world where neighbourliness is the currency'. The book is the
story of his first year there, full of local characters, customs and
history, lightly leavened with literary reference. On occasion
Gibbings's reminiscences wander to other parts of the river, to its
numerous Trout Inns, to Monkey Island at Bray, by then owned by
his son. But there is a continuous thread of naturalist observation.
In Chapter IV he describes the river in January:

It was a day of light. By the river everything shone,
luminous, insubstantial ... The dense curtain of reed plumes

Robert Gibbings's engraving of Footbridge Cottage, the Wittenham home from which he explored the Thames, and described in *Till I End My Song* (1957).

was like a froth of milk into which ochreous earths had been stirred. There was silence save for faint murmurs from the distant weir. Lapwings shimmered but made no sound as they passed overhead in scores. ...

Then as I watched the twitchings of the soil where a mole was working, there came to my ears, like chords to a tone poem by Sibelius, the long rhythmic beat of heavy wings, and looking up I saw close-knit in majestic flight six white swans following the course of the river.

Elsewhere in the book, Gibbings dilates on the mating and delicate colours of worms, battles between blackbirds, the structure of geese feathers, a tame drake that could tell the sex of human beings, a tamed robin that sat on a teapot, a collection of cuckoo's eggs perfectly matched to those in their host nests, the hundreds of house martins nesting under Clifton Hampden bridge. Finally he recalls how 'poets through the ages have sung the praises of rivers', and concludes that 'The quiet of an age-old river is like the slow turning of pages of a well-loved book.'

MAINLY ABOUT FISHING

Give me a punt, a rod, a line,
A snug arm-chair to sit on,
Some well iced punch, and weather fine,
And let me fish at DITTON.

Theodore Hook, 'Ode To Ditton', 1834

Fishing is a sport which tends to encourage observations of nature, some at least of it couched in prose or poetry. Holinshed recorded that the river at Richmond had such a supply of fish in Tudor times that there was 'no river in Europe able to exceed it' with salmon, shrimp, flounder, gudgeon, dace, lamprey and roach. Alexander Pope evidently enjoyed angling. These lines from his 'Windsor Forest' describe how on the Thames

The patient fisher takes his silent stand,
Intent, his angle trembling in his hand;
With looks unmov'd, he hopes the scaly breed,
And eyes the dancing cork, and bending reed.
Our plenteous streams a various race supply,
The bright-ey'd perch with fins of Tyrian dye,
The silver eel, in shining volumes roll'd,
The yellow carp, in scales bedrop'd with gold,
Swift trouts, diversify'd with crimson stains,
And pykes, the tyrants of the watry plains.

In his *Natural History of Oxfordshire* (1677) Dr Plot writes that in 1674 the river above Oxford 'gave so ample testimony of its great plenty that in the two days appointed for the fishing of Mr Mayor and the Bayliffe of the City it afforded betwixt Swithin's-Wear and Woolvercot Bridge (which I guess may be about three miles distant) fifteen hundred Jacks beside other fish.'

'Rivers and the inhabitants of the watery elements are made for wise men to contemplate and for fools to pass by without consideration' wrote Isaak Walton (1594–1683). He was a successful

London ironmonger who retreated to a small estate near Stafford after the Royalists were defeated at Marston Moor in 1644. From then on he devoted himself to writing biographies and fishing. *The Compleat Angler, or Contemplative Man's Recreation* (1653) is an affectionate description of a fishing expedition along the banks of the Lea, a tributary of the Thames. He also praises the Thames highly:

> This glorious river feeleth the violence and benefit of the
> sea more than any river in Europe; ebbing and flowing,
> twice a day, more than sixty miles; about whose banks are
> so many fair towns and princely palaces ... though some of
> our northern counties have as fat, and as large, as the river
> Thames, yet none are of so excellent a taste.

Green eels, he tells us, 'abound' in the Thames, and are best caught with one of the small lampreys which were as plentiful in the mud of the river 'as worms in a dunghill'. Walton made an annual visit to his friend the diplomat and poet Henry Wotton, who was Provost of Eton. Wotton had a fishing house on the bend in the Thames near Datchett known as Black Pots. *The Compleat Angler* includes a poem by Wotton which describes Walton fishing at Black Pots 'with patient skill, / Attending of his trembling quill' among swallows and nightingales:

> Already were the eaves possest
> With the swift Pilgrims' daubed nest:
> The Groves already did rejoice,
> In Philomel's triumphing voice:
> The showers were short, the weather mild,
> The morning fresh, the evening smil'd.[3]

Isaak Walton's *The Compleat Angler* was an account of a fishing trip along the Lea, a Thames tributary; he also described fishing in the Thames. Frontispiece by Arthur Rackham for the 1931 edition.

Fishing on the Thames had become well organised by the nineteenth century, and no busy lock was without fishing punts for hire and an expert to consult. Alfred J. Church's *Summer Days on the Thames: Recollections of Boating and Fishing between Henley and Oxford* (1890) is a chatty little memoir full of fishy tales. His first catch was a stickleback, near Caversham; it hooked him for life. His grandfather had great success in the Loddon, upstream of Henley, and he and his brother tied up to a footbridge at Bolney, near Shiplake, and caught 'not only a large weight of fish, but a specimen of every kind that swims in the Thames, excepting the trout only, and those rare denizens, the tench and the bream'. A friend caught a 23 lb pike in the weir pool at Sandford, below Oxford, which was also an excellent place for roach. The 'deep and quiet eddies' near Basildon Ferry were 'a very paradise of what I may call the professional bank-fisher', who comes on the earliest train with his two rods, one for roach, the other 'baited for gudgeon or small dace, for some wandering jack [pike] or perch'.

Church describes in details his own experiences at Basildon: learning to manage a punt, and to fix it for fishing by pinning it to the river bottom fore and aft with long 'rye-pegs'. He recommends to fellow anglers the Roebuck at Purley, a place which offered unrivalled variety for fishing: fine sand under 3 or 4 feet of swift current in one place, coarse gravel with 6 or 7 feet of slower water in another. Four-inch gudgeon abounded, because a nearby lockkeeper was illegally netting larger fish. 'Our largest bag was thirty-five dozen. ... In those days it was hardly possible to go astray, so plentiful were the gudgeon.'

William Morris had been fond of fishing ever since he traded his pet rabbits for a fishing rod while a schoolboy at Marlborough. At Oxford he alternated between reading voraciously and spending time out with rod or gun; in later years, he gave up shooting but remained a devoted angler. He knew all the best spots between Richmond and Windsor, and, Mackail tells us, 'it was his delight at all times of the year, and in all weathers, to

Edwin La Dell's 1951 lithograph for Lyons Tea Rooms, *Fishing at Marlow*, shows how the fishing punts favoured by Alfred Church were arranged.

escape from London for a day's fishing'; he also enjoyed cooking his catch. Fishing was even easier at Kelmscott, but his references to it, though frequent, are only brief. At Pangbourne, he recommends fly-fishing for trout in the Pang. He praises the beauties of Mapledurham, then deplores the ruthless trapping and shooting of the otter by Angling Societies that 'grudge it its tribute out of the coarse fish'.

Charles Cornish has two fine chapters on fish in the Thames, one of which describes the habits of chub. 'Drifting against a willow bush one day, the branches of which came right down over the water like a crinoline', he saw 'the backs of several chub pass as they cruised slowly up and down'. He manages to drop a hook concealed in a grasshopper among them.

What a commotion there was. The chub thought they were
all in a sanctuary and that no one was looking. I could see six
or seven of them, evidently all cronies and old acquaintances,
the sort of fish that have known one another for years and
would call each other by their Christian names. They were
as cocky and consequential as possible, cruising up and down
with an air, and staring at each other and out through the
screen of leaves between them and the river ...

The moment the grasshopper fell there was a regular
rush to the place .... They almost fought one another to get
a place. Flop! Splash! Wallop! My grasshopper, I think.' 'I
saw it first.' 'Where are you shoving to?' 'O – oh – what is
the matter with William?' I called him William because he
had a mark like a W on his back. But he was hooked fast and
flopping, and held quite tight by a very strong hook and gut,
like a bull with a ring and a pole fastened to his nose.

Arthur Ransome (1884–1967) is to fishermen less the author
of *Swallows and Amazons* than one of the finest fishing writers of
the twentieth century. His weekly 'Rod and Line' column ran in
the *Manchester Guardian* from 1925 to 1929, and selections from
it have filled four books. 'My Barbel' describes his tussle with
the pugnacious and famously elusive 'wild boar' of the river, 'the
hardest, most obstinate fighter of any of the coarse fish'. It was
the last day of a holiday spent fishing on the Thames, probably in
October 1927, when he and his wife stayed at the Rose Revived
at Newbridge. Ransome was expecting a roach or trout when he
dropped a few lobworms into what looked like a likely swim.
But suddenly

I was in battle with something tugging and boring far out
and deep down in the water ... I could do nothing with
him at all except run after him. We went a hundred yards
up river, and then he turned round and set off for London.
Trying to keep below and ahead of him to turn him, I
stumbled along in the dusk while he swam deep in the river,
now and then jerking the rod down by angry tugs. It grew

dark, when, after he had turned twice and gone up the river and down again, he began to weaken and allowed me at last to see my float.[4]

Only then did he see the droopy 'barbules' around the fish's jaw and realise that he had hooked a barbel rather than a huge trout.

In the twenty-first century, fishing became more a matter for competition than musings, and ecologists have become increasingly critical of 'the contemplative man's recreation'. But I suspect that many of those who patiently watch their rods by the side of the Thames see and record more of its natural beauties than those who tramp its increasingly bare banks or chug noisily between hostelries in cruisers.

SIX

DEAD
IN THE WATER

WRITERS, prominent among them Charles Dickens and Joseph Conrad, have always been fascinated by the Thames's dark side. Accidental drownings and suicides, battles at bridges and murders real and fictional have occurred all along its length, though nowhere more than in London. Peter Ackroyd goes so far as to describe the river as 'a great vortex of suffering', and calls one section of his *Thames, Sacred River*, 'River of Death'. He believes that the hundreds of human skulls severed from torsos and numerous sculpted heads found in the river were ancient ritual offerings. The stretch of the river at the Chelsea end of Battersea Bridge was described as a 'Celtic Golgotha' (Golgotha means a place of skulls) after H.S. Cuming published a paper about the many ancient crania unearthed when the bridge was rebuilt in the 1850s.[1] Were they relics of a battle, or of a macabre ceremony?

The gloomy literature of the Thames in Victorian times was a reflection of the deteriorating quality of the river itself. But the Thames's darkest hour came in the early 1940s with the blanket bombing of the river and the docks. A.P. Herbert, a Thames-loving author who stoically did what he could to defend his chosen territory in his motor cruiser *Water Gipsy*, immortalised the bravery and resourcefulness of Londoners and Estuary dwellers in print.

'The shrouded throng / Glide through the bolted doors and haste along / Where the black water Acherontic rolls': illustration by William Brown McDougall for Margaret Armour's 'Way for the Dead', in *Thames Sonnets and Semblances* (1897).

THE GREAT STINK

Blighted and baleful stream ! What wizard spell
Hath turned thy lucent wave to Stygian slime,
Altered thy voice to bated breath of crime,
Darkened thy smile to frown inscrutable?

Margaret Armour, 'Wharves at Night', 1897

By the middle of the nineteenth century, the water quality in London was so foul that it caused a cholera epidemic. Matthew Kneale's ironically titled historical novel *Sweet Thames* (1992) re-creates the nightmare 1849 world of 'miasmal airs' and cholera that swept the city until the powers that be realise it is the foul water of the river that is spreading disease. He describes the ramshackle wooden houses and rickety bridges of Jacob's Island, near Rotherhithe:

> Flowing beneath were a whole set of creeks and sewers, giving the neighbourhood the name of 'The Venice of the Drains'. We had earlier crossed one of the notorious of these, the Dock Head Creek, its waters – much affected by the dyes of the leather dressers – coloured scarlet, and covered with scum resembling a giant cobweb, through which loomed the patterned carcases of animals that had tumbled in, like so many ill-wrapped packages.

George Godwin's *Town Swamps and Social Bridges* (1859) remarked on a macabre phenomenon at Dead Men's Steps in Wapping. The currents there washed up an exceptional number of corpses, animal and human, again and again. He made a sketch showing the way in which a dead dog travelled:

> We thought he would get away: however, after a time, and after whirling and resting amongst the posts and barges, the dead dog came again in sight, moving against the tide, but much nearer to the shore; he turns off again towards the sea, and returns, this time much sooner than the last; and

Sketch by George Godwin showing a dead dog circling in the currents at the infamous Dead Men's Steps, in Wapping (*Town Swamps and Social Bridges*, 1859).

after describing various circles, as shown by the arrows in the sketch, he is deposited in the slime, together with other specimens of his own and allied families.

The river, even after the installation of Bazalgette's sewers in the 1870s, remained notorious. In 1884 there was a parody competition in *Truth* magazine. Competitors had to write about the filthy state of the Thames in the manner of Coleridge's *Ancient Mariner*. In the winning entry the narrator is buttonholed by 'an ancient lighterman':

Water, water everywhere
But offal foul can stink
The sweetest water anywhere.
And poison it for drink.

'For though there come both cats and dogs,
And corpses young and old.
The filth breast-high that's floating by
Is from some barge's hold.'

'God bless me! honest waterman.
You've told me quite enough.
Why look'st thou so? From my barge know
I shot the putrid stuff!'[2]

Margaret Armour published a series of relentlessly downbeat poems about the Thames in her *Thames: Sonnets and Semblances* (1897), with suitably gloomy illustrations by William McDougall. 'Wharves at Night' mourns the change in the river.

… foul-moored amid the slime,
Far boats loom out like monsters of the prime
Or blackened cairns of eld that, gruesome, heap
Horrid and dim memorials of crime.

The state of the river continued to deteriorate, and to provide authors with downbeat motifs, until its sewage works were enlarged in the 1970s. Dark fictions of the Thames continued to be written in the twentieth century, but their theme shifted from suicides and accidental deaths to murders – not just in London's river, but all along its course.

FOUND DROWNED

There was an old person of Ems,
Who casually fell in the Thames,
    And when he was found,
    They said he was drowned,
That unlucky old person of Ems.

Edward Lear, *The Book of Nonsense*, 1846

Until the Thames was efficiently controlled by pound locks and permanent weirs, travellers on its waters frequently drowned as they negotiated them. John Strype's 1720 revision of John Stow's Elizabethan *Survey of London* added several chapters describing the state of the Thames and its locks and weirs. He singled out Marlow's flash lock as particularly risky. 'The Streams were so strong and the Water had such a dismal fall that four Men within a short time were lost; three whereof drowned and a Fourth had his Brains dasht out.'

Dr Plot's *Natural History of Oxfordshire* describes a thunderstorm on 10 May 1666 which

> rather terrified Oxford, but was mischievous only at
> Medley, a well-known House; two scholars of Wadham
> College, alone in a Boat and newly thrust off shore to come
> homewards, being struck from the head of the Boat into the
> Water, the one of them stark Dead, and the other stuck fast
> in the Mud like a Post, with his Feet downward, and for the
> present so disturbed in his Senses, that he neither knew how
> he came out of the Boat, nor could remember either Thunder
> or Lightning that did effect it.

The Thames has long exerted a fatal attraction on would-be suicides. Samuel Pepys recorded one in his diary on 24 February 1666.

> This night going through bridge by water, my waterman told
> me how the mistress of the Bear tavern, at the bridge-foot,
> did lately fling herself into the Thames, and drowned herself;
> which did trouble me the more, when they tell me it was she
> that did live at the White Horse tavern in Lombard Street,
> which was a most beautiful woman, as most I have seen.
> It seems she hath had long melancholy upon her, and hath
> endeavoured to make away with herself often.

In 1763, the poet William Cowper, deeply depressed, tried to drown himself in the river at Customs House Quay. Fortunately for lovers of his wonderful poem *The Task* (1785), he failed.

> I left the coach upon the Tower Wharf, intending never to
> return to it; but upon coming to the quay I found the water

low, and a porter seated upon some goods there, as if on purpose to prevent me. This passage to the bottomless pit being mercifully shut against me, I returned back to the coach.

Mary Wollstonecraft made a more effective attempt. Deserted by her lover Gilbert Imlay, she went out on a rainy October night in 1795, and, once her clothes were thoroughly soaked, leapt off Old Fulham Bridge. However, a passer-by dived in to rescue her, and she survived to marry the political philosopher William Godwin. Their daughter Mary married Shelley and wrote *Frankenstein* (1818).

Thomas Hood (1799–1844) is famous for his comic verse, and the haunting 'I remember, I remember / The room where I was born'. Towards the end of his short life, however, he wrote long and moving ballads about the appalling conditions of London's poor. 'The Bridge of Sighs', the story of a destitute 'fallen woman' who drowns herself in the Thames is made particularly touching by its elegant rhyming scheme.

> One more Unfortunate,
> Weary of breath,
> Rashly importunate,
> Gone to her death! ...
> In she plunged boldly,
> No matter how coldly
> The rough river ran, –
> Over the brink of it,
> Picture it – think of it,
> Dissolute Man!
> Lave in it, drink of it,
> Then, if you can!
> Take her up tenderly,
> Lift her with care;

'One more Unfortunate, Weary of breath': a suicide hesitates before plunging into the Thames. Sketch made in 1871 by Gustave Doré for Thomas Hood's acclaimed poem 'The Bridge of Sighs'.

Fashion'd so slenderly,
Young, and so fair!
Ere her limbs frigidly
Stiffen too rigidly,
Decently, – kindly, –
Smooth, and compose them;
And her eyes, close them,
Staring so blindly!
Dreadfully staring
Thro' muddy impurity

It was widely anthologised, set to music and much illustrated, including etchings by Gustave Doré and John Everett Millais, and paintings by Augustus Egg (*Past and Present*) and G.F. Watts (*Found Drowned*). A bas relief of it decorates Hood's tomb in Kensal Green Cemetery.

Peering over the maelstrom of current that swirled around the middle arch of London Bridge, the hero of George Borrow's *Lavengro: The Scholar, The Gypsy, The Priest* (1851) is seized with awe.

Truly tremendous was the roar of the descending waters, and the bellow of the tremendous gulfs, which swallowed them for a time, and then cast them forth, foaming and frothing from their horrid wombs. ... To the right ... a maze of buildings, from which, here and there, shot up to the sky chimneys taller than Cleopatra's Needle, vomiting forth huge wreaths of that black smoke which forms the canopy – occasionally a gorgeous one – of the more than Babel city. Stretching before me, the troubled breast of the mighty river, and, immediately below, the main whirlpool of the Thames – the Maëlstrom of the bulwarks of the middle arch – a grisly pool, which, with its superabundance of horror, fascinated me. Who knows but I should have leapt into its depths?

But an old fruit-woman sitting on the bridge suddenly jumps up. 'Nay, dear! don't – don't!' said she. 'Don't fling yourself over – perhaps you may have better luck next time!'

Engraving by Ford Madox Ford for Dante Gabriel Rossetti's poem
'Downstream', the story of a seduced girl who drowns herself in the Thames
(*The Dark Blue* magazine, August/September 1871).

There is a macabre moment in Jerome's *Three Men in a Boat*
that had its basis in a true incident. It is even possible, R.R. Bol-
lard suggests, that the three friends were boating on the river at
Goring a year earlier when the body of Alice Douglas was found
on 11 July 1887. Jerome would certainly have read of it in the
papers. As they near Reading,

> George noticed something black floating on the water, and
> we drew up to it. George leant over, as we neared it, and laid
> hold of it. And then he drew back with a cry, and a blanched
> face.

It was the dead body of a woman. It lay very lightly on the water, and the face was sweet and calm. It was not a beautiful face; it was too prematurely aged-looking, too thin and drawn, to be that; but it was a gentle, lovable face, in spite of its stamp of pinch and poverty, and upon it was that look of restful peace that comes to the faces of the sick sometimes when at last the pain has left them. ...

We found out the woman's story afterwards. Of course it was the old, old vulgar tragedy. She had loved and been deceived – or had deceived herself ... With her last few shillings, [she] had taken a ticket and come down to Goring. ... She had wandered about the woods by the river's brink all day, and then, when evening fell and the grey twilight spread its dusky robe upon the waters, she stretched her arms out to the silent river that had known her sorrow and her joy. And the old river had taken her into its gentle arms, and had laid her weary head upon its bosom, and had hushed away the pain.

The hero of George Eliot's last novel *Daniel Deronda* (1876) is the ward of the wealthy Sir Hugh Mallinger. Desolate at having been rejected by his first love Gwendolen Harleth, Daniel has taken up the study of law in London, and keeps a boat on the river at Putney. Rowing from Putney to Richmond, he pauses near Kew to let a large barge overtake him, and absent-mindedly begins to sing the mournful gondolier's song from Rossini's *Otello*. Then he notices

a figure which might have been an impersonation of the misery he was unconsciously giving voice to: a girl hardly more than eighteen, of low slim figure, with most delicate little face, her dark curls pushed behind her ears under a large black hat, a long woolen cloak over her shoulders. Her hands were hanging down clasped before her, and her eyes were fixed on the river with a look of immovable, statue-like despair...

Embarrassed to realise that she has noticed him watching her, he rows on to Richmond, where he turns and drifts back with the tide as the sun sets.

> The approach of his favourite hour – with its deepening stillness and darkening masses of tree and building between the double glow of the sky and the river – disposed him to linger as if they had been an unfinished strain of music. He looked out for a perfectly solitary spot where he could lodge his boat against the bank, and, throwing himself on his back with his head propped on the cushions, could watch out the light of sunset and the opening of that bead-roll which some oriental poet describes as God's call to the little stars, who each answer, 'Here am I.' He chose a spot in the bend of the river just opposite Kew Gardens, where he had a great breadth of water before him reflecting the glory of the sky, while he himself was in shadow.

Then he sees the girl again, dipping her heavy cloak into the water, and realises that she is planning to drown herself. He rows over, and persuades her to let him take her to a friendly family he knows who live in Chelsea. He discovers she is Jewish, and has run away from her dissolute father in the hope of finding her mother and brother. Mirah will not only prove the love of his life, but be the agency by which he finds out that his own mother was Jewish, and leads him to embrace the faith himself.

Roni Horn's *Another Water (The Thames, for Example)* (2000) is a meditation on those found drowned in the river; terse notes and quotations fringe huge close-ups of the varied surface of its water. 'I am convinced the Thames itself is partly responsible for the suicides that end up there', she writes.

> The river evinces intimacy and fear. It possesses a monumentality without scale, and its surface is at once transparent and opaque. I took thousands of images of it, and I have come to see it as the ultimate metaphor, a mirror for our rights and wrongs, a surface in which we see ourselves.

'MR DICKENS'S OLD HORROR
OF THE DARK RIVER'

She was carried onward in a stream of life setting that
way, and flowing indifferently, past marts and mansions,
prisons, churches, market-places, wealth, poverty, good,
and evil, like the broad river side by side with it, awakened
from its dreams of rushes, willows, and green moss, and
rolling on, turbid and troubled, among the works and cares
of men, to the deep sea.

Charles Dickens, *Dombey and Son*, 1848

The Thames haunts the novels of Charles Dickens like an omen.
His early childhood was spent at Sheerness and Rochester, and
memories of the Kent countryside, the Medway marshes and trips
out into the Thames Estuary with his father John in the small
naval yacht *Chatham* are used in his first book, *The Pickwick
Papers* (1836). His lifelong ambition was to return there, and he
achieved this in 1856, when he acquired Gad's Hill Place on the
Old Dover Road, a house he had admired as a child. 'Cobham
Woods are behind the house, the distant Thames in front, the
Medway, with Rochester and its old castle and cathedral on one
side', he wrote proudly to his friend William de Serjat in 1858.

By then, however, Dickens had personal experience of the
river's dark side. In 1822 the family moved to Camden Town,
and when his father was put in a debtors' prison Charles was
set to work in a blacking factory by the river at Hungerford
Stairs, near Charing Cross; an experience he uses in *David
Copperfield* (1850).

Murdstone and Grinby's warehouse was at the waterside. It
was down in Blackfriars. Modern improvements have altered
the place; but it was the last house at the bottom of a narrow
street, curving down hill to the river, with some stairs at the
end, where people took boat. It was a crazy old house with a
wharf of its own, abutting on the water when the tide was in,

'A crazy old house with a wharf of its own, abutting on the water': Hungerford Stairs, site of the blacking factory where Charles Dickens worked as a boy (watercolour by George Harley, 1820).

and on the mud when the tide was out, and literally overrun with rats.

Towards the end of the book, David and Peggotty follow the repentant Martha to the river at Millbank. She walks slowly along the riverbank, looking for a place to drown herself.

Slimy gaps and causeways, winding among old wooden piles, with a sickly substance clinging to the latter, like green hair, and the rags of last year's handbills offering rewards for drowned men fluttering above high-water mark, led down through the ooze and slush to the ebb-tide. ... As if she were a part of the refuse it had cast out, and left to corruption and decay, [Martha] strayed down to the river's brink, and stood in the midst of this night-picture, lonely and still, looking at the water.

David and Peggotty prevent her from drowning, but she is still in a frenzy of misery.

'Oh, the river!' she cried passionately. 'Oh, the river!'
'Hush, hush!' said I. 'Calm yourself.'
But she still repeated the same words, continually exclaiming, 'Oh, the river!' over and over again.
'I know it's like me!' she exclaimed. 'I know that I belong to it. I know that it's the natural company of such as I am! It comes from country places, where there was once no harm in it – and it creeps through the dismal streets, defiled and miserable – and it goes away, like my life, to a great sea, that is always troubled – and I feel that I must go with it!'

In *Oliver Twist* (1839), the brutish Bill Sykes has his hideout on Jacob's Island. It is 'surrounded by a muddy ditch, six or eight feet deep and fifteen or twenty wide when the tide is in'. Once a thriving place, now

the houses have no owners; they are broken open, and entered upon by those who have the courage; and there they live, and there they die. They must have powerful motives for a secret residence, or be reduced to a destitute condition indeed, who seek a refuge in Jacob's Island.

In the chilling chapter in which Noah Claypole stalks Nancy to a flight of steps from London Bridge down to the river and overhears her telling Oliver's benefactors about the plot by Fagin's sidekick Monks to blacken the boy's name, Dickens makes the river foreshadow her doom:

> A mist hung over the river, deepening the red glare of the
> fires that burnt upon the small craft moored off the different
> wharfs, and rendering darker and more indistinct the murky
> buildings on the banks. The old smoke-stained storehouses
> on either side, rose heavy and dull from the dense mass of
> roofs and gables, and frowned sternly upon water too black
> to reflect even their lumbering shapes. The tower of old Saint
> Saviour's Church, and the spire of Saint Magnus, so long the
> giant-warders of the ancient bridge, were visible in the gloom.

As she tells them where to find Monks, Nancy is seized with foreboding. 'Look before you, lady', she says to Rose Maylie. 'Look at that dark water. How many times do you read of such as I who spring into the tide, and leave no living thing, to care for, or bewail them. It may be years hence, or it may be only months, but I shall come to that at last.' So she does: Sykes murders her after Claypole tells him that she has betrayed him.

London's river was 'an image of death in the midst of the great city's life', Dickens wrote in 'Down with the Tide', an 1853 article for *Household Words*, which described an evening spent on the river with the river police.

> A very dark night it was, and bitter cold; the east wind
> blowing bleak, and bringing with it stinging particles from
> marsh, and moor, and fen – from the Great Desert and
> Old Egypt, may be. Some of the component parts of the
> sharp-edged vapour that came flying up the Thames at
> London might be mummy-dust, dry atoms from the Temple
> at Jerusalem, camels' foot-prints, crocodiles' hatching-places,
> loosened grains of expression from the visages of blunt-
> nosed sphynxes, waifs and strays from caravans of turbaned
> merchants, vegetation from jungles, frozen snow from the
> Himalayas. O! It was very, very dark upon the Thames, and
> it was bitter, bitter cold.

He is introduced to the Searcher on Waterloo Bridge, a place much favoured for suicide, he is told, and he hears of the ingenious methods of the many water-thieves who smuggle and steal along the river, sometimes even taking the ships themselves.

Dickens's move to Gad's Hill in 1856 produced *Great Expectations* (1860), which begins dramatically in the marshlands near Rochester with a prisoner escaping from one of the prison hulks moored near the Kent shore.

> Ours was the marsh country, down by the river, within,
> as the river wound, twenty miles of the sea. My first most
> vivid and broad impression of the identity of things, seems
> to me to have been gained on a memorable raw afternoon
> towards evening. At such a time I found out for certain, that
> this bleak place overgrown with nettles was the churchyard;
> … and that the dark flat wilderness beyond the churchyard,
> intersected with dykes and mounds and gates, with scattered
> cattle feeding on it, was the marshes; and that the low leaden
> line beyond, was the river; and that the distant savage lair
> from which the wind was rushing was the sea; and that the
> small bundle of shivers growing afraid of it all and beginning
> to cry, was Pip.
> 'Hold your noise!' cried a terrible voice, as a man started
> up from among the graves at the side of the church porch.
> 'Keep still, you little devil, or I'll cut your throat!'

'Mr. Dickens's old horror of the dark river comes out again in the very first sentences', wrote the *Manchester Guardian*'s 1864 review of the first instalment of *Our Mutual Friend*. It opens with Gaffer Hexam hunting corpses in the river so that he could rob them, sitting in the prow of his boat 'like a roused bird of prey', while his daughter Lizzie rows. The body they recover and take to Rotherhithe, 'where the accumulated scum of humanity seemed to be washed from higher grounds, like so much moral sewage', is identified as that of the novel's hero John Harman, who is in fact not dead at all. Gaffer is wrongly accused of Harman's murder by

'He was a hook-nosed man, and with that and his bright eyes and his ruffled head, bore a certain likeness to a roused bird of prey': illustration by Marcus Stone for Charles Dickens's *Our Mutual Friend* (serialised 1864)

his former partner Rogue Riderhood, but is himself found dead the next night, having fallen overboard from his boat reaching for another corpse.

The Thames winds through the whole book. It will claim the lives of Riderhood and Bradley Headstone, the two villains of the piece, when during a life-or-death struggle they fall clinched together into an empty lock. But *Our Mutual Friend* also finds humour and hope in the river. An ancient waterside inn (identified as the still thriving Limehouse pub The Bunch of Grapes) is affectionately drawn as 'The Six Jolly Porters'.

Externally, it was a narrow lopsided wooden jumble of corpulent windows heaped one upon another as you might heap as many toppling oranges, with a crazy wooden verandah impending over the water.

Towards the end of the book, the idyllic setting of a paper mill on the upper Thames is used to signify renewed life: the macabre opening of the novel is balanced by Lizzie Hexam saving the decadent Eugene Wrayburn from Headstone's murderous attempt to drown him near the mill. Once recovered, Eugene sees the error of his attempts at her seduction and marries her.

The river can also offer escape. At the end of *David Copperfield*, the Micawbers, Peggotty, Martha and Emily set off from Gravesend to sail to Australia, a reminder that the Thames was an avenue to the opportunities then offered by the growing British Empire. David gets up early to see them off.

We went over the side into our boat, and lay at a little distance, to see the ship wafted on her course. It was then calm, radiant sunset. She lay between us, and the red light; and every taper line and spar was visible against the glow. A sight at once so beautiful, so mournful, and so hopeful, as the glorious ship, lying, still, on the flushed water, with all the life on board her crowded at the bulwarks, and there clustering, for a moment, bare-headed and silent, I never saw.

LIMEHOUSE LITERATURE

Imagine a person, tall, lean and feline, high-shouldered, with
a brow like Shakespeare and a face like Satan, a close-shaven
skull, and long, magnetic eyes of the true cat-green.

Sax Rohmer, The Mystery of Fu-Manchu, 1913

The early twentieth century was the heyday of trashy novels
warning of the 'yellow peril' and the 'infectious degeneracy'
of the opium and gambling dens in the Chinese quarter that
grew up in Limehouse to provide food, accommodation, laundry
services and entertainment for Asian seamen after the Blue Star
Line began regular steamer services between London and China
in the 1860s. At that time, China seemed immeasurably remote,

Engraving of the *Keyong*, a Chinese junk that arrived in the Thames in 1848,
bringing the exotic East to London. Books by Thomas Burke and Sax Rohmer
would soon demonise the so-called 'yellow peril' (Edward Walford, *Old and New
London*, 1890).

despite the popularity of its tea, silks and porcelain. When the *Keyong*, a Chinese junk laden with exotic articles, sailed up the Thames to Blackwall in 1848, it created a sensation. It belonged to an enterprising British captain who had sailed it from Hong Kong to London via New York, and was turning a pretty penny by exhibiting not just its contents but the seamen themselves. Charles Dickens described it in an article for *The Examiner* (24 June 1848). 'For the matter of eighteen pence, you are at the Chinese Empire', he marvelled, wondering how on earth this 'floating toyshop' had crossed three oceans.

> So narrow, so long, so grotesque; so low in the middle, so high at each end, like a Chinese pen-tray, with no rigging and nowhere to go aloft; with mats for sails, great warped cigars for masts, gaudy dragons and sea-monsters disporting themselves from stem to stern, and on the stern a gigantic cock of impossible aspect defying the world.

Even more bizarre were the Chinese mariners, 'without a profile among them, in gauze pinafores and plaited hair, wearing stiff clogs a quarter of a foot thick in the sole, and lying at night in little scented boxes, like backgammon men or chess-pieces, or mother-of-pearl counters'.

As Chinatown grew larger in the 1860s, there were alarmist reports of addiction to both opium and Chinese gambling games among working-class and middle-class Londoners, and wonder turned to fear. In 1870 Dickens began *The Mystery of Edwin Drood*, setting the first scene in a London opium den run by 'Princess Puffer' for both Asian and English addicts in search of oblivion. In Oscar Wilde's *The Picture of Dorian Gray* (1891), Dorian goes to Limehouse, where 'there were opium dens where one could buy oblivion, dens of horror where the memory of old sins could be destroyed by the madness of sins that were new':

> The moon hung low in the sky like a yellow skull. ... They passed by lonely brickfields. The fog was lighter here, and he

Many of Thomas Burke's books about Limehouse featured Quong Lee as narrator. Title page of the *Song Book of Quong Lee*, by C. Lovat Fraser (1920).

could see the strange, bottle-shaped kilns with their orange, fanlike tongues of fire. A dog barked as they went by, and far away in the darkness some wandering sea-gull screamed. The horse stumbled in a rut, then swerved aside and broke into a gallop. ... Over the low roofs and jagged chimney-stacks of the houses rose the black masts of ships. Wreaths of white mist clung like ghostly sails to the yards.

In Arthur Conan Doyle's Sherlock Holmes story 'The Man with the Twisted Lip' (1919), Dr Watson goes to an opium den in the East End of London to find Isa Whitney, who became addicted after reading Thomas de Quincy's *Confessions of an Opium Eater*, and experimenting with laudanum-laced cigarettes. He takes a hansom to 'a vile alley lurking behind the high wharves which line the north side of the river to the east of London Bridge'.

The heyday of Limehouse literature was between 1913 and the 1940s. Its two most famous exponents were Thomas Burke (1886–1945) and Arthur Ward (1886–1959). Burke adopts a remarkably sinophile viewpoint in the eye-popping tales that make up *Limehouse Nights* (1916). His child heroines are feisty protagonists eager to live life to the full for all their tender years, though they can be abused innocents, as in his most famous story, 'The Chink and the Child', which was made into a film by D.W. Griffith. *Broken Blossoms* starred Lillian Gish as Lucy, the daughter of Battling Burrows, a sadistic pugilist who regularly beats her up for fun, beating her to death when he finds she has taken refuge with the gentlemanly Chinaman Cheng Huan, who has long adored her from a distance. When Huan finds her corpse, he takes a typically subtle Oriental revenge, depositing a deadly snake on Burrows's couch, then taking away Lucy's body and committing suicide with her in his arms. The river is a constant dark presence.

> Down Wapping way, where the streets rush right and left
> to water-side and depot, life ran high. Tide was at flood,
> and below the Old Stairs the waters lashed themselves to
> fury. Against the savage purple of the night rose a few
> wisps of rigging and some gruff funnels: lyrics in steel and
> iron, their leaping lines as correct and ecstatic as a rhyming
> verse. Under the cold glare of the arc lights, gangs of
> Asiatics hurried with that impassive swiftness which gives
> no impression of haste. The acrid tang of the East hung on
> every breath of air. ('The Cue')

Under the pseudonym Sax Rohmer, Arthur Ward wrote a series of wild adventures in which the forces of good battle against a fiendish Oriental mastermind and his army of dacoits and thugs. The first collection was published as *The Mystery of Dr Fu-Manchu* in 1913. The upright English hero Nayland Smith describes Fu Manchu to his partner Dr Petrie as 'the most malign and formidable personality existing in the known world today',

'The most malign and formidable personality existing in the known world today': dust jacket of Sax Rohmer's *Mystery of Dr Fu-Manchu* (1913).

with 'the brains of any three men of genius' and 'all the resources of science past and present ... the yellow peril incarnate in one man'. The Thames is the line of communication along which Fu Manchu moves his mysterious forces:

> The opium den off Shadwell Highway, the mansion upstream ... the hulk lying off the marshes. Always he made his headquarters upon the river.

The villain in Rohmer's *Yellow Shadows* (1925) was not Fu Manchu but 'Burma Chang', a transparent allusion to Chan Nan, a real-life drug baron and womaniser popularly known as 'Brilliant Chang', who owned the Shanghai restaurant in Limehouse. He lived in an exotically furnished apartment on the river at 13 The Causeway, and was visited by a stream of addicted society women. Once the Defence of the Realm Act of 1914 criminalised drug-taking, Chang was watched by the police, especially after the death of a dance hostess who had been one of his dealers. In 1924 he was convicted of dealing himself, and sentenced to be transported. He was demonised in the popular press in both Britain and America as 'The Limehouse Spider', confirming all the public fears of international conspiracy that Sax Rohmer had raised. In actual fact, Chinatown was far from universally wicked. Arnold Bennett visited in 1925 and voted it 'rather flat'. 'We saw no vice whatever. The Inspector of Police gave the Chinese an exceedingly good character.' It was also very small, numbering around 100 in 1891, and not rising above 300 even at the peak of its notoriety in the 1920s.

The myth of Victorian Limehouse as a Thameside den of vice is enduring. Philip Pullman's playfully melodramatic *Ruby in the Smoke* (1985) is a modern homage to Limehouse literature. Pullman, who confesses to a love of Victorian penny dreadfuls, weaves his tale around the familiar trope of a priceless jewel pursued by villains from the east, deftly using the river Thames as the thread to link events. The villainous Mrs Holland lives in squalor at Hangman's Wharf, Wapping, and the heroine Sally Lockhart takes a train along the coast to the Estuary village of Swaleness to visit Major Marchbanks, who holds the key to the mystery of her past. The arch-villain Ah Ling arrives in the Thames Estuary on a P&O steamship, disguises himself as a Thames waterman in order to murder Sally's father's crooked business partner, then goes to Oxford to stab the only witness to the scuttling of her father's ship, and throw his bleeding corpse into the Thames at Port Meadow. The climax is back in London, a wharfside fight between Sally's allies and Mrs Holland's thugs, and a confrontation on London Bridge between Sally and Mrs Holland that ends with Mrs Holland, desperate to possess the ruby that Sally has thrown into the Thames, insanely plunging to her death in the river.

THRILLS AND SPILLS

The river, a sinister marvel of still shadows and flowing gleams mingling below in a black silence, arrested his attention. He stood looking over the parapet for a long time.

Joseph Conrad, *The Secret Agent*, 1907

For two centuries, writers of thrillers and detective novels have made chases along the Thames or corpses in it a familiar occurrence. In Arthur Conan Doyle's novel *The Sign of Four* (1890), the great detective, pepped up on cocaine, investigates the murder of Bartholomew Sholto with his faithful assistant Dr Watson. When the assassin attempts to flee London on the small steamer *Aurora*, Holmes and Watson follow in a police launch.

> We had shot through the pool, past the West India Docks, down the long Deptford Reach, and up again after rounding the Isle of Dogs. The dull blur in front of us resolved itself now into the dainty *Aurora*. ...At Greenwich we were about three hundred paces behind them. At Blackwall we could not have been more than two hundred and fifty ... never did sport give me such a wild thrill as this mad, flying manhunt down the Thames. Steadily we drew in upon them, yard by yard. It was a clear reach of the river, with Barking Level upon one side and the melancholy Plumstead Marshes on the other. ... It was a wild and desolate place, where the moon glimmered upon a wide expanse of marshland, with pools of stagnant water and beds of decaying vegetation.

In *Dracula* (1895), Bram Stoker makes the vampire Count lurk on the banks of the Thames until he can cross to Bermondsey from Purfleet Stairs at low tide; vampires can only cross running water when it is slack. After getting his boxed-up earth-filled coffin taken aboard the Black Sea-bound *Czarina Catherine*, he prevents the ship from leaving before full tide by creating a sinister fog around it.

A thin mist began to creep up from the river, and it grew, and grew; till soon a dense fog enveloped the ship and all around her. The captain swore polyglot – very polyglot – polyglot with bloom and blood; but he could do nothing. The water rose and rose; and he began to fear that he would lose the tide altogether. He was in no friendly mood, when just at full tide, the thin man came up the gang-plank again and asked to see where his box had been stowed. Then the captain replied that he wished that he and his box – old and with much bloom and blood – were in hell. ... On questioning other mariners who were on movement up and down on the river that hour, [the captain] found that few of them had seen any of fog at all, except where it lay round the wharf. The ship went out on the ebb tide.

The Thames is unfriendly and menacing in Joseph Conrad's *The Secret Agent: A Simple Tale* (1907). Anarchists plot to blow up Greenwich, assisted by the indolent Verloc, an unlikely secret agent. He uses Stevie, his mentally disabled brother-in-law, to carry the bomb, but Stevie stumbles on the way and is killed. Winnie Verloc, distraught when she discovers what happened, murders Verloc and then heads for the river to drown herself rather than face the gallows.

> She dragged herself painfully across the shop, and had to hold on to the handle of the door before she found the necessary fortitude to open it. She floundered over the doorstep head forward, arms thrown out, like a person falling over the parapet of a bridge. This entrance into the open air had a foretaste of drowning; a slimy dampness enveloped her, entered her nostrils, clung to her hair. It was not actually raining, but each gas lamp had a rusty little halo of mist.

She meets Ossipan, one of the anarchists, and greedy for her money, he persuades her to elope with him, but robs her in the train to the steamer and abandons her. Later that night he finds himself on Westminster Bridge, rightly imagining the lonely and penniless Mrs Verloc's midnight suicide on the steamer.

> The clock tower boomed a brazen blast above his drooping head. He looked up at the dial... Half-past twelve of a wild night in the Channel.

A.P. Herbert, novelist, barrister and MP for Oxford University, will appear later in this chapter as a hero of the river's darkest hour during the 1940s' Blitz. Twenty years earlier, he wrote *The House by the River* (1921), the story of the accidental murder of a housemaid by an arrogant young poet, and the disposal of her body in the Thames. The house of the title was Herbert's own, 12 Hammersmith Terrace. Herbert loved the river deeply, and never described its many moods more vividly than in this macabre story of betrayal.

> It was nearly high tide. Stephen Byrne stood at the end of his garden and regarded contentedly the River Thames. The warm glow of sunset lingered about the houses by Hammersmith Bridge and the tall trees on the Surrey side. The houses and the tall trees and the great old elms by William Morris' house stood rigid on their heads in the still water, and all that wide and comfortable reach between the Island and Hammersmith Bridge was beautiful in the late sun. There were a few small clouds flushed with pink in the southern sky, and these also lay like reefs of coral here and there in the water. The little boats in the foreground, moored in ranks in the tiny roads off Hammerton Chase, lay already deep in the shadow of the high houses of the Terrace, and the water about them was cool and very black. The busy tugs went by, hurrying up with the last of the flood, long chains of barges swishing delightfully behind them. The tug Maud went by, and Margaret, her inseparable companion. ... As they fussed away past the Island the long waves crept smoothly across the river and stole secretly under the little boats in the roads, the sailing-boats and the rowing-boats

and the motor-boats and the absurd dinghies, and tossed them up and heaved them about with pleasing chuckles; and went on to the garden-wall of the houses and splashed noisily under Stephen's nose and frothed back to the boats.

Historical whodunnits often picture the London Thames in past centuries, notably C.J. Sansom's Tudor-set *Dark Fire*, which has a spectacular climax in a Thameside warehouse, and Susanna Gregory's *Body in the Thames*, the sixth outing of her Restoration period inquiry agent Thomas Chaloner.

The Thames in London is not the only scene for fictional murder. Oxford is equally popular. One of the first was Ronald Knox's *Footsteps at the Lock* (1928) which gives pin-sharp descriptions of the river between Oxford and Shifford Lock.

Cushioned upon its waters, in punt or canoe, you see nothing but high banks on each side, deep in willow-herb and loose-strife, in meadow-sweet and deadly nightshade; or a curtain of willows cuts off the landscape from you; or deep beds of reeds stand up like forests between you and the sky-horizon, to meet haymakers in a field, to pass under one of the rare, purposeless iron bridges, makes you feel as if you had intersected an altogether different plane of life. Your fellow-citizens are the fishermen, incorrigible optimists who line the banks at odd intervals; the encampments of boy scouts, mud-larking in the shallows or sunning themselves naked on the bank; your stages are the locks, your landscape the glassy surface and the tugging eddies of the stream.

Shifford, disguised as 'Shipcote', Lock is the scene of the suspicious disappearance of one of a pair of brothers who go for a canoeing holiday up the river. Tadpole Bridge becomes Millington Bridge, and the Rose Revived at Newbridge is called The Gudgeon at Eaton. The dead brother had a gigantic insurance policy from which the surviving brother stands to benefit, and Miles Bredon, whom Knox had introduced in *The Viaduct Murder*

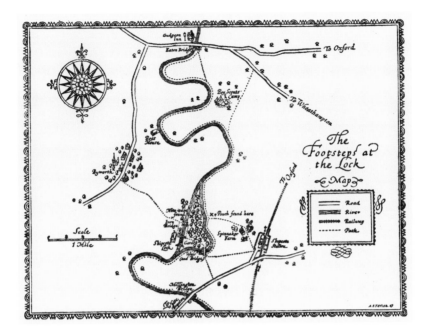

Map, based on Shifford Lock, near Newbridge, of the lock island where murder takes place in *The Footsteps at the Lock*, by Golden Age detective fiction writer Ronald Knox.

(1925), is asked to look into the incident by the insurance company. He and his wife take a room at the Gudgeon and begin their investigations by asking the lock-keeper about the travellers; he tells them about some puzzling naked footprints he noticed on the bridge to the island beside the lock. They began in the middle of the bridge, then went down to the island side. The footsteps are not the only clue to the mystery, an exceptionally tangled affair which will have you scratching your head and turning back to earlier pages rather too often.

A decade later Mavis Doriel Hay's *Death on the Cherwell* appeared. In it, the bursar of 'Persephone' College, a thinly disguised St Hilda's, is found dead in her canoe. Robert Robinson's Oxford frolic *Landscape with Dead Dons* (1956) has a wonderful scene in which naked scholars rush across the city in panic from the nude bathing station Parson's Pleasure.

Best known of modern Oxford murder mysteries are Colin Dexter's thirteen Inspector Morse novels, written between 1975 and 1999. Corpses are fished out of water several times, from the Cherwell in *The Jewel That Was Ours*, from the Oxford canal in *The Riddle of the Third Mile*, and from Duke's Cut, which links the Thames and the Oxford canal, in *The Wench Is Dead*. The latter is a Josephine Tey-style reconstruction of an unsolved Victorian murder which is solved by a hospitalised Morse; in it Dexter vividly re-creates the Victorian world of barge traffic. Television continuations of Morse and Lewis adventures rarely pass without a couple of eye-candy river scenes, preferably including a corpse slumped over its sculls, or bobbing under willows, and shots of Morse and Lewis enjoying a jar at The Trout at Godstow Bridge, the DI's favourite summer watering hole.

BENDS SINISTER

And the muddy tide of the Thames, reflecting nothing, and hiding a million of unclean secrets within its breast, – a sort of guilty conscience, as it were, unwholesome with the rivulets of sin that constantly flow into it, – is just the dismal stream to glide by such a city.

Nathaniel Hawthorne, *Our Old Home* (1863)

As the twentieth century dawned, cracks were appearing in the worldwide empire which had once been served by ships sailing out of and into the Thames Estuary. One of the earliest writers to see signs of decline was Nathaniel Hawthorne, who wrote in *Our Old Home*:

The aspect of London along the Thames, below Bridge, as it is called, is by no means so impressive as it ought to be, considering what peculiar advantages are offered for the display of grand and stately architecture by the passage of a river through the midst of a great city. It seems, indeed, as if the heart of London had been cleft open for the mere purpose of showing how rotten and drearily mean it had become. The shore is lined with the shabbiest, blackest, and ugliest buildings that can be imagined, decayed warehouses with blind windows, and wharves that look ruinous; insomuch that, had I known nothing more of the world's metropolis, I might have fancied that it had already experienced the downfall which I have heard commercial and financial prophets predict for it, within the century.

H.G. Wells ends his novel of a self-made man *Tono-Bungay* (1912) with a heavily symbolic journey down to the mouth of the Thames, freighted with comment on the ethics of Empire.

Light after light goes down. England and the Kingdom, Britain and the Empire, the old prides and the old devotions, glide abeam, astern, sink down upon the horizon, pass – pass. The river passes – London passes, England passes.

Wells would have read Joseph Conrad's *Heart of Darkness* (1899), a novella which was a radical indictment of white settlers' abuse of Africans. Conrad's tale develops into a more general condemnation of the darkness that lurks beneath the surface of even the most civilised human beings. Kurtz, the ivory trader at the centre of the story, is a 'universal genius' who becomes warped by fantasies of omnipotence and eventually destroyed by what he has himself set in motion. The story of Kurtz is told aboard a yawl moored off Tilbury by a trader called Charlie Marlow who went up the Congo river and discovered the trader's terrible fate. Conrad uses the Thames Estuary scenes to announce his intentions. Before Charlie begins his tale, the men on the yawl watch the sun set over the Essex marshes.

The gloom to the west, brooding over the upper reaches, became more sombre every minute, as if angered by the approach of the sun.

And at last, in its curved and imperceptible fall, the sun sank low, and from glowing white changed to a dull red without rays and without heat, as if about to go out suddenly, stricken to death by the touch of that gloom brooding over a crowd of men.

Conrad had pored over William Booth's stirring indictment of the London slums, *In Darkest England and the Way Out* (1890) and noted its deliberate parody of Henry Stanley's *In Darkest Africa*, published earlier that year. His narrator dwells complacently on the centuries of glorious maritime history evoked by the 'venerable stream' bathed 'in the august light of abiding memories', but Marlow abruptly changes the mood, suddenly saying, 'And this also ... has been one of the dark places of the earth.' He goes on to explain that he was thinking of the coming of the Romans:

> the military camp lost in a wilderness – cold, fog, tempests, disease, exile, and death. Or think of a decent young citizen in a toga – perhaps too much dice, you know – coming out here in the train of some prefect, or tax-gatherer, or trader even, to mend his fortunes. Land in a swamp, march through the woods, and in some inland post feel the savagery, the utter savagery, had closed round him, – all that mysterious life of the wilderness that stirs in the forest, in the jungles, in the hearts of wild men.

The tale Marlow goes on to tell is made as true to England as it is of Africa. In the closing scene, the gloom over London has spread to the east as well. 'The offing was barred by a black bank of clouds, and the tranquil waterway leading to the uttermost ends of the earth flowed sombre under an overcast sky – seemed to lead into the heart of an immense darkness.'

During the First and Second World Wars, the Thames between The Nore and London Bridge offered airborne enemies an appallingly visible silver highway meandering into the heart of London.

Jonathan Schneer's *Thames: England's River* (2005) aptly calls his chapter on the subject 'River of Fire'. Twenty-six miles of East London docks were appallingly vulnerable, first to Zeppelins and Gothas, then to Junker, Dornier and Heinkel bombers. In 1915 D.H. Lawrence described a Zeppelin airship raid in 1915 in a letter to Lady Ottoline Morrell.

> Last night when we were coming home the guns broke out, and there was a noise of bombs. Then we saw the Zeppelin above us, just ahead, amid a gleaming of clouds: high up, like a bright golden finger, quite small, among a fragile incandescence of clouds. And underneath it were splashes of fire as the shells from each burst. Then there were flashes near the ground – and the shaking noise. It was like Milton – then there was a war in heaven. But it was not angels. ... I cannot get over it, that the moon is not Queen of the sky by night, and the stars the lesser lights. It seems the Zeppelin is in the zenith of the night, golden like a moon, having taken control of the sky; and the bursting shells are the lesser lights.

There was no greater champion of the Thames in both peace and war than A.P. Herbert, author of *No Boats on the River* (1932), a forward-looking plea for waterbuses, and *The Thames* (1966), a survey of the river and its future. Herbert learned to row in London, and had a mooring for his little motor cruiser *Water Gipsy* behind his riverside house at Hammersmith In 1938 he volunteered for the River Emergency Services, and for the duration of the war he patrolled the lower waters of the river in *Water Gipsy*, painted battleship grey and equipped with 'a Hotchkiss machine-gun, two revolvers, a box of hand-grenades, and two cutlasses'. In *The War of Southend Pier* he tells the dramatic story of the river's first serious engagement with the enemy on 22 November 1939. The pier, an essential dropping off and loading point for ships, blazed away so furiously with Lewis guns, rockets and Verey lights that they downed one aeroplane and discouraged the Germans from ever repeating their attack. In a chapter on 'The Port in War' in *The Thames*, he describes his adventures in *Water Gipsy* during the sixty or so blitzes of the Battle of Britain, and the long later months of attacks on London's river. He braved a devastating attack on 7 September, 1940, navigating with a compass through towers of flame and smoke with a wet towel around his head in order to carry reels of wire to Woolwich, so that stricken barges could be towed clear of fires. Taking mail to and fro along the river, he saw 'a terrible brilliant bombardment' at Chatham,

> a concentration of flash and fireworks, the more frightful
> because, unless the wind was right, you could hear no
> sound. It was like seeing the silhouette of a murder behind a
> suburban blind.

The Thames also tells the story of London's watermen making 'Phoenixes', massive concrete components that would be towed round to be part of the Mulberry Harbours used in the Normandy landings, lighters converted into landing craft, and the huge reels known as 'conun-drums' that transported the pipes that would form PLUTO, the pipeline under the channel carrying fuel essential for the invasion.

After the war, Herbert continued to fight to improve the state of the river. He served for thirty years on the Thames Conservancy, and was an early champion of water buses and a Thames barrier. He was also president of the London Corinthian Sailing Club, which was conveniently close to his Hammersmith house. In 1968 he wrote *The Singing Swan*, a lively novel set at the start of the Second World War which satirises bureaucracy, affectionately records life aboard Thames barges, and describes the part they played in 1941, the year of Dunkirk, first supplying, and then rescuing, the beleaguered Allied forces.

Because of fears of the effect of global warming on rising seas, the flooding of London envisaged by Richard Jeffries is once again a popular fictional catastrophe. J.G. Ballard's *The Drowned World*

(1962) sees London swamped and in a pre-Triassic Age. Lucinda Roy imagines the river flooding London in her 1988 poem 'The Promised Flood Thames'.

> It will be the river's turn
> to dump upon the city
> with each brown rush
> the limbs of the forgotten dead ...
> At night, the sound will be a million tongues
> lapping at the sides of brick and mortar;
> and we will see a million tongues of flame
> in ripples captured by the moon.[3]

Chris Ryan offers a compelling imagining of what it would be like to be caught in such a disaster in *Flash Flood* (2006), the first in his Code Red series, all of which feature teenage Ben Tracy getting caught up in extreme conditions. During a school trip to London, a sudden tidal surge and a freak thunderstorm result in the Thames Barrier being breached. With streets underwater, communications down, rats pouring up out of the sewers, and thousands of people in a state of panic, the schoolboys have to use all their resourcefulness to escape.

POLY-OLBION

GREAT BRITAINE

RHYMING
THE RIVER

T HE chapters in this book have been generously laced with
quotations from poems about the Thames. This one is
devoted to verse. Fun and culturally revealing as it often is, it is
rarely very good, and few anthologies have been devoted to the
subject. The best are Jocelyn Herbert's *Sweete Themmes* (1951),
which includes prose as well as poems, and Anna Adams's *Thames:
An Anthology of River Poems* (1999), which has some ancient
favourites, but is mainly refreshingly modern. In his preface to
it, Iain Sinclair calls the shift over the centuries in how poets
have described the river

> a process of reverse alchemy – from Spencer's 'silver-
> streaming Thames', through Pope's 'sunbeams trembling on
> the floating tides' to our lead-coloured drift. It's not the tides
> that have changed, but our way of seeing them.

My selection of Thames verses is divided into two main catego-
ries: poems which attempt a sweep from source to sea, and those
pinned to a particular place or part of the river. The source-to-sea
poems are presented chronologically to mirror the changes through
the centuries in literary style and poetic imagination; poems of
place follow the course of the river from the source to London,
and from London to The Nore regardless of date, and say as much
about the character of the poet as the place described.

Britannia in a robe embroidered with rivers, which Michael Drayton used as
guides in his 'chorographical' poem *Poly-Olbion*: title page of the 1612 edition.

FROM SOURCE TO SEA

Great is the love of English poets for rural and secluded
places. Greater still their love of rivers. In Drayton's Poly-
Olbion, the roar of rivers is almost deafening.

Henry Longfellow, *Poems of Place*, 1877

Michael Drayton's *Poly-Olbion* was published in 1612, declaring
its ambitious scope with a 64-word subtitle:

*A chorographical description of tracts, rivers, mountains, forests,
and other parts of this renowned isle of Great Britain: with
intermixture of the most remarkable stories, antiquities, wonders,
rarities, pleasures, and commodities of the same: digested in a
poem by Michael Drayton, Esq. With a table added, for direction
to those occurrences of story and antiquity, whereunto the course of
the volume easily leads not.*

With tortuous ingenuity, its 15,000 alexandrine couplets use the
kingdom's rivers as guides. The Thames is, naturally, a major
theme, and Drayton describes its entire length. In Song XIV,
we read of its source at Trewsbury Mead to London, and of its
tributaries.

But eas'ly from her source as Isis gently dades;
Unto her present aid, down through the deeper slades,
The nimbler-footed Churne, by Cissder [Cirencester] doth slide;
And first at Greeklade gets pre-eminence, to guide
Queen Isis on her way, ere she receive her train.
Clear Colne, and lively Leech, so down from Cotswold's Plain,
At Leechlade linking hands, come likewise to support
The Mother of great Tames. When, seeing the resort,
From Cotswold Windrush scours; and with herself doth cast
The train to overtake, and therefore hies her fast
Through the Oxfordian fields; when (as the last of all
Those Floods, that into Tames out of our Cotswold fall,
And farthest unto the north) bright Einlode forth doth beare.

By spelling Cricklade 'Greeklade', Drayton nods at the old legend that the town pre-dated Oxford as a centre of Greek learning; whether doctors thronged 'Leechlade' is left a mute point. He ends with a peroration on the river's arrival in London (Song XVII).

> And on by London leads, which like a crescent lies,
> Whose windows seem to mock the star be-freckled skies;
> Beside her rising spires, so thick themselves that show,
> As do the bristling reeds within his banks that grow.
> There sees his crowded wharfs, and people pest'red shores,
> His bosom overspread with shoals of lab'ring oars

Two centuries later, the poet and novelist Thomas Love Peacock (1785–1866) tried his hand at celebrating the course of the Thames. The source, dominated then by a huge pump that fed the nearby Thames and Severn Canal, was a disappointment. In a letter to his friend Edward Hookham he wrote:

> A satirist might exclaim: The rapacity of Commerce, not
> content with the immense advantages derived from this river
> in a course of nearly 300 miles, erects a ponderous engine
> over the very place of its nativity, to suck up its unborn
> waters from the bosom of the earth and pump them into a
> navigable canal![1]

The fruit of Peacock's excursion was *The Genius of the Thames*, published in June 1810. Conceived in epic style, the first half, written before he explored the river himself, is a prolix description of Britain's and indeed the world's, other major rivers, dismissing them all as inferior on economic and democratic grounds. He then offers an overblown account of the Romans' defeat of the Druids and the Celtic race he liked to think of as his own (he had just met the Welsh girl he would eventually marry); then of the Romans' defeat in turn by Saxons, Danes and Picts. At last we get back to the Thames itself, where 'crystal waters wind along, /

Thomas Love Peacock deplored the 'ponderous engine' that sucked up the 'unborn waters' of the Thames and pumped them into the Thames and Severn Canal, but he described the source lyrically in his *Genius of the Thames* (illustration by Joseph Farington, 1794).

Responsive to the wild bird's note, / Or lonely boatman's careless song'. His lyrical description of the source betrays nothing of the disappointment voiced in his letter to Hookham.

> Let fancy lead from Trewsbury Mead,
> With hazel fringed and copsewood deep,
> Where scarcely seen, through brilliant green,
> Thy infant waters softly creep,
> To where the wide-expanding Nore
> Beholds thee, with tumultuous roar,
> Conclude thy devious race,
> And rush, with Medway's confluent wave,
> To seek, where mightier billows rave,
> Thy giant-sire's embrace.

James Bird (1788–1839) was a Yoxford bookseller with a philosophical bent who had some success with narrative poems about his native Suffolk, and had two plays put on in London. He may have been there to enjoy the Sadlers Wells Theatre's first — and last — night of his play *The Smuggler's Daughter* when he penned his 'Metropolitan Sketches' in 1835. One of the best of them vigorously debunked the river.

Old Thames! thou babbler! noisy tyrant! proud
Thou art, and mighty in thy devious course!
Methinks thou need'st not be so rudely loud —
Look to the tiny dribbling of thy source!
But thou art like the wild and noisy crowd,
Vain and tumultuous rushing on with force,
Regardless of the mud from which, forlorn,
A puny thing thy Rivership was born! ...

And after all thy tumult and thy strife,
What are thy waters to the boundless sea?
A viewless drop! Can Neptune and his Wife
Extend their empire by the help of thee,
Thou slight humidity? Upon my life,
Thou scarce would'st fill the kettle for their tea.

The soaring popularity of the Thames in the second half of the nineteenth century led to new attempts to characterise the entire river. *The Thames, a Poem* (1878) by John Stapleton is very long and best read with friends after a few glasses of wine. Bathos is to the fore, but there are nice touches: I like the idea of a coracle twirling out of the Thames and Severn Canal, and swans' wings resembling 'half-reefed sails'. Two quatrains, one about the reach below Oxford, one about riverside villas near Pangbourne, give the flavour of the tortured whole:

Some trim the sail, some paddle all alone,
Some guide great boats which many oars propel,
Some, skilful steersmen, clear each jutting stone,
Though threatening squalls arise, and gusts their canvas swell

And many a villa hugs the river-side,
Some wealthy citizen's much-cherished home,
Where wife and daughter undisturbed reside,
Whilst dangerous and far his speculations roam.

Richard Hippisley Domenichetti's *The Thames* (1885) won the prestigious Newdigate Prize for poetry. He excells in descriptions of misty morning effects on the river near Oxford, and celebrates the river's literary connections – the mention of Shakespeare may refer to Falstaff's ducking in the river in *The Merry Wives of Windsor*:[2]

Is not each haunt a place of memories,
A poet-altar lit with godlike flame,
A centred glory and a deathless name?
Here Chaucer lived, and faery Spenser sang;
By thee the wizard harp of Shakespeare rang;
Here Pope wrought out, instinct with fire divine,
And stiff with classic gold, the splendid line.

He mentions 'wild-eyed Shelley' wandering in Oxford, and his 'twin spirit' Keats, who 'with weary steps, trod those dark London streets, / By the same river'. Also in London, he imagines a 'wretched wanderer' stumbling through the city's 'paths of hell' to leap into the river, a 'loathsome under-stream' that flows 'beneath life's glitter and false dream'. After a salute to J.M.W. Turner, whose 'strange alchemy … touched our northern city, and sullen stream, / With magic wand and colours of his dream … and dip't his brush in all those lights that die, / At morn and eve'. Finally comes a rather grand finale, embellished with a phrase from Psalm 42:

Triumphantly, the hurrying river nears
Loud ocean, and deep calleth out to deep.
The white stars die, and on the waters sweep
In broader tide; the ships like ghosts steal by,
And ocean scents drift upwards, as draw nigh

'Ships like Ghosts': Domenichetti's *The Thames* makes The Nore Lightship a striking seamark for mariners and poets alike of the point where the Thames met the ocean, 'and deep calleth out to deep' (Tombleson and Fearnside, *Eighty Picturesque Views of the Thames and Medway*, 1840).

> A sound of many waters, and a light
> From verge to verge of dawning infinite.

Rudyard Kipling's rollicking 'The River's Tale: Prehistoric' is only about the tidal Thames in prehistoric times, but it can't be left out. Like 'The Reeds of Runnymede' it was written for C.R. Fletcher's 1911 *A School History of England* for schoolchildren (see Chapter 1).

> Twenty bridges from Tower to Kew —
> (Twenty bridges or twenty-two) —
> Wanted to know what the River knew,
> For they were young, and the Thames was old
> And this is the tale that River told: —

'I walk my beat before London Town,
Five hours up and seven down.
Up I go till I end my run
At Tide-end-town, which is Teddington.
Down I come with the mud in my hands
And plaster it over the Maplin Sands.
But I'd have you know that these waters of mine
Were once a branch of the River Rhine,
When hundreds of miles to the East I went
And England was joined to the Continent.

'I remember the bat-winged lizard-birds,
The Age of Ice and the mammoth herds,
And the giant tigers that stalked them down
Through Regent's Park into Camden Town.
And I remember like yesterday
The earliest Cockney who came my way,
When he pushed through the forest that lined the Strand,
With paint on his face and a club in his hand.
He was death to feather and fin and fur.
He trapped my beavers at Westminster.
He netted my salmon, he hunted my deer,
He killed my heron off Lambeth Pier.
He fought his neighbour with axes and swords,
Flint or bronze, at my upper fords,
While down at Greenwich, for slaves and tin,
The tall Phoenician ships stole in,
And North Sea war-boats, painted and gay,
Flashed like dragon-flies, Erith way;
And Norseman and Negro and Gaul and Greek
Drank with the Britons in Barking Creek,
And life was gay, and the world was new,
And I was a mile across at Kew!
But the Roman came with a heavy hand,
And bridged and roaded and ruled the land,
And the Roman left and the Danes blew in –
And that's where your history-books begin!

'There is a persistent refrain that the great river poem has yet to be written' writes John Eade in the comprehensive survey of poems about the Thames given on his website.[3] I agree, fond though I am of James Bird's subversive contribution and Kipling's 'River's Tale'. But Carol Ann Duffy's Jubilee poem comes close, and honourable mention must be made of Andrew Motion's elegant 'Fresh Water: In memory of Ruth Haddon'. Ruth was a friend who died in 1989 when the riverboat *Marchioness* sank after a collision with a dredger. He begins with a visit to the source,

> ... a red-brown soft-lipped cleft
> with bright green grass right up to the edge
> and the water twisting out like a rope of glass.

Then he recalls joining a friend in a punt at Lechlade.

> ... The hills rise behind him
> in a gradual wave so that he seems at the centre
> of an enormous amphitheatre.

Next he remembers standing on Folly Bridge in Oxford, watching police divers search for, we presume, a body in the river near Christ Church meadow. Finally he takes his children to visit the Tower of London, and a question from one of them ('do people drown in the river?') makes him think of the death of Ruth, and he imagines her

> swimming back upstream, her red velvet party dress
> flickering round her heels as she twists through the locks
> and dreams round the slow curves, slithering on for miles

and slipping 'over the bright green grass and into the small wet mouth of the earth'.

POETS AND PLACES

Towery city and branchy between towers;
Cuckoo-echoing, bell-swarmèd, lark-charmèd, rook-racked,
　　river-rounded;
The dapple-eared lily below thee

　　　　Gerard Manley Hopkins, 'Duns Scotus's Oxford', 1918

Versifiers are scarce on the 'stripling Thames', but Radcot Bridge
was the subject of a bouncy ballad by Joseph Ashby-Sterry.

On Radcot Bridge, I'd have you know
They fought like demons years ago!
Here brave De Vere was put to flight,
And left his troops in sorry plight:

To-day, in place of swordly clash,
The boom of bee, the fishes' plash,
Is all the sound you hear, I ween,
To break the silence of the scene!

And now a winsome maid I see,
Who 'holds the bridge' with laughing glee,
Above its pointed arch she stands,
And archly points with small brown hands!

　　　　　　　　　　'The River Rhymer', 1913

Bablockhythe, where once a chain-hauled ferry carried walk-
ers, horses, waggons and, in the twentieth century, cars across
the river, has always been loved by those enchanted by the quiet
romance of the Thames above Eynsham Lock. 'There is some
very noble, still, quiet scenery at, and just above and below,
Bablockhythe', wrote Charles Harper.

The water runs with a deep and silent stealthiness, and the
bushy poplars and pendant weeping willows are reflected
with such startling faithfulness that the reflection in the water
beneath looks more solid — much more real than the foliage
above. It is an illusion of the weirdest kind.

The best-known mention of the crossing is Matthew Arnold's sighting there of the elusive 'Scholar Gipsy',

> ... who has been seen
> In hat of antique shape, and cloak of grey ...
> Crossing the stripling Thames at Bab-lock-hithe,
> Trailing in the cool stream thy fingers wet,
> As the slow punt swings round.
>
> *The Scholar Gipsy*, 1853

My own favourite is Laurence Binyon's poem 'Bablockhythe', which captures the scene as seen from the water.

> In the time of wild roses
> As up Thames we travelled
> Where 'mid water-weeds ravelled
> The lily uncloses...
> High woods, heron-haunted
> Rose, changed, as we rounded
> Old hills greenly mounded.
> To meadows enchanted

The Evenlode joins the Thames between Swinford Bridge and King's Lock. Hilaire Belloc captures its remote mystery in a poem, which recalls exploring it during his time at Oxford.

> I will not try to reach again,
> I will not set my sail alone,
> To moor a boat bereft of men
> At Yarnton's tiny docks of stone.
>
> But I will sit beside the fire,
> And put my hand before my eyes,
> And trace, to fill my heart's desire,
> The last of all our Odysseys ...
>
> A lovely river, all alone,
> She lingers in the hills and holds
> A hundred little towns of stone,
> Forgotten in the western wolds.

The romantic legend of Henry II's murdered mistress Rosamund, who was buried at Godstow Nunnery, inspired numerous poems, among them Samuel Daniel's 'Complaint of Rosamund' (1592) and Thomas Deloney's 'Fair Rosamund' (1612); at that time the ruins were much more extensive than they are today. Most are insufferably moralising and bedecked with vocatives and exclamation marks. I'm going to settle for the beginning of Gascoigne Mackie's 'Godstow' (1867), which also celebrates the Trout Inn.

> And once we rowed together up the river
> To many-gated Godstow, where the stream
> Splits, and upon a tongue of land there stands
> An Inn with willow bowers: – it is a spot
> Where still the flavour of old Merry England
> Lingers. And softly flowed the silver Thames
> Beside the garden, while we fed the fish.
> There 'mid the twilight and the trellised roses
> We sang the ballad of fair Rosamund:
> And when at last we loosed the boat, we saw
> Above the ruined Nunnery where she sleeps
> A star: and from the reeds a mournful gust
> Whispered and rippled round the shallow prow
> And passed: and all was quiet.

In his blank verse autobiography *Summoned by Bells* (1960), John Betjeman describes a school trip to Oxey Mead, just upstream of Godstow.

> The skiffs were moored above the lock,
> They bumped each other side to side:
> I boarded one and made her rock.
> 'Shut up, you fool,' a master cried.
> By reed and rush and alder-bush
> See soon our long procession glide.

He looks into the water, and sees 'Deep forests of the bladed reed / Whose wolves are rats of slimy coat', and notices how 'hideous larva from the mud / Clung to a reed with patient hold' before turning into 'an aeroplane of green and gold'.

Oxford, as you would expect of such a word-obsessed place, has spawned more poems than any Thames location outside London. J.B. Firth admits in the preface to his plump anthology of poems relating to Oxford, *The Minstrelsy of Isis* (1908), that 'if only verses of high excellence had been admitted, this book would have been considerably smaller'. Unlike Firth, I will omit the dross; I also limit myself to mentions of the Thames, or Isis, and the Cherwell.

The Isis gets a mention in Wordsworth's sonnet on Oxford (1820). After apostrophising Oxford's spires, its 'air of liberty' and 'light of truth,

> ... rushing on a bold exchange,
> I slight my own beloved Cam, to range
> Where silver Isis leads my stripling feet;
> Pace the long avenue or glide adown
> The stream-like windings of that glorious street

John Bruce Norton (1815–1883) was a Merton undergraduate, later a lawyer, who wrote two poems to celebrate his days in Oxford. 'Memories of Merton' sets the college between two rivers.

> Gay with June's livery of liveliest green,
> By daisies crimson-edged and cowslip-dyed,
> Smile Merton meadows in their summer pride,
> While far-off Isis glints back steely sheen,
> Yon stately avenue's tall trees between.
> Like flash of casque and spear when warriors ride.
> Sweet Cherwell's waters edge the nearer side.

'Isis the River' describes the Thames between Godstow and Nuneham with Augustan pomp, but I like this vivid picture of rowing the river:

> Or up or down, I cleft my swift-oared way
> Nightly, alone, with little heed or care,

Through the full stream with racing cutters gay;
Oft laughing at the imperious steersman's shout,
As from his very bows I glided out!

The quintessential Oxford poet is Matthew Arnold (1822–1888), who was the University's Professor of Poetry from 1857 to 1867. Although he is famous for his apostrophe to the city in the preface to his *Essays on Criticism* as an 'Adorable Dreamer … the home of lost causes and forsaken beliefs', he was most inspired by the hills to the west of Oxford. 'On Friday I got out to Hinksey and up the hill to within sight of the Cumner [*sic*] firs', he wrote to his son in 1885. 'I cannot describe the effect which this landscape always has upon me, the hillside with its valleys, and Oxford in the great Thames valley below.'

Both his most famous Oxford poem *The Scholar Gipsy* and its companion piece *Thyrsis* are written as if the poet is roaming high in the Cumnor hills, looking down on 'that sweet city with her dreaming spires'. That, and these following lines, are from *Thyrsis*, which was written in memory of his friend Arthur Hugh Clough, with whom he walked the hills when they were students.

I know what white, what purple fritillaries
The grassy harvest of the river-fields,
Above by Eynsham, down by Sandford, yields;
And what sedged brooks are Thames's tributaries…
Where is the girl, who, by the boatman's door,
Above the locks, above the boating throng,
Unmoor'd our skiff, when through the Wytham flats,
Red loose-strife and blond meadow-sweet among,
And darting swallows, and light water-gnats,
We track'd the shy Thames shore?

Two days after he matriculated, Gerard Manley Hopkins went out on the upper river with James Strachan-Davidson. He recorded that they

In April 1863, Gerard Manley Hopkins and a friend 'took a sailing boat, skulled up and sailed down' the upper river. Illustration: 'Sailing at Godstow' from *The Royal River* (1885).

took a sailing boat, skulled up and sailed down. We then took canoes. I know nothing so luxuriously delicious as a canoe. It is a long, light covered boat, the same shape both ways, with an opening in the middle where you recline, with your feet against one board, your back against a cushion on another ... The motion is Elysian.[4]

Hopkins haunted the rivers around Oxford, enjoying walks along the banks to the ferries at Bablockhythe and Marston, and swimming in the Cherwell at Parson's Pleasure, where nude swimming had long been a tradition. The river is mentioned in two of his best and most quoted poems. 'Binsey Poplars (Felled 1879)', an elegy for the great black poplars that lined the Thames on the Binsey side of Port Meadow, and 'Duns Scotus's Oxford'.

Less well known as an Oxford versifier is Oscar Wilde, who read Greats at Magdalen from 1874 to 1878. In 1881, he began his 'Burden of Itys' with panache:

This English Thames is holier far than Rome,
Those harebells like a sudden flush of sea
Breaking across the woodland, with the foam
Of meadow-sweet and white anemone
To fleck their blue waves, – God is likelier there
Than hidden in that crystal-hearted star the pale monks bear!

Those violet-gleaming butterflies that take
Yon creamy lily for their pavilion
Are monsignores, and where the rushes shake
A lazy pike lies basking in the sun,
His eyes half shut, – he is some mitred old
Bishop *in partibus*! look at those gaudy scales all green and gold.

I love the piscine bishop. But the poem drags on for 345 lines, off to Kent one minute and Arcadia the next, dwells on Tempe, Ariadne and Troy, and returns only sporadically and unconvincingly 'in rapturous threnody' to the Thames.

J.R.R. Tolkien (1892–1973) spun quite a few verses in his student days, among them 'From Iffley', which he wrote in 1911. Only one of its stanzas survives:

From the many-willow'd margin of the immemorial Thames,
Standing in a vale outcarven in a world-forgotten day,
There is dimly seen uprising through the greenly veiled stems,
Many-mansion'd, tower-crowned in its dreamy robe of grey,
All the city by the fording: aged in the lives of men,
Proudly wrapt in mystic mem'ry overpassing human ken.[5]

On a hill a mile or so from Dorchester is the most unusual of all poems connected to the Thames. It was carved on a tree that overlooked the Thames from the summit of Wittenham Clumps between 1844 and 1845 by Joseph Tubb of Warborough. The tree itself died in the 1990s, but a stone with a reproduction of the poem taken from a 1965 tracing of Tubb's time-swollen lettering was erected close to it in 1994. The rotted trunk finally collapsed in 2012.

Oxford's lovely riverside setting inspired poets galore. Joseph Mallord William Turner, *South View of Christ Church from the Meadows* (1789).

As up the hill with labr'ing steps we tread
Where the twin Clumps their sheltering branches spread
The summit gain'd, at ease reclining lay
and all around the wide spread scene survey
Point out each object and instructive tell
The various changes that the land befel.
Where the low bank the country wide surrounds
That ancient earthwork form'd old Murcia's bounds.
In misty distance see the barrow heave,
There lies forgotten lonely Culchelm's grave.
Around this hill the ruthless Danes intrenched,
and these fair plains with gory slaughter drench'd,
While at our feet where stands that stately tower
In days gone by, uprose the Roman power
And yonder, there where Thames smooth waters glide

In later days appeared monastic pride.
Within that field where lies the grazing herd
Huge walls were found, some coffins disinter'd
Such is the course of time, the wreck which fate
And awful doom award the earthly great.

The greatest menace to poetic musings by the riverside were
the steam launches that had become an inescapable nuisance in
the more popular stretches of the river by the 1880s. Virginia
Woolf's cousin James Kenneth Stephen (1859–1892) wrote this
splendid rant in 1891:

Shall we, to whom the stream by right belongs,
Who travel silent, save, perchance, for songs;
Whose track's a ripple, – leaves the Thames a lake,
Nor frights the swan – scarce makes the rushes shake;

Who harmonize, exemplify, complete
And vivify a scene already sweet:
Who travel careless on, from lock to lock,
Oblivious that the world contains a clock,

With pace commensurate to our desires,
Propelled by other force than Stygian fire's;
Shall we be driven hence to leave a place
For these, who bring upon our stream disgrace:

The rush, the roar, the stench, the smoke, the steam,
The nightmare striking through our heavenly dream;
The scream as shrill and hateful to the ear
As when a peacock vents his rage and fear;

Which churn to fury all a glassy reach,
And heave rude breakers on a pebbly beach:
Which half o'erwhelm with waves our frailer craft,
While graceless shop-boys chuckle fore and aft:

Foul water-toadstools, noisome filth-stained shapes,
Fit only to be manned by dogs and apes:
Blots upon nature: scars that mar her smile:
Obscene, obtrusive, execrable, vile?

And so onwards to Windsor, childhood home of Alexander Pope (1688–1744), who first won fame with his epic poem 'Windsor Forest' (1713). It begins with a rapturous description of the Eden-like peace of the forest, then introduces the Thames, the 'great father of the British floods', on whose shores 'future navies' (in the shape of oak trees) appear. He summarises the past glories and more recent political chaos witnessed by Windsor and the Thames, finally arriving at his own age, when 'great Anna said "Let Discord cease!" ... the World obey'd, and all was Peace!' Enter Father Thames and his attendant tributaries, each aptly characterised.

> In that blest moment, from his oozy bed
> Old Father Thames advanced his reverend head;
> His tresses dropp'd with dews, and o'er the stream
> His shining horns diffused a golden gleam ...
> Around his throne the sea-born brothers stood,
> Who swell with tributary urns his flood;
> First the famed authors of his ancient name,
> The winding Isis and the fruitful Thame:
> The Kennet swift, for silver eels renown'd;
> The Loddon slow, with verdant alders crown'd;
> Cole, whose dark streams his flowery islands lave;
> And chalky Wey, that rolls a milky wave;
> The blue, transparent Vandalis [Wandle] appears;
> The gulfy Lee his sedgy tresses rears;
> And sullen Mole, that hides his diving flood;
> And silent Darent, stain'd with Danish blood.

Pope ends by prophesying the time when 'unbounded Thames shall flow for all mankind, / Whole nations entering with each swelling tide', but quietly bows out himself, explaining that his own humble muse prefers to 'paint the green forests and the flow'ry plains / Where Peace descending bids her olives spring'.

Thomas Gray (1716–1771) recalled his schooldays in his 'Ode on a Distant Prospect of Eton College' (1747). After saluting the 'silver-winding way' of the 'hoary Thames' on which the boys 'cleave / With pliant arm thy glassy wave', it shifts abruptly from idyll to omen. 'Alas, regardless of their doom, / The little victims play', concluding forlornly, 'where ignorance is bliss, / 'Tis folly to be wise.' The poem most popularly associated with Eton is, however, the boating song written in 1863 by William Johnson Cory, then a tutor at the school. Here is the atmospheric second verse:

> Skirling past the rushes,
> Ruffling o'er the weeds,
> Where the lock-stream gushes,
> Where the cygnet feeds,
> Let us see how the loving cup flushes,
> At supper on Boveney meads,
> Let us see how the loving cup flushes,
> At supper on Boveney meads.

Downstream of Windsor, Cooper's Hill rises high above the meadows of Runnymede. For two centuries, the most acclaimed poem associated with the Thames was the Royalist Sir John Denham's 'Cooper's Hill' (1642). It set a fashion for a new kind of didactic local poetry, one that not only celebrated the vista spread before the poet, but moralised about its historical associations. Dryden described it as 'a poem which for majesty of style is, and ever will be, the standard of good writing',[6] and Pope's 'Windsor Forest' gives it a reverential nod: 'Here his first lays majestic Denham sung'. Written at the height of the Civil War, 'Cooper's Hill' is as much a disquisition on the need for balance of power as praise of the Thames as it strays 'among wanton valleys ... Hasting to pay his tribute to the sea, / Like mortal life to meet eternity'. Looking west to Windsor inspires a whistle-stop catalogue of monarchs from Arthur onwards; the sight below him of the riverside ruins of Chertsey Abbey brings a condemnation of the Reformation. Then comes fulsome praise of the river itself, a symbol of good kingship, which Denham claims (quite wrongly)

Sir John Denham's long-famous poem 'Cooper's Hill' (1642) was composed looking down to the Thames. *View of Runnymede from Cooper's Hill with a Distant View of Windsor Castle*, by Edmund John Niemann (1876).

never floods but only offers 'unwearied bounty'. Cue the poem's most quoted quatrain:

> O could I flow like thee, and make thy stream
> My great example, as it is my theme!
> Though deep, yet clear, though gentle, yet not dull,
> Strong without rage, without o'er-flowing full.

A stag hunt symbolic of the Parliamentarians' pursuit of Charles I ends at Runnymede, where Denham recalls that 'Here was that Charter sealed wherein the crown / All marks of arbitrary power lays down'. Finally, he likens the Parliamentary forces to greedy husbandmen who try to get more than their due from the river, ending with a thunderous warning:

> If with bays and dams they strive to force
> His channel to a new or narrow course,
> No longer then within his banks he dwells;
> First to a torrent, then a deluge swells;
> Stronger and fiercer by restraint he roars,
> And knows no bound, but makes his power his shores.

Oscar Wilde was living near the river in Tite Street, Chelsea, when he derided James Whistler's 1876 *Nocturne in Blue and Silver: Old Battersea Bridge*, saying it was 'worth looking at for about as long as one looks at a real rocket, that is, for somewhat less than a quarter of a minute'.[7] However, his own word picture of the river at dawn, 'Impressions de Matin' (1881), is clearly indebted to Whistler's hazy vista. Interestingly, in 1892, Whistler's painting was renamed *Nocturne in Blue and Gold*.

> The Thames nocturne of blue and gold
> Changed to a Harmony in grey:
> A barge with ochre-coloured hay
> Dropt from the wharf: and chill and cold
> The yellow fog came creeping down
> The bridges, till the houses' walls
> Seemed changed to shadows and St. Paul's
> Loomed like a bubble o'er the town.
> Then suddenly arose the clang
> Of waking life; the streets were stirred
> With country waggons: and a bird
> Flew to the glistening roofs and sang.
> But one pale woman all alone,
> The daylight kissing her wan hair,
> Loitered beneath the gas lamps' flare,
> With lips of flame and heart of stone.

The Thames is also an element in Wilde's 1889 'Symphony in Yellow'.

> Big barges full of yellow hay
> Are moored against the shadowy wharf,
> And, like a yellow silken scarf,
> The thick fog hangs along the quay.
>
> The yellow leaves begin to fade
> And flutter from the Temple elms,
> And at my feet the pale green Thames
> Lies like a rod of rippled jade.

LONDON TO THE NORE

The boat light-skimming stretched its oary wings;
While deep the various voice of fervent toil
From bank to bank increased; whence, ribbed with oak
To bear the British thunder, black, and bold,
The roaring vessel rushed into the main.

James Thomson,
The Seasons, 1772

London's river has inspired poetry of all kinds through the centuries: triumphant, nostalgic, joyful, and most recently what Iain Sinclair calls 'lead-coloured drift'. One of the earliest poems to mention the Thames is John Gower's *Confessio Amantis*, a book finished in 1390 which he described enticingly as 'somewhat of lust, somewhat of lore'. In its preface, he claims that he was rowing in the river when he met his 'liege lord' Richard II.

In Temse whan it was flowende
As I by bote cam rowende,
So as Fortune hir tyme sette,
My liege lord par chaunce I mette;
And so bifel, as I cam neigh,
Out of my bot, whan he me seigh,
He bad me come into his barge.
And whan I was with him at large,
Amonges othre thinges seyde
He hath this charge upon me leyde,
And bad me doo my busynesse
That to his hihe worthinesse
Som newe thing I scholde booke,
That he himself it mighte looke
After the forme of my writyng.

A century later, William Dunbar (*c.*1465–*c.*1530) praised the Thames in his 'In Honour of the City of London' (1501).

'Earth has not anything to shew more fair': this mid-eighteenth-century painting of Westminster Bridge by an unknown artist shows it as Wordsworth would have known it when he composed his famous sonnet in 1807.

Above all rivers thy river hath renown,
Whose beryl streams, pleasant and preclare,
Under thy lusty walls runneth down;
Where many a swan doth swim with wingès fair,
Where many a barge doth sail, and row with oar,
Where many a ship doth rest with top-royal.

William Wordsworth (1770–1850) wrote 'Composed upon Westminster Bridge' in 1807, recalling a visit to London five years earlier, with his sister Dorothy. She, as was her wont, recorded their experiences in her journal.

31 July 1802. We left London on Saturday morning at half past 5 or 6, the 31st July (I have forgot which); we mounted the Dover Coach at Charing Cross. It was a beautiful morning. The City, St Pauls, with the River & a multitude of little Boats, made a most beautiful sight as we crossed Westminster Bridge. The houses were not overhung by their cloud of smoke & they were spread out endlessly, yet the sun shone so brightly with such a pure light that there was even something like the purity of one of nature's own grand Spectacles.

William may have used it as an aide-memoire, when he came to write his sonnet.

Earth has not any thing to shew more fair:
Dull would he be of soul who could pass by
A sight so touching in its majesty:
This City now doth like a garment wear
The beauty of the morning; silent, bare,
Ships, towers, domes, theatres, and temples lie
Open unto the fields, and to the sky;
All bright and glittering in the smokeless air.
Never did sun more beautifully steep
In his first splendour, valley, rock, or hill;
Ne'er saw I, never felt, a calm so deep!
The river glideth at his own sweet will:
Dear God! the very houses seem asleep;
And all that mighty heart is lying still!

Hilaire Belloc's mother Bessie Rayner Parkes (1829–1925) was a prominent Victorian journalist, feminist and poet, who founded the influential *Englishwoman's Journal*. She had a wide literary acquaintance, including George Eliot, Dante Gabriel Rossetti and Christina Rossetti. 'Up the River' is an eccentrically scanned account of a steamer trip from Westminster to Richmond, 'all for half-a-crown'.

See there the line of distant hills, and where the blue is faintest,
The brown sails of the barges lie slanting in the sun.
Here's a steamer – now we're in it – one is passing every minute;
There's the palace of St. Stephen, which they call 'a dream
  in stone';
But I think, beyond all question, it was in an indigestion
That the architect devised those scrolls whose language is
  unknown.

London's docks were vividly conjured up by James Thomson in 'The Seasons: Autumn':

Then commerce brought into the public walk
The busy merchant; the big warehouse built;
Raised the strong crane; choked up the loaded street
With foreign plenty; and thy stream, O Thames,

Large, gentle, deep, majestic, king of floods!
Chose for his grand resort. On either hand.
Like a long wintry forest, groves of masts
Shot up their spires; the bellying sheet between
Possessed the breezy void; the sooty hulk
Steered sluggish on; the barge along
Rowed, regular, to harmony; around
The boat, light skimming, stretched its oary wings;
While deep the various voice of fervent toil
From bank to bank increased

George Gordon, Lord Byron, was much less respectful in *Don Juan* (1819).

A mighty mass of brick and smoke and shipping,
Dirty and dusky, but as wide as eye
Could reach, with here and there a sail just skipping
In sight, then lost amidst the forestry
Of masts; a wilderness of steeples peeping
On tiptoe through their sea-coal canopy;
A huge, dun cupola, like a foolscap crown
On a fool's head, – and there is London Town!

Wilfred Owen (1893–1918) always preferred London's East End to its West End. He wrote this atmospheric imagining of a night walk in Wapping while he was stationed in Scarborough in 1918, just before he returned to France to die shortly before the signing of the Armistice; it conveys the acute sense of unreality experienced by soldiers on leave.

I am the ghost of Shadwell Stair.
Along the wharves by the water-house,
And through the cavernous slaughter-house,
I am the shadow that walks there.

Yet I have flesh both firm and cool,
And eyes tumultuous as the gems
Of moons and lamps in the full Thames
When dusk sails wavering down the Pool.

Shuddering, a purple street-arc burns
Where I watch always. From the banks
Dolorously the shipping clanks
And after me a strange tide turns.

I walk till the stars of London wane
And dawn creeps up the Shadwell Stair.
But when the crowing sirens blare
I with another ghost am lain.

Robert Louis Stevenson's great friend William Henley (1849–1903), the inspiration for Long John Silver, is most famous for the lines 'I am the master of my fate, / I am the captain of my soul' that close his defiant poem 'Invictus' (1875), which was written just after he lost a leg to a tubercular infection. He also wrote 'London Voluntaries', a poem about the city which included this sensuous vision of dawn on the lower reaches of the river:

What miracle is happening in the air,
Charging the very texture of the gray
With something luminous and rare?
The night goes out like an ill-parcelled fire,
And, as one lights a candle, it is day.
The extinguisher, that perks it like a spire
On the little formal church, is not yet green
Across the water: but the house-tops nigher,
The corner-lines, the chimneys – look how clean,
How new, how naked! See the batch of boats,
Here at the stairs, washed in the fresh-sprung beam!
And those are barges that were goblin floats,
Black, hag-steered, fraught with devilry and dream!
And in the piles the water frolics clear,
The ripples into loose rings wander and flee,
And we – we can behold that could but hear
The ancient River singing as he goes,
New-mailed in morning, to the ancient Sea.

John Davidson (1857–1909) never found fame in his lifetime, but was much admired by contemporaries such as W.B. Yeats and

Oscar Wilde. 'Possibly a great man', said Frank Harris, 'certainly a man of genius'. His subjects were unusual. 'In The Isle of Dogs' the sound of a street organ takes the listening poet back in time and place to his Scottish island childhood. The first lines evoke the industrial slum that was then Millwall.

> While the water-wagon's ringing showers
> Sweetened the dust with a woodland smell,
> 'Past noon, past noon, two sultry hours,'
> Drowsily fell
> From the schoolhouse clock
> In the Isle of Dogs by Millwall Dock.
> Mirrored in shadowy windows draped
> With ragged net or half-drawn blind
> Bowsprits, masts, exactly shaped
> To woo or fight the wind,
> Like monitors of guilt
> By strength and beauty sent,
> Disgraced the shameful houses built
> To furnish rent.

T.S. Eliot admired Davidson and acknowledged his influence on *The Waste Land*. In its third part, 'Fire Sermon', he juxtaposes a patchwork of images, some sordid, some lyrical, to create arrestingly modern songs for Thames nymphs borrowed from Edmund Spenser's tale of the marriage of Thames and Isis, *Prothalamium*.

London's largely hidden rivers fascinate many writers. The best poem about them is by the late great U.A. Fanthorpe (1929–2009). 'Rising Damp' (1980) begins with an epigram: 'A river can sometimes be diverted but is a very hard thing to lose altogether (Paper to the Auctioneers' Institute, 1907).' Then off she goes, spinning together the story of the lost streams and ending with a reminder of ancient underworld rivers.

> At our feet they lie low,
> The little fervent underground

Rivers of London
Effra, Graveney, Falcon, Quaggy,
Wandle, Walbrook, Tyburn, Fleet

Whose names are disfigured,
Frayed, effaced.

These are the Magogs that chewed the clay
To the basin that London nestles in.
These are the currents that chiselled the city,
That washed the clothes and turned the mills,
Where children drank and salmon swam
And wells were holy.

They have gone under
Boxed, like the magician's assistant.
Buried alive in earth.
Forgotten, like the dead.

They return spectrally after heavy rain,
Confounding suburban gardens. They infiltrate
Chronic bronchitis statistics. A silken
Slur haunts dwellings by shrouded
Watercourses and is taken
For the footing of the dead.

Being of our world, they will return
(Westbourne, caged at Sloane Square,
Will jack from his box).
Will deluge cellars, detonate manholes,
Plant effluent on our faces,
Sink the city.
Effra, Graveney, Falcon, Quaggy,
Wandle, Walbrook, Tyburn, Fleet

It is the other rivers that lie
Lower, that touch us only in dreams
That never surface. We feel their tug
As a dowser's rod bends to the source below.
Phlegethon, Acheron, Lethe, Styx.

Another unusual take on the Thames in London is 'The River Goddess in the A–Z' (1999), in which Anna Adams contrasts the 'blue contours of a living limb' with the 'ruled geometry of streets' on the street guide's pages. The river is 'a liquid-muscled snake', an illegal immigrant from Amazonian, African and Asian waters, 'more cosmopolitan than the great town she jigsaws, mirrors, joins … the wilderness at large in town'.

The moment when the Thames merges with the North Sea is fancifully described in the copious source-to-sea verse already mentioned. How much perceptions of that moment have changed over the centuries can be seen in my two final poems. In 'Ovid's Banquet of Sense' (1595), George Chapman likens Ovid's hesitation before creeping up on his adored Corinna while she is bathing to that of the Thames as it flirtatiously comes to the sea.

> Forward and backward went he thus,
> Like wanton Thamysis that hastes to greet
> The brackish coast of old Oceanus:
> And as by London's bosom she doth fleet,
> Casts herself proudly through the bridge's twists,
> Where, as she takes again her crystal feet,
> She curls her silver hair like amourists,
> Smooths her bright cheeks, adorns her brow with ships,
> And, empress-like, along the coast she trips
> Till coming near the sea, she hears him roar,
> Tumbling his churlish billows in her face,
> Then, more dismay'd than insolent before,
> Charged to rough battle for his smooth embrace,
> She croucheth close within her winding banks,
> And creeps retreat into her peaceful palace;
> Yet straight high-flowing in her female pranks
> Again she will be wanton, and again,
> By no means staid, nor able to contain.

Ruth Pitter's (1897–1992) 'The Estuary' is a much more personal vision. She grew up in Ilford, Essex, and lived in London until

1954, She wrote while she was working in Morgan's Crucible Works close to the Thames at Battersea during the Second World War.

Light, stillness and peace lie on the broad sands,
On the salt-marshes the sleep of the afternoon.
The sky's immaculate; the horizon stands
Steadfast, level and clear over the dune.

There are voices of children, musical and thin
Not far, nor near, there in the sandy hills;
As the light begins to wane, so the tide comes in,
The shallow creek at our feet silently fills:

And silently, like sleep to the weary mind,
Silently, like the evening after the day,
The big ship bears inshore with the inshore wind,
Changes her course, and comes on up through the bay,

Rolling along the fair deep channel she knows,
Surging along, right on top of the tide.
I can see the flowery wreath of foam at the bows,
The long bright wash streaming away from her side:

I can see the flashing gulls that follow her in,
Screaming and tumbling, like children wildly at play,
The sea-born crescent arising, pallid and thin,
The flat safe twilight shore shelving away.

Whether remembered or dreamed, read of or told,
So it has dwelt with me, so it shall dwell with me ever:
The brave ship coming home like a lamb to the fold,
Home with the tide into the mighty river.

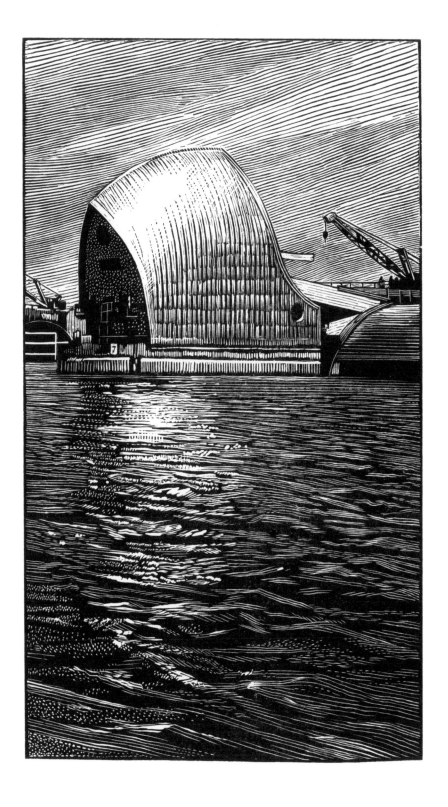

WRITING THE THAMES TODAY

W HAT does Thames literature amount to in the twenty-first century? The 2012 Diamond Jubilee Pageant in honour of the 60th anniversary of Queen Elizabeth II's reign was an exceptional reminder of the Thames as 'liquid history'. We are nervous these days about what was once proudly called 'Our Island Story'. Although the hundreds of historic craft were splendid, the BBC's commentators were lamentably ignorant of their importance, concentrating instead on celebrity-spotting. Patriotism was to the fore again, however, in March 2015, when hundreds of thousands of people packed the bridges and banks to watch the 50th anniversary re-enactment of the 1965 voyage of the *Havengore*, the launch that carried Winston Churchill's Union Jack-draped coffin from St Paul's Cathedral to Waterloo. Today times have changed: the lofty cranes on the Surrey bank that spontaneously dipped in slow salute as the launch went past them in 1965 have disappeared. Happily, Barbara Daniels reminds us of them in her poem 'Homage'.

> The complex traffic of this river's flow
> forms patterns on the waves: bright pleasure boats
> set off for Greenwich as a seagull floats.
> I watch the up-and-down, the to-and-fro,

The Thames Barrier, wood engraving by Simon Brett for *Reflections on the River Thames* (2000).

the skimming, chugging, churning, fast and slow;
small craft beneath the bridge, the blurred, remote
outline of larger ships and wharves. My throat
catches. That day, so many years ago,
saw one lone barge, black-draped, carry its load
in silence for a battle fought and won.
as we recalled his words, the way he led.
Even the sceptics knew how much they owed.
And then the final tribute: one by one
tall cranes in Dockland bowed their metal heads.[1]

What of topography and tourism? West of London, the river is a parking place for motor cruisers that move as rarely as the majority of caravans; the further upstream you go, the fewer voyagers there are of any kind, and in winter the river is almost deserted. The riverbanks between Tower Bridge and the great silver helmets of the Thames Barrier are now boom areas for ritzy residential developments intended as investments for global capital rather than homes. Downstream of the Barrier is an industrial desert, with polluted wastelands, a scatter of marshy islands and down-at-heel towns. And yet the urge to explore that the Thames has always aroused endures. Every year, thousands of enthusiasts follow in the footsteps of the early topographers and artists. Thanks to the establishment of an official Thames Path, there are accounts galore of expeditions along and beside the river, some in print, some on film, most in the form of blogs. The Thames Meander is now a Wikipedia entry; the river can be rowed, run, swum or bicycled either in competition or for pleasure.

Facilitated by the digital revolution, more records in words and pictures have been devoted to such expeditions in the last three decades than in all previous centuries put together. The most comprehensive topographical survey of the river is not a book but a website. John Eade is a retired vicar who has been a lifelong aficionado of the river, exploring as far upstream in his punt *Pax* as Cricklade, and downstream to Teddington. The website also covers the tidal Thames, with its fascinating historic bridges and races. Although Eade now lives in Dorset, he still regularly visits the river in the second of two punts he has built himself; in 2015 *Pax* was even coaxed through the jungle of Oxford backwaters around and under the Botley Road as far as The Fishes at North Hinksey. A developing interest is the tides and their graphical online presentation. 'Where Thames Smooth Waters Glide' can be summoned up by typing in Thames John Eade, or thames.me.uk. It is an unrivalled treasure house of facts, literary reference and artworks that is constantly being added to and updated.

Only the most successful modern authors can now afford to buy retreats on the Thames itself, and they guard their privacy jealously. But in recent decades creative writers have flourished in the East London borough of Hackney. It isn't on the Thames but some of its best authors seem to be umbilically attached to the river. The writing of Iain Sinclair (1943–) has been neatly summed up by reviewer Tobias Hill as 'a cross between Betjeman and William Burroughs'. His *Downriver* (1991) is a series of extravagantly Gothic and frequently surreal scenes that contrast London's West End with the Thames badlands; like Eliot's *The Waste Land*, it is threaded with ironic literary reference.

> Wooden stumps in the mud. The ruins of a jetty. The tide was turning: a slime-caked causeway, plastered in filth and sediment, pointed at Gravesend. [Bobby] often boasted, without much justification, that Magwitch faltered here, escaping from the hulks, and was brought to shore. The last pub in the world, the World's End.

Set in the last years of Margaret Thatcher's premiership, and fuelled by Sinclair's resentment of her policies in general and the gentrification of his 'Rose-Red Empire' in Hackney in particular, the book is a biting satire on the obscene extremes of wealth and poverty. Sinclair's trademark is movement: walking London's river and the city's environs and recording what he sees with

Iain Sinclair and Andrew Kötting in the swan-shaped pedalo in which they voyaged up the Thames and the Lea in 2012.

Blakean zest. There is a cinematic exactness in his descriptions of his journey along the Thames from Tilbury to Hackney, as if the chance details of London life that he documents have been freeze-framed. *Downriver* also takes a sideswipe at imperialism, tellingly guyed in twelve bizarre photographic postcards, supposedly found in a Tilbury junkshop, which are put in order and called 'Joblard's Heart of Darkness'. To Sinclair's mind, London's river has become as savage and wild as Marlow had imagined it to have been in the time of the Romans.

Sinclair has now fled the abhorred fashionistas. 'I can't live in Hackney any more', he says, from a bolt-hole in St Leonards, which he jokingly calls Hackney-on-Sea. His latest waterbourne escapade was recorded in the documentary film *Swandown* (2012). He and the film's director, Andrew Kötting, propelled a swan-shaped pedalo 160 miles from Hastings to the Olympics site on the River Lea to make a protest about the commercialization of the games. The absurd voyage neatly referenced seventeenth-century poets' love of symbolic swans gliding down the Thames. The pedalo was not allowed to navigate in the Estuary, however; instead Sinclair and his companion loaded it onto a Thames tug until they reached the mouth of the River Lea.

Patrick Wright's *A Journey Through Ruins* (1991) ranges from Docklands back to his Hackney home, where he likens Dalston Lane to 'a clogged river of junk flowing through the city'. More recently he wrote the refreshingly acerbic *The Thames in Our Time* (1999), a record of a television series in which he fought the corner of the neglected estuarial reaches of the river, and rejected the complacent nationalist fable on which the heritage industry thrives. Telling the epic story of the dockers' fight for decent working conditions, he argues that John Burn's famous phrase 'liquid history' was less about the Thames than the 'river of progress and solidarity surging through the hearts and minds of generations of militants and activists'. He cites Jack Lindsay's dockland drama *Rising Tide* (1953) and Jack Dash's autobiographical *Good Morning, Brothers* (1969) as elements in 'the idealized river of socialist aspirations', and notes that the downfall of the dockers under Margaret Thatcher saw the decline of the defiant East End patriotism that helped Britain to win the war. Something at least of their spirit survives, Wright is pleased to find, in the 'stiff history lesson' of the commentary delivered by John Potter, captain of the cruise boat *Princess Pocohontas*, rich in 'acid put-downs' against 'the new powers that have colonized the riverside and ripped its heart out'.

FOLLOWING SPREAD Patrick Wright's *The Thames in Our Time* explores the neglected stretches of the Thames Estuary.

What of messing about on the river? If Henry James were writing his *English Hours* today, he would remark on England's 'mighty population' taking to cars rather than boats 'on the smallest pretext of a holiday or fine weather'. Those who still go afloat include frenetic rowers in rapier-thin craft, retirees in narrowboats and motor cruisers, and a great many canoe and kayak paddlers. Punts remain popular on the Cherwell in Oxford; they also race at several river clubs further downstream. The annual championships take place at Maidenhead. Punts have their chronicler in R.T. Rivington, whose lively and generously illustrated *Punting, Its History and Techniques* was published in 1983. The Thames sailing clubs flourished after the wartime inventions of plywood and synthetic glues made putting together kit dinghies like the Mirror and the British Moth a hobby for Everyman. Oxford, Henley and Richmond still hire out punts and rowing skiffs.

Accounts of adventurous boating expeditions on the river abound. Easily the best and the funniest is *The Unlikely Voyage of Jack de Crow: A Mirror Odyssey from North Wales to the Black Sea* (2002). The Thames is only one of the many rivers along which its author A.J. ('Sandy') McKinnon voyaged. He set off from Ellesmere in a Mirror dinghy, and rowed and sailed along the Severn to Gloucester. He wore a pith helmet, sang sea shanties and, being by profession a teacher of English literature, quoted copiously from Tennyson, Shelley, Arthur Ransome, John Masefield and other literary greats. He frequently came to grief, but was saved time and again by passing boats and helpful riparians who repaired the increasingly battered *Jack de Crow* and fortified its captain with potent cordials. He enjoyed himself so much that he rowed on – down the Kennet and Avon Canal, to the Thames at Reading. There he turned upstream and headed not just to Oxford but beyond it, describing in ebullient detail the mystic attraction of the quiet stretches of the river between Oxford and Lechlade, the limit of powered navigation. He even struggled on to Hannington Bridge.

Ash and osier and willow closed in overhead, thick sedge and reeds clogged the river's course and where they did so the current trebled in strength, making it all but impossible to work my way upstream … Finally I came to Hannington Bridge, a lonely stone bridge half-hidden in trees. Here the stream ambled swiftly down over a shallow rocky bed beneath the arch, chattering between fallen lumps of rubble and masonry, and five attempts to propel *Jack* up and into the quieter pool proved fruitless. As I rested on my oars after the fifth time a kingfisher, dragonfly blue, came skimming upstream, flashed past me and vanished into the darkened arch. An omen? A sign to struggle on through? A herald leading me beyond the Wasteland, past the Dark Tower, beyond the River Gate to the land of the Fisher King himself?

Possibly. But let some later Childe Roland do the finding. *Jack* and I were weary, and besides, it had begun to rain again. 'Out oars for Narnia', I cried, turned *Jack*'s nose, and started the long haul downstream.

After spending a little time in Oxford, he scudded downstream on a favourable westerly to London, whence he sailed across the Channel, down the Rhine, numerous canals and the Danube to the Black Sea.

Similarly enterprising and entertaining is *Circle Line* (2012), yachting journalist Steffan Hughes's 70-mile mini-odyssey around the London waterways in a 15-foot sailing dinghy, via the Thames itself, the Brent, the Grand Union Canal and the Lea, 29 locks, 189 bridges, two tunnels, two aquaducts and the tidal barrier. Capsizes, a recalcitrant outboard, and a broken rowlock impede progress. Although on occasion he bolts for his Holloway home, Hughes is dependent, like McKinnon, upon the kindness of strangers. Lock-keepers and boat people offer local insights. Near Southall, a narrowboat-dwelling carpenter repairs his boat while explaining that the numerous coconuts and occasional saris floating in the river are part of Hindu post-cremation rituals

'Early sunlight shines across the lake in the middle of the meadow, making the plumage of the widgeon glow with warm colours': Port Meadow, photograph by Richard Mayon-White for *Exploring the Thames Wilderness* (2013).

that substitute the canal for the Ganges. It's a notion that Peter Ackroyd would perhaps enjoy, regarding the Thames as he does as a sacred river, akin to the Ganges as a place of pilgrimage and of spiritual renewal, and the Brent as one of its supplicant tributaries.

In 1957 the Thames in London was declared biologically dead by the Natural History Museum. Fortunately, matters improved from then on, not least because of vociferous protests from environmentalists. Today, appreciation of the river's ecology has never been greater, and the destruction dealt to its flora, fauna and fish by motor craft, overfishing and insensitive riverside development in the twentieth century is, though not over, slowing up. However, most of the eloquent and adventurous new generation

of nature writers find the Thames too tame a subject; they seek out wildernesses to provide what the American novelist and environmentalist Wallace Stegner calls 'a geography of hope'[2] to set against the hectic modern pace of life, and the omnipresent urban sprawl, industrial wastelands, motorways and railways. The Thames and its tributaries do occasionally creep in. Richard Mabey's *The Unofficial Countryside* (1973) is a quest for signs of hope in the neglected spaces between places on London's fringes. Walking a patch of as yet unused development land on the edge of the Thames, Mabey discovers in a rubbish dump 'a veritable spice garden: Cumin, fenugreek, coriander, dill, fennel – you could have flavoured a whole Indian meal'. Exploring the Colne Valley Park, where flooded gravel pits appear as 'a vast cone of blue on the map' and the Thames tributary divides into eight separate water courses, he sees 'fledgling swifts racing crazily above the pits … They arch their wings above their heads, sometimes until they are almost touching, making for themselves a combined parachute, balance and brake.' He discovers a pair of crested grebes that had 'put together their reedy nest on top of one of the old car tyres which had been dumped in great numbers in the pit'.

In *Waterlog: A Swimmer's Journey through Britain* (2000), the naturalist Roger Deakin salutes both the Thames and William Morris by taking a dip in a pool between Kelmscott and Buscot Lock in what Morris used to call the 'baby Thames'.

> The water was clear enough just above the lock to see the dark shapes of tench weaving lazily among the lily stalks. … Swimming in a big circle around the pool, I was observed by several swans, and surrounded by tall, untidy old crack willows. These were the very trees that inspired Morris, on his daily fishing trips aboard his punt, to design his 'Willow Boughs' wallpaper.

In 2013 the ecology of the Thames was presented in an inspiring way in *Exploring the Thames Wilderness* by Richard Mayon-White and Wendy Yorke. Much of the information in it came from the River Thames Society's numerous volunteer river wardens who divide guardianship of the river between them in conveniently walkable stretches. Richard Mayon-White led the complex project, and Wendy Yorke managed it on behalf of the Thames Rivers Trust. Mayon-White first fell in love with the Thames when he was working at St Thomas's Hospital as a medical student in the 1960s. Over the last fifty years, many of them spent working in Oxford University's Department of Public Health and Primary Care, he and his wife Valerie explored the length of the river in boats of all kinds, on foot and by bicycle. The river, he argues, is not only 'our living heritage', but 'an open green corridor that runs right across southern England … a revitalising way of escaping from the ruck and rumble of everyday stresses'.

The book is generously furnished with photographs, maps and walking routes. It explores the river in ten sections, beginning at the source, and ending at The Nore. Each has an introduction about the character and history of that part of the river, and describes the wildlife in and beside the river and in the many nature reserves now established along its course. The style is appropriately down to earth, and the authors' deep affection for the river is unmistakeable. There is a lyrical passage about wintertime on Port Meadow, often referred to as Oxford's natural lung:

> Early sunlight shines across the lake in the middle of the meadow, making the plumage of the widgeon glow with warm colours, contrasting with the nip of an easterly wind. The ducks talk to one another with piping calls, while geese give their haunting honk as they fly in to graze. The swans look elegant, as they always do. Across the meadow, the Thames makes its curving course from the Cotswolds on its way to the East Coast. Here you are connected with Nature.

The final chapter appeals to readers of the book to get involved in the river's conservation themselves, offering a tempting range of opportunities for volunteers. This is a book to be used and to treasure.

There are fewer accidental deaths in the Thames these days, but literary sleuths go from strength to strength. Claire Curzon's Mike Yeading investigations are set in the Thames Valley, though only *Close Quarters* (1997) involves a corpse in the river. Deborah Crombie's Scotland Yard detective duo Kincaid and Crombie are twice faced with Thames murders. In *Leave the Grave Green* (1996) a body is found in a lock on the middle Thames, which is, it emerges, related to the death in the river of a young boy long ago. *No Mark Upon Her* (2011) centres around a young woman DCI and champion rower who sets out at dusk from the Leander Club at Henley and is found murdered.

The record in river body counts is undoubtedly held by Sharon Bolton's shiver-a-minute Lacey Flint series, in which she uses the

Thames as a constant and usually ominous presence as deftly as did Dickens. Bolton knows both the river in London and Victorian Gothic novels well, and excels in menacing and macabre descriptions. *Now You See Me* (2011) is about a reborn Jack the Ripper who leaves mutilated female corpses on its shores, and almost succeeds in drowning Flint; *Like This Forever* (2013), prefaced with a quotation from *Dracula*, offers a series of murdered young boys left on the banks of the Ravensbourne and the Thames itself. In *A Dark and Twisted Tide* (2014), Flint is living in a houseboat in Deptford Creek, and working with the river police. The book starts with an epigram about mermaids from *Our Mutual Friend*, and a prologue set in a Rotherhithe pumping station that is being used by a serial killer as a grim temporary morgue. In the opening chapter, Flint, wild swimming from her houseboat, tangles with a shroud-wrapped corpse.

Finally, and in a class all its own, Ben Aaronovitch's *Rivers of London* (2011) is an exuberant and bloody fantasy of murderous magic threaded through with the history and mythology of the Thames. Father and Mama Thames are at war over territory, and their spirited offspring Ash, Brent, Lea, Fleet, Ty and Oxley, with his wife Isis, are set on creating chaos and havoc.

Such modern rhymers of the river as U.A. Fanthorpe, Anna Adams, and Carol Ann Duffy have been saluted in earlier chapters. But in pride of place among river rhymers and among all the books so far mentioned should stand the longest and greatest literary tribute that the Thames has received, Peter Ackroyd's *Thames, Sacred River*. Although it looks like narrative, Ackroyd's writing has such a spring in its step, and such breath-taking aptness in its phrasing that it is not far-fetched to call the book a prose poem. After all, Ackroyd began his literary life as a poet, just as Edward Thomas began his as a prose writer. Edward Thomas famously shifted to poetry when Robert Frost told him that in *Pursuit of Spring* he was already writing poetry 'but in prose form'. Ackroyd did the opposite, shifting to novels, biographies and histories, into all of which he instils the economic aptness and gnomic wisdoms of poetry. *Thames, Sacred River* is a book to be sipped meditatively rather than swallowed whole. Packed with facts, it will also fill up your senses. I revisit it with pleasure again and again, always finding challenging ideas, thoughts that linger.

> Water reflects. It has no meaning. So we may say that the Thames is in essence a reflection of circumstances …
>
> The Thames represented the city's destiny. It was how London was imagined …
>
> Bridges reach across the void, prompting the wanderer onwards …
>
> To look at rain falling into the river is like watching flames within a general fire; it is the delectation of watching an elemental force mingling with itself …

Ackroyd has never felt that there need be rigid boundaries between the mediums. Remembering Mary Oliver's 'the prose horse is in harness … while the poetry horse has wings',[3] there is something of Pegasus about *Thames, Sacred River*. The book's last sentence is 'The song of the Thames had ended.'

NOTES

ONE

1. Translated by Joseph Stevenson, 1875.
2. William Leigh, *Queene Elizabeth, paraleld in her princely vertues, with Dauid, Iosua, and Hezekia 1 With Dauid her afflictions, to build the Church 2 With Iosua in her puissance, to protect the Church 3 With Hezechia in her pietie, to reforme the Chureh [sic]. In three sermons, as they were preached three seuerall Queenes dayes. By William Leigh, Bachelor of Diuinitie*, Thomas Creed, London, 1612 (Early English Books Online).
3. The two versions of Sharp's letter are in MS. Harley 6798, article 18, London, British Library, and *The Cabala, Mysteries of State, in Letters of the Great Ministers of K. James and K. Charles*, 1654. They are compared line for line in Janet M. Green, '"I My Self": Queen Elizabeth I's Oration at Tilbury Camp', *The Sixteenth Century Journal*, vol. 28, no. 2 (Summer 1997), pp. 421–45.
4. Quoted in Garrett Mattingley, *The Defeat of the Spanish Armada*, Jonathan Cape, London, 1959.
5. 'Thamasis's Advice to the Painter, from her frigid zone, etc, printed by G. Croom, on the river of Thames'.
6. Quoted in William Andrews, *Famous Frosts and Frost Fairs*, Redway, London, 1887.

TWO

1. Preface of *The laboryouse journey [and] serche of Johan Leylande, for Englandes antiquitees*, printed by S. Mierdman for John Bale, London, 1549.
2. The *Polychronicon* was written in Latin in the fourteenth century, and translated into English in 1387. Higden wrote: 'Tamisia videtur componi a nominibus duorum fluminium, quae sunt Thama et Ysa aut Usa'. Peter Ackroyd, *Thames, Sacred River*, Chatto, London, 2007, p. 26.
3. In 1610, a new edition was given the informative subtitle *A chorographical description of the most flourishing kingdoms, England, Scotland, and Ireland, and the islands adjoining, out of the depth of antiquity beautified with maps of the several shires of England: written first in Latin by William Camden Clarenceux K of A. Translated newly into English by Philémon Holland Doctor of Physic: finally, revised, amended, and enlarged with sundry additions by the said author.*
4. Flower de lice is an iris; cowslips of Jerusalem are pulmonaria; and cloves of Paradise are pinks.

5. Jack B. Oruch, 'Spenser, Camden, and the Poetic Marriages of Rivers', *Studies in Philology*, vol. 64, no. 4 (July 1967), pp. 606–24.

6. Egan's first literary success was *Life in London, or the Day and Night Scenes of Jerry Hawthorn, esq., and his elegant friend, Corinthian Tom, accompanied by Bob Logic, the Oxonian, in their rambles and sprees through the Metropolis* (1821). Soon dramatised, Tom and Jerry became bywords for young men about town, long before they were immortalised in the 1940 Tom Cat and Jerry Mouse cartoon.

7. 'Odcombian shoes': a reference to Thomas Coryat, who was given the nickname 'the Odcombian leg-stretcher' after he walked all over Europe in search of gastronomic curiosities, which he described in *Crudities, hastily gobled up in five moneths travells in France, Savoy, Italy, Rhetia commonly called the Grisons country, Helvetia alias Switzerland, some parts of high Germany and the Netherlands; newly digested in the hungry aire of Odcombe in the county of Somerset, and now dispersed to the nourishment of the travelling members of this kingdome* (1611).

8. Abraham Cowley, *Discourse by way of Vision concerning the Government of Oliver Cromwell* (1661).

9. *Oxford Dictionary of National Biography* entry for Samuel Carter Hall.

10. This was demolished six years later, but the chains were reused for the Clifton Suspension Bridge.

THREE

1. The Bun House, in Grosvenor Row, was run by several members of a family named Hand. It also had a Museum of Curiosities. The often quoted figure of a quarter of a million buns sold on Good Friday 1829 is probably apocryphal, but the buns themselves sound wonderful: 'a zephyr in taste, fragrant as honey'.

2. Quoted on the Twickenham Museum website, www.twickenham-museum. org.uk/detail.asp?ContentID=184.

3. A letter to Robert Digby in 1722 showed that he and Bathurst had had visions of a canal linking the Thames and the Severn sixty years before it was begun. 'The Thames and Severn', Pope wrote, 'are to be led into each other's embrace thro' secret caverns of not above twelve or fifteen miles, till they rise and openly celebrate their marriage in the midst of an immense amphitheatre, which is to be the admiration of posterity a hundred years hence'.

4. Letter to H.S. Conway, 1747. The line is actually borrowed from Pope's *Epistle to Mr Addison occasioned by his Dialogues on Medals*.

5. Preface to his 'Pastoral Dialogue', June 1727, www.online-literature.com/ swift/poems-of-swift/58.

6. Interview for the Oxford Canal Heritage Project, 2015.

7. William Morris, The Expedition of The Ark, www.morrissociety.org/publications/JWMS/SP77.3.3.Baissus.pdf; *Collected Letters of William Morris 1848–1880*, ed. Norman Kelvin, Princeton University Press, 1984.

FOUR

1. *Picturesque rides and walks, with excursions by water, thirty miles round the British metropolis; illustrated in a series of engravings, coloured after nature; with an historical and topographical description of the country within the compass of that circle*, London, 1818.

2. J.B. Firth, ed., *The Minstrelsy of Isis: Poems Relating to Oxford*, Chapman & Hall, London, 1908, p. 217.

3. The play was originally titled *The Houseboat*. However, Barrie discovered at the last minute that there had already been a play with that title, so gave his play its odd but arresting title ('Walker', originally Hookey Walker, is Victorian slang for 'you must be joking').

4. Cuthbert Bede was the pen name of the novelist Edward Bradley (1827–1889). He had spent a year at Oxford after taking his degree at Durham. He illustrated the book himself.

5. R.R. Bolland, *In the Wake of 'Three Men in a Boat'*, Parapress, Tunbridge Wells, 1995, p. 33.

6. Recorded in Shepard's introduction to the 1951 Methuen edition.

FIVE

1. Although Compton's advice was frequently sought by such contemporaries as Soane and Evelyn, his surviving literary works only concern theology. Thirteen acres of the original much more extensive gardens survive, and are open to the public.

2. Quoted in Martin Andrews, *The Life and Work of Robert Gibbings*, Primrose Hill Press, Bicester, p. 226.

3. Henry Wotton, 'On a Bank as I Sat Fishing', in *The Book of Elizabethan Verse*, ed. W. Braithwaite, Chatto, London, 1988.

4. Arthur Ransome, 'My Barbel', *Rod and Line*, 1929.

SIX

1. *Journal of the British Archaeological Association*, 1857.

2. *Truth*, 11 September 1884.

3. Lucinda Roy, 'Thames', from *Wailing the Dead to Sleep*, Bogle L'Ouverture Press, London, 1988; *Callaloo* 36 (Summer 1988).

SEVEN

1. Thomas Love Peacock, *Letters to Edward Hookham and Percy B. Shelley, with Fragments of Unpublished Mss*, Forgotten Books, London, 2013, pp. 28–9. (Original work published 1910.)

2. W. Harper, *Shakespeare and the Thames*, London, 1890.

3. http://thames.me.uk.

4. Letter to his mother, 22 April 1863, in *Gerard Manley Hopkins: Complete Poetical Works*, Delphi, 2013.

5. *Stapeldon Magazine*, vol. 4, no. 3 (December 1913), quoted in Arne Zetterstan, *J.R.R. Tolkien's Double Worlds and Creative Process: Language and Life*, Palgrave Macmillan, Basingstoke, 2011.

6. Brendan O Hehir, *Harmony From Discords: A Life of Sir John Denham*, University of California Press, Berkeley CA, 1968, p. vii.

7. Quoted in Richard Dorment and Margaret MacDonald, *James McNeill Whistler*, Tate Gallery, London, 1994, p. 130.

EIGHT

1. *The River Thames in Verse: An Illustrated Anthology of New Poems (from the River Thames Society's Open Poetry Competition in the Winter of 2002/03)*, ed. Val Mason, River Thames Society, London, 2004.

2. Letter to David E. Pesonen, 3 December 1960.

3. Mary Oliver, *Long Life: Essays and Other Writings*, Da Capo Press, Cambridge MA, 2004.

FURTHER
READING

Although I have listed printed editions here, a great many sources for this book are also available online.

GENERAL

Ackroyd, Peter, *Thames, Sacred River*, Chatto, London, 2007.

Anon., *Royal River: The Thames from Source to Sea, Descriptive, Historical, Pictorial*, Cassell, London, 1885.

Atterbury, Paul, ed., *Nicholson's Guide to the Thames*, Nicholson, London, 1969.

Barton, Nicholas, *The Lost Rivers of London*, Leicester University Press, London, 1962.

Batey, Mavis, Henrietta Buttery, David Lambert and Kim Wilkie, *Arcadian Thames*, Barn Elms, London, 1994.

Belloc, Hilaire, *The River of London*, Foulis, Edinburgh, 1912.

————, *The Historic Thames*, Dent, London, 1914.

Benson, Don, and David Miles, *The Upper Thames Valley*, Oxford Archeology, Oxford, 1974.

Besant, Walter, *The Thames*, Black, London, 1903.

Brett, Simon, *Reflections on the River Thames*, Smith Settle, 2000.

Burstall, Patricia, *The Golden Age of the Thames*, David & Charles, London, 1981.

Cairns, A.J., *The Book of Marlow*, Barracuda Books, Chesham, 1976.

Carpenter, Humphrey, and Mari Prichard, *A Thames Companion*, Oxford University Press, Oxford, 1975.

Carter Hall, Samuel, and Anna Maria Fielding, *Book of the Thames from Its Rise to Its Fall*, Viture, London, 1859.

Clyde, Eddy, *Voyaging Down the Thames*, Frederick A. Stokes, New York, 1938.

Cooke, William, *Views on the Thames*, Cooke, London 1822.

Curtis, Roy, *Thames Passport: A Guide to the Non-tidal River*, Macmillan, London, 1970.

Dix, Frank L., *Royal River Highway*, David & Charles, Newton Abbott, 1985.

Dougill, John, *Oxford in English Literature: The Making, and Undoing, of 'The English Athens'*, University of Michigan Press, Ann Arbor MI, 1998.

Eade, John, 'Where Thames Smooth Waters Glide', http://thames.me.uk.

Evelyn, John, *Diary*, ed. William Bray, Dunne, London, 1901.

Fidler, Kathleen, *The Thames in Story*, Epworth, London, 1971.

Firth, J.B. (ed.), *The Minstrelsy of Isis*, Chapman & Hall, London, 1908.

Gedge, Paul, *Thames Journey*, Harrap, London, 1949.

Goodsall, R.H., *The Widening Thames*, Constable, London, 1965.

Harrison, William, *An Historicall Description of the Islande of Britayne*, London, 1587.

Hawthorne, Edward, *Electric Boats on the Thames, 1889–1914*, Sutton, Stroud, 1995.

Higgins, Walter, *Father Thames*, Gardner, London, 1922.

Household, Humphrey, *The Thames and Severn Canal*, David & Charles, Newton Abbot, 1969.

Hutton, W.H., *By Thames and Cotswold*, Holden, London, 1908.

Jenkins, Alan, *The Book of the Thames*, Macmillan, London, 1983.

Jones, S.R., *Thames Triumphant*, The Studio, London, 1943.

Leslie, G.D., *Our River*, Bradbury, London, 1881.

———, *Letters to Marco*, Macmillan, London, 1893.

———, *Riverside Letters*, Macmillan, London, 1896.

Mackay, Charles, *The Thames and Its Tributaries*, Bentley, London, 1840.

Mare, Eric de, *London's Riverside*, Reinhardt, London, 1958.

———, *Time on the Thames*, Architectural Press, London, 1952.

Maxwell, Donald, *A Pilgrimage of the Thames*, Centenary Press, London, 1932.

Maxwell, G.S., *The Authors' Thames*, Palmer, London, 1924.

Pepys, Samuel, *Diary*, online edition, www.Pepysdiary.com.

Pilkington, *Small Boat on the Thames*, Macmillan, London, 1966.

Robertson, E.A., *Thames Portrait*, Nicolson, London, 1937.

Robertson, H.R., *Life on the Upper Thames*, Virtue Spalding, London, 1875.

Rolt, L.T.C., *The Thames from Mouth to Source*, Batsford, London, 1951.

Runciman, J., *Royal River: Gravesend to The Nore*, London, 1885.

Schama, Simon, *Landscape and Memory*, Fontana, London, 1995.

Shrapnel, Norman, *A View of the Thames*, Collins, London, 1977.

Sinclair, Mick, *The Thames, A Cultural History*, Signal, Oxford, 2007.

Thames Guardian, Journal of The River Thames Society.

Thacker, F. S., *The Stripling Thames*, privately printed, London, 1909.

———, *The Thames Highway*, 2 vols, London 1914 and Kew 1920.

Tomlinson, H.M., *London River*, Cassell, London, 1925.

Vickers, Miranda, *Eyots and Aits: Islands on the River Thames*, History Press, Stroud, 2012.

Waters, Brian, *Thirteen Rivers to the Thames*, Dent, London, 1964.

Williams, Alfred, *Folk Songs of the Upper Thames*, Duckworth, London, 1923.

———, *Round About Middle Thames*, Alan Sutton, Stroud, 1982.

———, *Round About the Upper Thames*, Duckworth, London, 1922.

Wilson, D.G., *The Making of the Middle Thames*, Spurbooks, Bourne End, 1977.

———, *The Victorian Thames*, Alan Sutton, Stroud, 1993.

———, *The Thames: Record of a Working Waterway*, Batsford, London, 1987.

ONE

Akenside, Mark, *Poetical Works*, ed. Alexander Dyce, George Bell & Sons, London, 1886.

Andrews, William, *Famous Frosts and Frost Fairs*, Redway, London, 1887.

Aske, James *Elizabetha Triumphans*, T. Orwin for T. Gubbin & T. Newman, London, 1588.

Belloc, Hilaire, *Historic Thames*, Dent, London, 1907.

Caesar, Julius, *Commentaries on the Gallic Wars*, trans. W.A. MacDevitt, Everyman's Library, Dent, London, 1915.

Camden, William, *Britannia, or, a chorographical description of Great Britain and Ireland, together with the adjacent islands*, ed. E.G. Matthews, London, 1722.

Cassius Dio, *Roman History*, Book 40, Loeb Classical Library, Harvard University Press, Cambrdge MA, 1924.

Churchill, Winston, *A History of the English Speaking Peoples*, 4 vols, Cassell, New York, 1956.

Deloney, Thomas, 'Miscellaneous Ballads', in *The Works of Thomas Deloney*, ed. Frances Oscar Mann, Clarendon Press, Oxford, 1912.

Denman, John, *Cooper's Hill: A poem*, London, 1766.

Duffy, Carol Ann (ed), *Jubilee Lines*, Faber, London, 2012.

Fletcher, C.R.L., and Rudyard Kipling, *A School History of England*, Clarendon Press, Oxford, 1911.

Foot, William, *The Battlefields That Nearly Were: Defended England 1940*, Tempus, Stroud, 2006.

Graves, Robert, *Claudius the God*, Penguin, London, 1935.

Henty, G.A., *The Dragon and The Raven*, Blackie, London, 1908.

Heywood, Thomas, *If You Know Not Me, You Know Nobody*, London, 1633.

Irwin, Margaret, *The Stranger Prince*, Chatto & Windus, London, 1938.

Jerome K. Jerome, *Three Men in a Boat*, Arrowsmith, London, 1889.

Macaulay, Thomas Babington, 'Armada: A Fragment', in *Lays of Ancient Rome*, Longmans, London, 1842.

Mattingley, Garrett, *The Defeat of the Spanish Armada*, Cape, London, 1959.

Melrose Chronicle (1270), see *A Mediaeval Chronicle of Scotland*, ed. Joseph Stevenson, Felinfach, Llanerch, 1991.

The names of the nobility, gentry, and others, who contributed to the defence of this country at the time of the Spanish invasion, in 1588, Printed for Leigh & Sotheby, London, 1798.

Polyaenus, *Stratagems of War*, trans. E. Shepherd, London, 1793.

Ramsay, Sir James Henry, *The Foundations of England, Or Twelve Centuries of British History (B.C. 55–A.D. 1154)*, Volume 2: *1066–1154*, Swan Sonnenschein, London, 1898.

Stevens, C.E., *History Today*, vol. 9, no. 9, 1959.

Tupper, M., ed., *The Poems of King Alfred*, Hall & Virtue, London, 1850.

Vincent, Nicholas, *Magna Carta*, Bodleian Library, Oxford, 2015.

Wilson, John Maurius, *Imperial Gazeteer of England and Wales*, 1870–72.

Woolf, Virginia, *Orlando: A Biography*, Hogarth Press, Richmond, 1933.

TWO

Brownell, Morris R., 'William Gilpin's "Unfinished Business": The Thames Tour (1764)', *Volume of the Walpole Society*, vol. LVII (1993/94), pp. 52–78.

Burke, Edmund, *Enquiry into the Origins of the Sublime and Beautiful*, in Edmund Burke, *Works*, vol. I, Nimmo, London, 1887.

Camden, William, *Britannia*, trans. Philemon Holland, London, 1610.

Combe, William, *An History of the River Thames*, Boydell, London, 1794–96.

Currie, Ian, *Frost, Freezes and Fairs – Chronicles of the Frozen Thames since 1000 AD*, Frosted Earth, Coulsdon, 1996.

Defoe, Daniel, *A Tour Thro' the Whole Island of Great Britain*, Faulkner, Dublin, 1724.

Drayton, Michael, *Poly-Olbion. Or a Chorographicall Description of Tracts, Rivers, Mountaines, Forests*, Humphrey Lownes, London, 1612.

———, 'Song to Beta', in *England's Helicon* (1600), ed A.H. Bullen, London 1887.

Egan, Pierce, *The Pilgrims of the Thames*, Strange, London, 1838.

Fisher Murray, John, *Picturesque Tour of the River Thames in its Western Courses, including particular descriptions of Richmond, Hampton Court and Windsor*, Bohn, London, 1845.

Gilpin, William, *Observations, relative chiefly to picturesque beauty, made in the year 1772*, R. Blamire, London, 1788.

Hall, Mr, and Mrs S.C., *The Book of the Thames*, Hall Virtue, London, 1859.

Harrison, William, *Description of England*, quoted in *Elizabethan England*, ed. Lothrop Withington, Scott, London, 1910.

Ireland, Samuel, *Picturesque Views on the River Thames*, Clarke, London, 1792.

Leland, John, *Preface of The laboryouse journey [and] serche of Johan Leylande, for Englandes antiquitees*, Printed by S. Mierdman for John Bale, London, 1549.

————, *John Leland's Itinerary*, ed. John Chandler, Alan Sutton, Stroud, 1993.

————, 'Κύκνειον ᾆσμα' ['Cantio Cygnea'] (1545). A hypertext edition by Dana F. Sutton, University of California, 2006, www.philological.bham. ac.uk/swansong.

Leyland, John, *The Thames Illustrated: A Picturesque Journeying from Richmond to Oxford*, Newnes, London, 1897.

Mitton, G.E., *The Thames*, Black, London, 1906.

Oruch, Jack B., 'Spenser, Camden, and the Poetic Marriages of Rivers', in *Studies in Philology*, vol. 64, no. 4 (July 1967), pp. 606–24.

Peele, George, 'Farewell to Sir John Norris and Sir Francis Drake', in *Works*, ed. Alexander Dyce, Pickering, London, 1817.

Read, Susan, ed., *The Thames of Henry Taunt*, Alan Sutton, Gloucester, 1989.

Spenser, Edmund, *The Faerie Queen*, ed. Thomas Wise, George Allen, London, 1897.

————, 'Prothalamion', in John Morley, *English Men of Letters*, Macmillan, New York, 1879.

Taunt, Henry, *Guide to Goring, Streatley and the Neighbourhood*, Oxford, 1894.

Thorne, James, *Rambles by Rivers*, Knight, London, 1847.

Vallans, William, 'The tale of two swans', quoted in 'Spenser and the Tradition: English Poetry 1579–1830', VirginiaTech database, www.lib.vt.edu/find/ databases/S/spenser-and-the-tradition-english-poetry-1579–1830.html.

Vergil, Polydore, *Anglica Historia*, in *Polydore Vergil's English history, from an early translation preserved among the MSS of the Old Royal Library in the British Museum*, Volume I: *Containing the first eight books, comprising the period prior to the Norman Conquest*, ed. Sir Henry Ellis, Camden Society, London, 1846.

THREE

Ackroyd, Peter, *The Life of Thomas More*, Chatto, London, 1998.

Allingham, William, *A Diary*, ed. H Allingham, Macmillan, London, 1908.

Beccles Wilson, Anthony, *Strawberry Hill: A History of the Neighbourhood*, Strawberry Hill Residents Association, Twickenham, 1991.

Brayley, E., et al., *The Beauties of England and Wales, or Delineations Topographical, Historical and Descriptive of Each County: Middlesex*, Longman, London, 1816.

Beerbohm, Max, *Zuleika Dobson*, Heinemann, London, 1911.

Bowack, John, *Antiquities of Middlesex*, London, 1705.

Burney, Frances, *The Diary and Letters of Madame D'arblay*, vol. 1, London, 1890.

Carroll, Lewis, *Alice's Adventures in Wonderland*, MacMillan, London, 1865.

The Correspondence of Thomas Carlyle and John Ruskin ed. George Allan Cate, Stanford University Press, Stanford CA, 1982.

Davis, Mark, *Alice in Waterland: Lewis Carroll and the River Thames in Oxford*, Signal, London, 2010.

Dougill, John, *Oxford in English Literature: The Making, and Undoing, of 'The English Athens'*, University of Michigan Press, Ann Arbor MI, 1998.

Dryden, John, *Epilogue Spoken to the King at the Opening of the Playhouse at Oxford, 1681*, John Johnson at the Clarendon Press, Oxford, 1932.

Gray, Thomas, *Poems and Letters of Thomas Gray*, Priestley, London, 1820.

Hamilton, Walter, *Parodies of the Works of English and American Authors*, vol. 5, Reeves & Turner, London, 1888.

Hardy, Thomas, *Jude the Obscure*, Osgood, McIlvaine & Co., London, 1896.

Hood, Thomas, *The Beauties of England and Wales*, Vernor & Hood, London, 1801.

James, Henry, *English Hours*, Heinemann, London, 1905.

Johnson, Samuel, *Lives of the Poets*, London, 1781.

Keats, John, *Selected Letters*, ed. Robert Gittings, Oxford University Press, 1995.

Leigh Hunt, James, *Lord Byron and some of his Contemporaries, with Recollections of the Author's Life, and of his Visit to Italy*, H. Colburn, London, 1828.

———, *The Town: Its Memorable Characters and Events. St Paul's to St James's*, Smith Elder, London, 1848.

Mackail, John, *The Life of William Morris*, vols 1 and 2, Longmans, London, 1899.

More, Thomas, *Dialogue of Comfort against Tribulation*, *Works of Thomas More*, vol. 12, ed. Louis L. Martz and Frank Manley, Yale University Press, New Haven CT, 1976.

Morris, William, 'The Expedition of The Ark', www.morrissociety.org/publications/JWMS/SP77.3.3.Baissus.pdf.

———, *News from Nowhere*, Reeves & Turner, London, 1890.

Pope, Alexander, *Windsor Forest*, Lintoft, London, 1713.

———, *The Rape of the Lock*, Lintoft, London, 1714.

Ransome, Arthur, *Bohemia in London*, Chapman & Hall, London, 1907.

Shelley, Percy Bysshe, *The Revolt of Islam*, Ollier, London, 1818.

Tagholm, Roger, *Walking Literary London*, New Holland Publishers, London, 2001.

Thomson, James, *The Seasons*, Clark, Edinburgh, 1772.

Vansittart, Peter, *London: A Literary Companion*, John Murray, London, 1993.

Walpole, Horace, *Memoirs of Horace Walpole and his contemporaries, including numerous original letters, chiefly from Strawberry Hill*, ed. Elias Warburton, Colburn, London, 1852.

Woolf, Virginia, *Night and Day*, Hogarth Press, London, 1919.

FOUR

Ashby-Sterry, Joseph, *A Tale of the Thames, with illustrations in verse by the author*, Bliss Sands, London, 1896.

———, *The River Rhymer*, Ham-Smith, London, 1913.

Barrie, J.M., *Walker London: A Farcical Comedy in Three Acts*, French, London, 1907.

Bede, Cuthbert (pseud.), *The Adventures of Mr Verdant Green*, Cooke, London, 1853.

Beerbohm, Max, *Zuleika Dobson*, Heinemann, London, 1911.

Betjeman, John, *New Bats in Old Belfries*, John Murray, London, 1945.

Bolland, R.R., *Victorians on the Thames*, Oast, Tunbridge Wells, 1974.

Chandler, John H., ed., *Travels through Stuart Britain: The Adventures of John Taylor, the Water Poet*, Sutton, Stroud, 1999.

Church, Alfred, *Summer Days on the Thames: Recollections of Boating and Fishing between Henley and Oxford*, Seely, London, 1890.

Coke, Desmond, *Sandford of Merton: A Story of Oxford Life*, Aldens, Oxford, 1903.

———, *In the Wake of 'Three Men in a Boat'*, Parapress, Tunbridge Wells, 1995.

Dickens, Charles, Jr, *A Dictionary of the Thames*, Macmillan, London, 1887.

Domenichetti, Richard Hippisley, *The Thames: Newdigate Prize Poem*, privately published, Oxford, 1885.

Firth, J.B., ed., *The Minstrelsy of Isis: Poems Relating to Oxford*, Chapman & Hall, London.

Forester, C.S., *Hornblower and the Atropos*, Gollancz, London, 1953.

Grahame, Kenneth, *The Wind in the Willows*, Methuen, London, 1951.

Gauger, Anne, *The Annotated Wind in the Willows*, W.W. Norton, New York, 2009.

Hawthorne, Nathaniel, *Our Old Home*, Smith Elder, London, 1863.

Herbert, A.P., *The House by the River*, Methuen, London, 1920.

Herrick, Robert, *Hesperides, and Noble Numbers*, ed. A.W. Pollard, Lawrence, London, 1891.

Hewlett, Joseph, *Peter Priggins, the College Scout*, 3 vols, ed. Theodore Hook, Henry Colburn, London, 1841.

Hughes, Thomas, *Tom Brown at Oxford*, Macmillan, London, 1861.

Ionides, Cyril, *A Floating Home*, illustrated by Arnold Bennett, Chatto & Windus, London, 1918.

James, Henry, *English Hours*, Heinemann, London, 1905.

Jerome, Jerome K., *Three Men in a Boat*, Arrowsmith, London, 1889.

————, *My Life and Times*, Hodder & Stoughton, London, 1926.

Larkin, Philip, *A Girl in Winter*, Faber, London, 1947

Mitchell, Charles (ed.), *Hogarth's Peregrination*, Clarendon Press, Oxford, 1952.

Morris, William, *News from Nowhere*, London, 1891.

————, *Collected Letters*, Vol. 1, ed. Norman Kelvin, Princeton, 2014.

Peacock, Thomas Love, *Crotchet Castle*, T. Hoockham, London, 1831.

Pennell, Joseph, and Elizabeth Robins, *The Stream of Pleasure*, Fisher Unwin, London, 1891.

Pullman, Philip, *His Dark Materials*, Scholastic, London, 2001.

Reynolds, Clifton, *Sailing Small Waters*, John Lane, London, 1946.

Sayers, Dorothy, *Gaudy Night*, Gollancz, London, 1939.

Taylor, John, *The Works of John Taylor, the Water Poet*, Simms, Manchester, 1869.

Wack, H.W., *In Thamesland*, Putnams, New York, 1906.

Wells, H.G., *The History of Mr Polly*, Odhams, London, 1910.

————, *The Secret Places of The Heart*, Macmillan, London, 1922.

West, Rebecca, *The Return of the Soldier*, Daily Express, London, 1918.

Whitman, James, 'Down the Thames in a Birchbark Canoe', *Harpers Monthly*, January 1881.

Williams, Howard, *Diary of a Rowing Tour from Oxford to London via Warwick, Gloucester, Hereford & Bristol in 1875*, Alan Sutton, Gloucester, 1982.

Wordsworth, Charles, *Annals of My Early Life, 1806–1846*, Longman, London, 1891.

FIVE

Andrews, Martin, *The Life and Work of Robert Gibbings*, Primrose Hill Press, Bicester, 2003.

Church, Alfred, *Summer Days on the Thames: Recollections of Boating and Fishing between Henley and Oxford*, Seeley, London, 1890.

Cornish, C.J., *The Naturalist on the Thames*, Seeley, London, 1902.

Cowper, William, *The Task*, Charles Whittingham, London, 1817.

Darwin, Erasmus, *The Botanic Garden*, J. Johnson, London, 1791.

Gibbings, Robert, *Sweet Thames Run Softly*, Dent, London, 1940.

————, *Till I End my Song*, Dent, London, 1957.

Herbert, A.P., *The Singing Swan*, Methuen, London, 1968.

Hadfield, John, 'A Man of Hills and Rivers', *Picture Post*, 14 October 1944.

Hook, Theodore, 'Ode to Ditton', in *The Mirror of Literature, Amusement, and Instruction*, vol. 24, ed. Thomas Byerley, London, 1834.

Jefferies, Richard, *Nature Near London*, Chatto & Windus, London, 1883.

————, *After London*, Cassell, London, 1885.

————, 'The Modern Thames', *Pall Mall Gazette*, 1885.

Lock to Lock Times, London, 1888–99.

Miller, Philip, *Gardeners Dictionary; Containing the Methods of Cultivating and Improving the Kitchen, Fruit and Flower Garden, as also, the Physick Garden, Wilderness, Conservatory and Vineyard*, printed for the author, London, 1731.

Plot, Robert, *The Natural History of Oxfordshire*, Sheldonian Theatre, Oxford, 1677.

Pope, Alexander, *Windsor Forest*, Lintoft, London, 1713.

Pulteney, Richard, *Historical and biographical sketches of the progress of botany in England from its origin to the introduction of the Linnæan system*, T. Cadell, London, 1790.

Ransome, Arthur, *Rod and Line*, Jonathan Cape, London, 1929.

————, *Mainly About Fishing*, Jonathan Cape, London, 1959.

————, *Arthur Ransome on Fishing*, ed. J. Swift, Jonathan Cape, London, 1994.

————, *Fair Cops and Glow Worms: More of Arthur Ransome's Fishing Articles from 1910 to 1935 Together with Thoughts and Stories from Other Fishing Writers, Ancient, Contemporary and Modern*, ed. Paul Crisp, Amazon Publications, 2011.

Sloane, Hans, *A Voyage to the Islands Madeira, Barbados, Nieves, S. Christopher and Jamaica*, London, 1707–25.

Thomas, Edward, *Richard Jefferies, His Life and Work*, Hutchinson, London, 1909.

Tradescant, John, *Musaeum Tradescantianum*, Grismond, London, 1656.

Walton, Isaak, *The Compleat Angler*, London, 1653.

White, Gilbert, *The Natural History of Selborne*, Benjamin White, London, 1789.

SIX

Armour, Margaret, *Thames: Sonnets and Semblances*, Elkin Matthews, London, 1897.

Bennett, Sharon, *A Dark and Twisted Tide*, Bantam, London, 2014.

Borrow, George, *Lavengro: The Scholar, the Gypsy, the Priest*, John Murray, London, 1851.

————, *The Song Book of Quong Lee*, Allen & Unwin, London, 1920.

Boulton, J., ed., *Selected Letters of D.H. Lawrence*, Cambridge University Press, Cambridge, 2000.

Burke, Thomas, *Limehouse Nights*, Grant Richards, London, 1916.

Conan Doyle, Arthur, *The Sign of Four*, Spencer Blackett, London, 1890.

————, *The Adventures of Sherlock Holmes*, George Newnes, London, 1892.

Conrad, Joseph, *The Heart of Darkness*, Blackwoods Magazine, London, 1899.

————, *The Secret Agent*, Methuen, London, 1907.

————, The Mirror of the Sea: Memories and Impressions, Dent, London, 1923.

Cowper, Thomas, *Life and Works of Thomas Cowper*, ed. Robert Southey, Baldwin, London, 1836.

Dexter, Colin, *The Riddle of the Third Mile*, Pan, London, 1983.

————, *The Wench is Dead*, Pan, London, 1989.

————, *The Jewel That Was Ours*, Pan, London, 1991.

————, *Daughters of Cain*, Pan, London, 1994.

Dickens, Charles, *Dombey and Son*, Chapman & Hall, London, 1848.
————, *David Copperfield*, Bradbury &Evans, London, 1849.
————, 'Down with the Tide', *Household Words*, London, 5 February 1853.
————, *Great Expectations*, Chapman & Hall, London, 1861.
————, *Our Mutual Friend*, Chapman & Hall, London, 1865.
————, *Letters of Charles Dickens*, Chapman & Hall, London, 1880.
Eliot, George, *Daniel Deronda*, Blackwood, Edinburgh, 1876.
Fletcher, C.R.L., and Rudyard Kipling, *A School History of England*, Clarendon Press, Oxford, 1911.
Godwin, George, *Town Swamps and Social Bridges*, Routledge, London, 1859.
Harper, C.G., *Thames Valley Villages*, Chapman & Hall, London, 1910.
Harper, W., *Shakespeare and the Thames*, 1890.
Hawthorne, Nathaniel, *Our Old Home*, Smith Elder, London, 1863.
Herbert, A.P., *The House by The River*, Methuen, London, 1920.
————, *The Water Gipsies*, Methuen, London, 1930.
————, *The War Story of Southend Pier*, County Borough of Southend, 1945.
————, *The Thames*, Weidenfeld & Nicolson, London, 1966.
Horn, Roni, *Another Water*, Scalo, Zurich, 2000.
Hood, Thomas, *Poetical Works*, Springer, New York, 1873.
Kneale, Matthew, *Sweet Thames*, Sinclair Stevenson, London, 1992.
Knox, Ronald, *Footsteps at the Lock*, Methuen, London, 1928.
Pullman, Philip, *The Ruby in the Smoke*, Oxford University Press, Oxford, 1985.
————, *Northern Lights*, Scholastic, London, 1995.
Rohmer, Sax, *The Mystery of Dr Fu-Manchu*, Methuen, London, 1913.
Roy, Lucinda, *Wailing the Dead to Sleep*, Bogle-L'Ouverture Press, London, 1988.
Schneer, Jonathan, *The Thames, England's River*, Yale University Press, New Haven CT and London, 2005.
Stoker, Bram, *Dracula*, Constable, London, 1897.
Stow, John, *A Survey of the Cities of London and Westminster*, ed. John Strype, 2 vols, printed for A. Churchill, London, 1720.
Wells, H.G., *Tono-Bungay*, Macmillan, London, 1909.
Wilde, Oscar, *The Picture of Dorian Gray*, Ward Lock, London, 1891.

SEVEN

Adams, Anna, *Thames: An Anthology of River Poems*, Enitharmon, London, 1999.
Arnold, Matthew, *The Scholar Gipsy*, Macmillan, London, 1905.
Ashby-Sterry, Joseph, *The Lazy Minstrel*, T. Fisher Unwin, London, 1887.
————, *Tale of the Thames*, Bliss Sands, London, 1896.
Betjeman, John, *Summoned by Bells*, John Murray, London, 1960.
Binyon, Lawrence, *Collected Poems*, MacMillan, London, 1931.
Bird, James, *Frances Abbott, the Recluse of Niagara and Metropolitan Sketches*, London, 1835.
Blyth, Caroline, ed., *Decadent Verse: An Anthology of Late-Victorian Poetry, 1872–1900*, Anthem, New York, 2009.
Byron, Lord, *Don Juan*, Penguin, Harmondsworth, 1986.
Chapman, George, *Ovid's Banquet of Sense and other poems, 1595*, Scolar Press, Menston, 1970.
Davidson, John, *Poems*, Akros, Edinburgh, 1895.
Domenichetti, Richard Hippisley, *The Thames: Newdigate Prize Poem*, privately published, Oxford, 1885.
Drayton, Michael, *Poly-Olbion*, Humphrey Lownes, London, 1612.

Dunbar, William, *Life and Poems of William Dunbar*, Nimmo, Edinburgh, 1860.
Fanthorpe, U.A., *Standing To: Poems by U.A. Fanthorpe*, Peterloo Poets, London, 1999.
Gower, John, *Confessio Amantis*, ed. Russell A. Peck, University of Toronto Press, Toronto, 1980.
Gray, Thomas, *Poems by Mr Gray*, J. Dodsley, London, 1768.
Henley, William, *Poems*, David Nutt, London, 1898.
Herbert, Jocelyn, *Sweete Themmes*, Parrish, London, 1951.
Hill, David, *Turner on the Thames*, Yale University Press, New Haven CT and London, 1993.
Hopkins, Gerard Manley, *Poems of Gerard Manley Hopkins*, ed. Robert Bridges, Oxford University Press, London, 1918.
————, *Complete Poetical Works*, Delphi, 2013.
Longfellow, Henry, *Poems of Places*, MacMillan, London, 1877.
Mackie, Gascoigne, *Charmides and Other Poems Chiefly Relating to Oxford*, Blackwell, Oxford, 1912.
Motion, Andrew, *Salt Water*, Faber, London, 1997.
Norton, John Bruce, *Memories of Merton*, Smith, Elder, London, 1861.
Owen, Wilfred, *The Poems of Wilfred Owen*, ed. Jon Stallworthy, Chatto & Windus, London, 1990.
Rayner Parkes, Bessie, *Ballads and Songs*, Bell & Daldy, London, 1863.
Peacock, T.L., *The Genius of the Thames*, Hookham, London, 1812.
————, *Letters to Edward Hookham and Percy B. Shelley*, Forgotten Books, London, 2013.
Pitter, Ruth, *The Bridge: Poems, 1939–1944*, Cresset Press, London, 1945.
Pope, Alexander, *Windsor Forest*, Lintoft, London, 1713.
Stapleton, John, *The Thames, a Poem*, Kegan Paul, London, 1878.
Stephen, James, 'Steam Launches on the Thames', in Caroline Blyth, *Decadent Verse*.
Thomson, James, *The Seasons*, Clark, Edinburgh, 1772.
Wilde, Oscar, *Poems of Oscar Wilde*, Buckles, New York, 1906.
Wordsworth, William, *Poems in Two Volumes, 1807*, ed. Helen Darbishire, Clarendon Press, Oxford, 1952.

EIGHT

Aaronovitch, Ben, *Rivers of London*, Gollancz, London, 2011.
Deakin, Roger, *Waterlog: A Swimmer's Journey through Britain*, Vintage, London, 2000.
Hughes, S., *Circle Line*, Summersdale, Chichester, 2012.
Mason, Val, ed., *The River Thames in Verse – An illustrated Anthology of New Poems*, River Thames Society, London, 2004.
Mayon-White, R., and Wendy Yorke, *Exploring the Thames Wilderness*, Adlard Coles, London, 2013.
McKinnon, A.J., *The Unlikely Voyage of Jack de Crow: A Mirror Odyssey from North Wales to the Black Sea*, Seafarer, Woodbridge, 2002.
Rivington, R.T., *Punting*, Rivington, Oxford, 1983.
Sinclair, Iain, *Downriver (or, The Vessels of Wrath): A Narrative in Twelve Tales*, Vintage, London, 1991.
Wright, Patrick, *A Journey Through Ruins: The Days of London*, Radius, London, 1991.
————, *The River: The Thames in Our Times*, BBC Books, London, 1999.

ACKNOWLEDGEMENTS

IMAGES

COVER © The British Library Board. Author photo Georgina Ferry.
ii   © Trustees of the British Museum
4   Oxford, Bodleian Library, MS. Gough Gen. Top. 16
9   © Ashmolean Museum, University of Oxford, HCR7231
13   Wikimedia Commons
19   © Trustees of the British Museum, London
24   Oxford, Bodleian Library, MS. Rawl. A. 195A
26   © Museum of London
32   © Trustees of the British Museum, London
34   University of Bristol Library, Special Collections
39   Oxford, Bodleian Library, MS. Bodl. 764, fol. 58v (detail)
43   Oxford, Bodleian Library, J-J Drayton d.35, pp. 235–7
47   © The Victoria and Albert Museum, London
49   Oxford, Bodleian Library, Vet. A5 b.82 (v.1) opp p190
64   © Canterbury Museums and Galleries
66   Courtesy of The Lewis Walpole Library, Yale University
69   © The Victoria and Albert Museum, London
70   © Museum of London
77   © Heritage Image Partnership Ltd/Alamy
79   Reproduced by permission of Chatsworth Settlement Trustees/
     © Devonshire Collection, Chatsworth/Bridgeman Images
82   Courtesy of The Lewis Walpole Library, Yale University
87   Oxford, Bodleian Library, Harcourt adds. Box 11, 1 of 4
89   Oxford, Bodleian Library, Vet. A5. b.82
90   Oxford, Bodleian Library, 2527 d.1551
101 Delaware Art Museum, Wilmington, Samuel and Mary R. Bancroft
     Memorial/Bridgeman Images
104 Oxford, Bodleian Library, Kelmscott Press e.9
106 © TfL from the London Transport Museum collection
111 © Trustees of the British Museum
114 © Hamburger Kunsthalle/bpk, photo Elke Walford
143 Oxford, Bodleian Library, MS. Eng. misc. d. 281
146 © Ashmolean Museum, University of Oxford, WA1898.8
150 © The British Library Board, London

163 University of Reading, Special Collections/© Estate of Robert Gibbings and the Heather Chalcroft Literary Agency
166 University of Reading, Special Collections/© Estate of Robert Gibbings and the Heather Chalcroft Literary Agency
168 Oxford, Bodleian Library, 18956 d.93
171 Gwen Hughes Gallery, © Tom and Maria La Dell
174 Oxford, Bodleian Library, 280 e.1852
181 © Victoria and Albert Museum
187 © Museum of London
197 Oxford, Bodleian Library, 25611 e.2325
210 Oxford, Bodleian Library, J-J Drayton d.35
214 © UK Government Art Collection
217 Oxford, Bodleian Library, G.A. Gen. top. 4° 25
227 © Ashmolean Museum, University of Oxford, WA1850.48
231 Anglesey Abbey, Cambridgeshire/National Trust Photographic Library/Bridgeman Images
234 © The Victoria and Albert Museum, London
242 © Simon Brett
246 Film still of Iain Sinclair & Andrew Kotting in *Swandown*. Courtesy of Fly Film Company Limited. Photo: Anonymous Bosch
248 © Gordon Scammell/Alamy
252 © Richard Mayon-White

QUOTATIONS

33 'The Thames, London 2012' by Carol Ann Duffy reproduced by permission of Rogers, Coleridge and White
133 & 222 excerpts from John Betjeman's *New Bats in Old Belfries* (John Murray, 1945) and *Summoned by Bells* (John Murray, 1960) reproduced by permission of Aitken Alexander Associates
209 Lucinda Roy, 'Thames', from *Wailing the Dead to Sleep* (Bogle-L'Ouverture, 1988), reprinted by permission of Lucinda Roy
226 'From Iffley', first published in *Stapeldon Magazine*, vol. 4, no. 3 (December 1913), © The Tolkien Estate Limited 1913, 2011
238 'Rising Damp' from U.A. Fanthorpe's *New and Collected Poems* (Enitharmon Press, 2010), reproduced by kind permission of Dr R.V. Bailey
244 'Homage' reproduced by kind permission of Barbara Daniels

INDEX

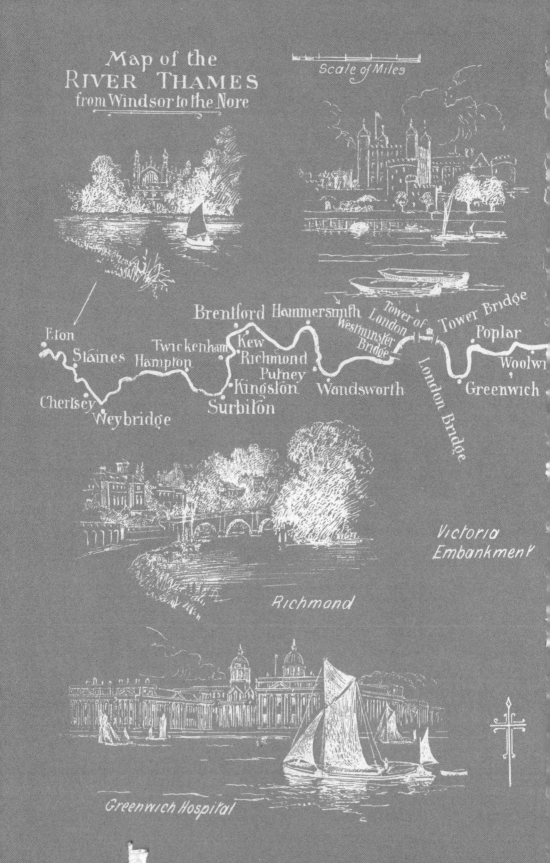

Map of the
RIVER THAMES
from Windsor to the Nore

Scale of Miles

Eton
Staines
Chertsey
Weybridge
Hampton
Twickenham
Kew
Richmond
Putney
Kingston
Surbiton
Brentford
Hammersmith
Wandsworth
Westminster Bridge
Tower of London
London Bridge
Tower Bridge
Poplar
Woolwich
Greenwich

Victoria Embankment

Richmond

Greenwich Hospital